SOCIAL IMPACT ASSESSMENT
An Introduction

C. J. Barrow
Senior Lecturer in Development Studies,
University of Wales Swansea

A member of the Hodder Headline Group
LONDON
Co-published in the United States of America by
Oxford University Press Inc., New York

First published in Great Britain in 2000 by
Arnold, a member of the Hodder Headline Group,
338 Euston Road, London NW1 3BH

http://www.arnoldpublishers.com

Co-published in the United States of America by
Oxford University Press Inc.,
198 Madison Avenue, New York, NY 10016

British Library Cataloguing in Publication Data
A catalogue record for this book is available from the British Library

Library of Congress Cataloging-in-Publication Data
A catalog record for this book is available from the Library of Congress

ISBN 0 340 74217 8 (hb)
ISBN 0 340 74218 6 (pb)

1 2 3 4 5 6 7 8 9 10

Production Editor: Wendy Rooke
Production Controller: Bryan Eccleshall
Cover Design: Terry Griffiths

Typeset in 10/12pt Palatino by
J&L Composition Ltd, Filey, North Yorkshire
Printed and bound in Great Britain by
MPG Books, Bodmin, Cornwall

CONTENTS

PREFACE

During the last 30 years or so, planners and decision-makers have increasingly accepted that 'social' impacts need to be considered along with environmental and economic: because they are often important, or closely interrelated with them; as a response to the growth in the West of a popular desire for 'social responsibility'; and for improved environmental management and sustainable development, which demand a precautionary approach.

Social impact assessment (SIA) runs parallel with, overlaps, or is used by: environmental impact assessment (EIA); risk and hazard assessment; technology assessment; project, programme and policy monitoring and evaluation; and a number of other planning and management fields. Increasingly, governments, funding agencies and non-governmental organizations (NGOs) seek to improve development efforts by establishing likely effects in advance, so that they can be avoided, or mitigation and contingency measures put in place. Social and socio-economic problems cause misery, waste money and hinder efforts to establish stable governance and sustainable development. In an increasingly crowded world, SIA can help to avoid such problems. These efforts are being applied to a huge range of situations, so the public, planners, administrators, lawyers, engineers, technicians, conservationists and many others – as well as social scientists – are all likely to get involved in SIA, a field that is still evolving.

I undertook to write this book, aware of the complexity of the subject, and conscious that I am not a 'mainstream' social studies specialist. However, objective synthesis and review may usefully be conducted by those who dispassionately distance themselves from a subject. Also, SIA is an evaluative process that uses descriptive and analytical tools which are often derived from the natural sciences, economics and planning. Furthermore, SIA should integrate closely with EIA, planning, management, economics and other non-social studies disciplines.

I make no attempt to offer a training volume, nor an in-depth handbook; my aim is to offer a clear and comprehensive introduction.

C.J. Barrow
University of Wales Swansea

ACKNOWLEDGEMENTS

I wish to thank the staff of the Library, University of Wales Swansea for their help. I am also most grateful to all the editorial and production staff of Arnold.

Permission to use copyright material in this book is acknowledged in the text. Every effort has been made to trace the copyright holders of material produced in this book. Any rights not acknowledged here, and/or inappropriate attributions, will be rectified in subsequent editions if notice is given to the publisher.

1

INTRODUCTION

THE CHARACTER, PRINCIPLES AND AIMS OF SIA

Wise rulers and politicians who wish to prosper have always tried to foresee, and either prevent or prepare for, social and economic impacts.[1] It has been claimed, that as far back as the seventeenth century there were anthropologists and social psychologists doing something like SIA.[2,3] Becker (1997: 23) argued that Johan de Witt conducted what was essentially an SIA in The Netherlands in 1640 and, in France, the Marquis de Condorcet made an assessment of the likely impacts of a proposed canal in the Somme Valley between 1775 and 1776. Condorcet identified enough problems to ensure that the canal was never built; he has also been credited with the concept that social action might be quantifiably analysed and reliably predicted (Wilson, 1998: 16). Modern SIA is a field that draws on over three decades of theoretical and methodological development to improve foresight of future change and understanding of past developments.

Many books on SIA start by trying to define what is meant by a 'social

[1] A 'social impact' may be defined as an adaptation on the part of a social system to external agents of change and/or endogenous change. Another definition might be 'the social consequences of actions, including change to norms, beliefs, perceptions, values, etc.'. There are many categories of impact, some overlapping others. For example, economic (income, employment, taxes, etc.); demographic; institutional; displacement and relocation; community cohesion (see Glossary); lifestyle or well-being; beliefs; health and so on.

[2] SIA has been used as an abbreviation for 'social impact assessment' since roughly 1970. However, within the last decade or so, others have adopted the same acronym. It is now used in medicine (subcutaneous infusion anaesthesia; strip immunoblot assay), chemistry (stepwise isothermal analysis), biochemistry (sialylated antigens; sialic acid), impact assessment (sustainability impact assessment) and a number of other fields (scientific information activity; scientific-industrial associations; Singapore International Airlines).

[3] I use the term 'assessment' rather than 'analysis', 'appraisal' or 'evaluation'. 'Analysis' implies precise, accurate, repeatable results, something SIA does not provide. 'Appraisal' or 'evaluation' have come to mean something different to mainstream SIA.

impact' (*see* Glossary); for example, a definition might be: 'a significant or lasting change in people's lives brought about by a given action or actions'.[1] I broadly interpret SIA to be systematic, iterative (*see* Glossary), ideally ex-ante (*see* Glossary), assessment of such changes. There has been a tendency for SIA, like EIA, to stress negative (unwanted) impacts rather than positive ones. Advance warning of any probable impacts can be very useful, so effective SIA should address both negative and positive. Some recognize 'outcomes' as something distinct from 'impacts'. The former are less obvious; for example, a group may undertake a legal action and fail to win or lose much, so there is little impact. However, the group may have gained valuable experience and confidence in the process, and in future may fight much more effectively for its wishes to be heeded – a positive outcome.

The 'roots' of SIA lie, in part, in research carried out since the 1950s by anthropologists and sociologists who feared that proposed developments might have serious negative side-effects; for example, on indigenous peoples (Green, 1986). By the early 1970s it was being argued that if socio-economic impacts could be reliably identified in advance of development they might well be avoided or mitigated.

It is difficult to agree upon a single precise definition of SIA, or a universally accepted list of its aims (some suggestions are offered in Box 1.1). The goal of SIA, many would accept, is that 'it seeks to help individuals, groups, organizations and communities understand possible social, cultural, or economic impacts of change, or better-still impacts of proposed change'. SIA should go beyond anticipating possible impacts to suggest development alternatives to avoid, reduce or mitigate problems and maximize benefits. It can also play a crucial role in shaping ongoing monitoring (*see* Glossary) and evaluation, and may also be a means for public involvement and empowerment, and for improving the accountability of planners and administrators. Certain points recur in definitions and statements of aim, so there are commonly accepted qualities: it is a 'process' for 'systematic' assessment; it is 'anticipatory', it 'aids understanding', 'planning' (*see* Glossary) and (so far, not often enough) 'policy making'; it is 'iterative', i.e. adding depth and detail as it proceeds through its successive stages. Increasingly SIA, and related fields like strategic environmental assessment (SEA), are being explored as aids to achieving sustainable development.

SIA can mean different things to different people. For example, it can be a research technique, often *ad hoc* in approach; or it is applied as a 'technocratic' planning or management tool, seeking to be 'scientific'; or as a policy instrument shaped by agreed laws and frameworks for application (Anon, 1993: 240); others see it as a means of ensuring participation or even the empowerment of people in the development process. There are several ways in which SIA can be interpreted and applied (*see* Chapter 3). Some focus SIA on social systems affected by 'external' forces of change (Shields, 1975), others explore 'internal' factors as a cause of impacts – for example, alterations of perception or aspiration. Sometimes the focus is social, sometimes more socio-economic or socio-cultural. Generally, SIA aims to be multidisciplinary or interdisciplinary in approach, using a combination of objective and subjective assessment and ethical judgement, and considering external and internal changes. Those from a science background should note that it has been argued that detached observation alone is not enough if seeking to understand a social context (*see* Glossary).

SIA is often part of the EIA process, and some seek to incorporate it as a subfield (Gismondi, 1997). If EIA and SIA are laid out as a 'spectrum', then there are extremes where each is clearly distinct in terms of approach, methodology and technique, background of practitioners, and literature; however, there is also a great deal of overlap. There is clearer separation in historical terms, EIA and SIA having had reasonably different evolutions, and in respect of legislative and financial support – in which SIA has been more neglected.

Usually the aims of SIA are more practical than theoretical; Burdge (1995: 9) observed that it offers opportunities for social scientists to contribute in a meaningful way to solving interdisciplinary problems. Tester and Mykes (1981: 11) recognized three SIA objectives: to inform the public about proposals and their implications; to assemble information from locals; to solicit public opinion on proposals, alternatives, trade-offs, etc. Some feel that 'social assessment' (SA) is a better term than SIA, because it avoids the negative associations of the word 'impact'. In 1998 the National Environmental Policy Act (NEPA) defined SA as: '. . . an analysis of the community designed to ascertain how the community is organized, how its people relate to one another, how decisions are made, and other factors. These data can help . . . anticipate issues and establish effective ways to resolve them. The SA describes current conditions, but, unlike SIA, it does not attempt to forecast outcomes if things change' (NEPA 'call in' internet site, *see* Further reading and resources at the end of this chapter).

A good deal of SIA is applied after a decision has been made to act, so mainly serves to 'stock-take' and clarify what has already happened, although it might also suggest what may take place in the future. Such retrospective SIA adds to hindsight experience and understanding of how change takes place. Although there may be situations where anticipatory (ex-ante) SIA predictions are impossible or impractical (e.g. with complex, rare, random or unexpected events), if it is undertaken before an action or policy is firmly formulated, or at the first sign of some worrying trend, it can greatly benefit decision-making, policy formulation, choice of technology, implementation and management. Adopting an anticipatory but piecemeal approach is not enough, because developments can be complex, can change over a long period, and can affect a wide area. In addition, developments may alter as time progresses, and the people affected are also likely to change attitudes, adapt, acquire and lose abilities, alter their tolerance, etc. Constantly changing external factors may also impinge. Therefore, in addition to being anticipatory, SIA should be systematic, ongoing (seeking more than a single temporarily and spatially limited 'snapshot' view) and adaptive (Geisler, 1993: 332; Holling, 1978).

Box 1.1 Selected definitions and aims of SIA

- The process of assessing or estimating in advance the social consequences that are likely to follow from specific policy actions or project development.
- The definition offered by the Inter-organizational Committee on Guidelines and Principles for Social Impact Assessment: '. . . efforts to assess or estimate, *in advance*, the social consequences that are likely to follow from specific policy actions (including programs, and the adoption of new policies), and specific government actions (including buildings, large projects, and leasing large tracts of land for resource exploitation) . . .' (Burdge *et al.*, 1995: 12).
- Describe and analyse the real or potential effects of proposed developments upon specific groups of people.
- The goal is to balance science and politics in policy formulation and implementation (Rickson *et al.*, 1990: 9).
- SIA aims to help structure development so it responds to people's needs and is compatible with sociological conditions.
- The identification, analysis and evaluation of the social impacts resulting from a particular event. A social impact being a significant improvement or deterioration in people's well-being or a significant change in an aspect of community concern (Dietz, 1987: 54).
- The purpose of SIA is to answer the following question: 'Will there be a measurable difference in the quality of life in the community as a result of the proposed action?'
- The practical goal of SIA is to anticipate likely impacts and utilize the information in the planning process, and thereby ensure appropriate mitigation.
- The process of assessing or estimating in advance, the social consequences that are likely to follow from specific policy actions, project development, environmental impacts, commerce, altered tastes, media activity, social movements, etc.
- The systematic analysis in advance of the likely impacts a development or event will have on the everyday life of persons and communities.
- The process of identifying the future consequences of a current or proposed action which are related to individuals, organizations and social macro-systems.
- A method of policy analysis that offers great potential for integrating scientific policy analysis into a democratic political process (Dietz, 1987: 54).
- Efforts to identify, assess and summarize significance of the full range of effects/consequences that may result from some future development (the development being a new project, policy, environmental change, social change, etc.).
- A process examining proposed projects, programmes and policies for their possible effects on individuals, groups and communities (Buchan and Rivers, 1990: 97).
- Prediction and evaluation of the social effects of a policy, programme or project while it is in the planning stage – before the effects have occurred (Wolf, 1980: 27).
- Analysis of past and present impingements upon social conditions and processes and a projection of likely future consequences of proposed interventions (Burdge, 1994: 78).
- A systematic assessment of social and cultural impacts for a proposed development.

Note: most of these definitions are paraphrased, rather than direct quotations.

A given impact, or combination of impacts is likely to affect various social, ethnic, gender or age groups differently, though perhaps not simultaneously (these are known as 'differential impacts'). A given impact might quickly advantage one group, slowly damage another and leave others unaffected. There may also be difficulties defining social units that may not be fixed. Finsterbusch (1995: 230) noted that '. . . Weber [in the late 1950s] attributed the rise of capitalism in the West to the impacts of Calvinistic Protestantism. Most of us sociologists, if we had done an SIA at the time, would have missed these impacts.' These difficulties tend to prompt an issues-oriented approach that tries to explore off-site or downstream impacts, indirect impacts and cumulative impacts (*see* Chapter 5).

SIA needs to be 'continuous', or at least repeated regularly, with ex-ante (anticipatory or proactive) blending into ex-post (retrospective or reactive) *see* Glossary) assessment; possibly as a sort of life-cycle approach that considers impacts at planning, implementation, function, decommissioning and rehabilitation stages, or at succeeding stages in a project, programme, or policy (*see* Glossary for definitions of 'project', 'programme' and 'policy'), or during social change (Ellis, 1989; Geisler, 1993). Many practitioners would agree that the goal of SIA is to monitor and predict changes in quality of life, although it is difficult to make precise, quantifiable, reliable forecasts of such complex scenarios.

Some have tried hard to ensure that SIA deals with quantifiable data, perhaps to gain better acceptance from engineers and other non-social studies specialists who may fail to appreciate the value of qualitative data, and who might otherwise dismiss it as 'soft science'. These efforts can end up obscuring useful observations and usually hide the way in which assessments have been arrived at; they may also waste time and money for little real gain in objectivity or precision. It is best to accept that SIA is as much an art as a science, and that it relies a great deal on the professional judgement of researchers, so that qualitative measurements are useful. Torgerson made a careful examination of the character of SIA, concluding that it was not a science, but a 'social process', which itself has social impacts (1980: 2). (For discussion of SIA as a 'social phenomenon' and the impacts it can itself cause, *see* Chapter 5.)

Increasingly, EIA is being called upon to advise those seeking sustainable development, but it is not enough to assess physical impacts, one must also consider the social, cultural and socio-economic issues that are interrelated with them, and that control exploitation (Harrop and Nixon, 1999). SIA can provide information on social institutions, social capital and social change which may have huge importance in determining whether sustainable development happens in practice. The value of SIA for those seeking sustainable development and social development is discussed in Chapter 2. O'Riordan (1976) suggested that EIA comprised 'value judgements of a policy-making kind superimposed on the findings of pure scientists'; the same thing may be said of SIA, only more so. Some SIA may be quite objective, but it is wise to bear in mind that it is seldom wholly free from pressures, and is often part of political manoeuvring. Special interest groups may use SIA to legitimize and support their own wishes unless care is taken to ensure it is independent (Rickson *et al.*, 1990).

While a 'core' of SIA remains distinct, there is much overlap with other impact assessment fields. SIA has drawn a good deal on environmental sociology (Dunlap and Catton, 1979), human ecology, social evaluation, studies of social indicators (*see* Glossary), and other social science fields; however, as Freudenburg (1986: 463) observed, it is '. . . not merely an area of empirical social science; it also draws from and contributes to the policy-making process'.

SIA, it must be stressed, is still evolving theoretically and in its practice. Critics argue that:

- it still needs more conceptual development
- it is desirable it be better integrated with EIA, technology assessment and other impact assessment fields
- it must better relate with recent social theory and research
- practitioners must understand what happens to knowledge in the political process of applying it to development if SIA is to improve
- there is a need to better apply SIA to programme and policy levels of decision-making and planning.

The relationship between SIA and other impact assessment fields, notably EIA, has been rather uncertain (*see* Figure 1.1). Some have seen it as an integral component of EIA, others hold it to be a separate process (Kirkpatrick and Lee, 1997: 7). SIA has developed more slowly than EIA and, even though the stated policy in the USA and elsewhere is to integrate the two, this has often not been effective. A late-1980s study of environmental impact statements (EISs) – the 'results' of impact assessments in the USA – revealed that many had little, if any, 'social' component (Culhane *et al.*, 1987). SIAs worldwide have often been of poor quality and have had little impact on project, programme or policy decision-making. This is due to a variety of reasons, including: uncertainty in some countries about its legal status; problems comparing results because of a plethora of methodologies; and the ability of special interest groups to manipulate findings and to side-line what they do not agree with. SIA has also been slow to make use of what is known about community (*see* Glossary) and cultural change. Freudenburg (1986: 452) felt that SIA tended to focus on the consequences of technical change and environmental change and should widen its coverage.

Some authorities seek to combine social and economic impact assessment (SEIA); however, this is not a common approach. NEPA argues that the two are distinct (*see* http://www.gsa.gov/pbs/pt/call-in/factshet/1098b/10_98b_3.htm (May, 2000). More widespread at present is a tendency to integrate SIA with EIA, usually with SIA in a 'minor' and EIA a 'major' role. This is more likely with policy-makers and those concerned with legislation.

Well-established and expanding fields – evaluation research, social evaluation, or evaluation – focus on projects programmes and policies (Gosling

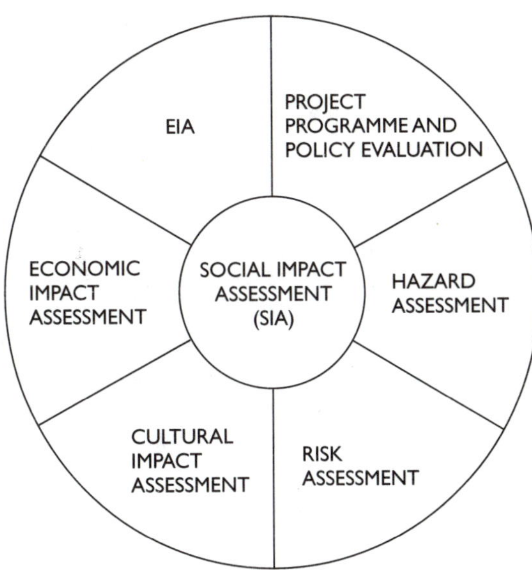

FIGURE 1.1 The relationship of SIA with other impact assessment fields
Although the 'core' of SIA is relatively discrete, it overlaps other impact assessment fields and evaluation studies, sharing techniques, expertise, literature and so on. The segments are drawn as discrete fields, but most overlap with some, if not all, other fields. Some fields are not included in Figure 1.1 through lack of space – for example: technology assessment; strategic environmental assessment; social soundness analysis; social assessment; futures studies; and monitoring.

and Edwards, 1995). There is a tendency for evaluation practitioners to talk of conducting 'impact assessment'; however, this is seldom the structured, anticipatory and iterative process recognized by most impact assessors. Evaluation, like SIA, may cover economic, social, cultural, psychological and other social studies fields, but the end product is usually a report to the commissioning body (rather than an SIA-type impact statement). Project appraisal is another well-established allied field, and one in which a large number of non-governmental organizations (NGOs) and consultants are active (Fernandes, 1990; Lee, 1996). Evaluation and project, programme or policy appraisal can be said to deal with 'existing' projects, programmes and policies, assessing expected and intentional change, often checking to see whether goals have been accomplished and are being maintained; whereas SIA is more concerned with predicting the unexpected impacts of 'proposed' developments. Evaluation is thus more retrospective (post-development studies), concerned with taking stock of the situation after something has been set in motion; and SIA is, ideally, anticipatory (pre-development studies). A glance through any of the periodicals devoted to project, programme or policy evaluation or appraisal reveals the use of many techniques familiar to the SIA practitioner, although some, like log-frame analysis (*see* Chapter 6) are of less value for anticipatory impact assessment. Some of the techniques developed by evaluation studies for collecting data on difficult-to-measure processes, and for establishing how NGOs and other bodies network and communicate, are of value to SIA. Evaluation also overlaps with monitoring (systematic and continuous assessment of progress), which also interrelates with SIA (Gosling and Edwards, 1995).

A 'social audit' is an assessment of the social impact and ethical behaviour of an organization, project, programme or policy in relation to its objectives and those of the people involved. A social audit has more in common with eco-auditing than SIA, and tends to use indicators proposed by the stakeholders to make an assessment. There is less stress on forecasting than with SIA. So, SIA (if well conducted) is of greater value as a planning tool, because it has the potential to prevent problems. A 'social assessment' (SA) is an assessment of the community, designed to ascertain how its people relate to one another, and how decisions are made. An SA describes current conditions; unlike SIA, it does not attempt to forecast outcomes and impacts.

SIA, it must be stressed, is imperfect; even if it accurately predicts many direct impacts it may miss others, together with some (or even all) indirect and cumulative effects (*see* Chapter 5). There is thus a risk that those unfamiliar with SIA may be given a false sense of security. It should be noted that there may be situations where the application of SIA (and EIA) can have positive and negative impacts, changing how people react, triggering speculation, etc.

The weaknesses of SIA may not be as serious as they first appear, Burdge (1995: 5) argued that being sensitive to social impacts is as important (perhaps more important) than being able to identify them precisely. A less than detailed and accurate SIA may, then, be useful. Improved accuracy of assessment is a goal, but so must be the ability to get the findings accepted and acted upon by decision-makers and planners. Half-hearted SIA must not be allowed to placate decision-makers, official watchdogs or the public.

The principles of SIA

Between the early 1970s and 1995 there was little uniformity in approach or methodology. Proposals from the Interorganizational Committee on Guidelines and Principles for Social Impact Assessment have helped shape and guide SIA since the mid-1990s (Burdge *et al.*, 1995). Seebohm (1997) provided a precis of those principles (*see* Box 1.2), however he was critical of some, and noted that they contain contradictions (in particular, points 9 and 6). In the USA guidelines and principles for SIA currently adopted by the government are based on those of the Interorganizational Committee on Guidelines and Principles for Social Impact Assessment. These have been published on the internet (*see* Box 1.3), and should be consulted by anyone seriously interested in SIA.

Box 1.2 Aims of SIA

1. Identify the main features of the proposed development project, programme, policy, or whatever.
2. Identify the types and numbers of people involved.
3. Identify data sources: use published scientific literature, secondary data and primary data from the affected area (*see* Glossary for definitions of primary and secondary data).
4. Plan for gaps in the data.
5. Identify the impacts the proposed development will have on various segments of the population.
6. Involve the public: identify and involve all the potentially affected groups and individuals.
7. Analyse impact equity: identify who are 'winners' and who are 'losers', and emphasize the vulnerability of under-represented groups.
8. Focus the assessment: deal with the issues and concerns that really count, not those that are easy to handle.
9. Identify methods and assumptions and define significance in advance: define how the SIA was conducted, what assumptions were used and how significance was selected.
10. Provide feedback on social impacts to project planners and identify problems that can be solved with changes to the proposed action or alternatives.
11. Establish monitoring and mitigation programmes: manage uncertainty by monitoring and mitigating adverse impacts.
12. Make development more socially sound.

Source: various (including Seebohm, 1997: Figure 1, p. 239)

The history of SIA

Attempts to appraise the existing and possible future social consequences of development and change are not new. Some argue that SIA is a part of policy analysis and has in large part (conceptually) evolved independently of EIA (Dietz, 1987: 54). Although there had been studies of the social impacts of development and change before the 1969 National Environmental Policy Act (NEPA) was passed by the US Congress in January 1970, virtually all were retrospective and mostly *ad hoc* (Colson, 1971; Cottrell, 1951; Sharp, 1952). The expression 'social impact assessment' (and its abbreviation SIA) seem to have first appeared in 1973 (Burdge, 1995: 14) during discussions on the Trans-Alaska (oil) Pipeline. NEPA was clearly an important catalyst.[4] A

[4] NEPA called upon US federal agencies to ensure that, before any activity 'likely to significantly affect the quality of the human environment', a balanced, interdisciplinary and publicly available assessment of the likely impacts be undertaken. NEPA does not require assessment to make a 'best decision' or to veto development, it does, however, insist that identified impacts and available development options be disclosed to the public, and that the EIS be considered by policy-makers. It should also be noted that of the four and a half pages of NEPA, only one half page discusses impacts on people, the rest focuses on environmental impacts (Burdge, 1994: 65). The relevant section of NEPA regulations

Box 1.3 An outline of NEPA's suggested principles for structuring SIA

1. Involve the diverse public: basically, involve all groups in decision-making, even those that are reluctant or marginalized.
2. Analyse impact equity: establish who 'wins' and who 'loses'.
3. Focus the assessment: through scoping (*see* Chapter 3); ensure that SIA deals with the issues that really matter, rather than those that are easy to assess or politically correct.
4. Identify methods and assumptions: an SIA must report clearly what assumptions it makes, and describe the methods and techniques it uses.
5. Define significance: make explicit what is deemed significant and why.
6. Provide feedback to project planners: this should be active, co-ordinated feedback between SIA assessors and planners/commissioners.
7. Use proper SIA practitioners: it is vital to use social scientists with the appropriate skills, experience, education/training for the type of assessment being undertaken.
8. Establish monitoring and mitigation programmes: SIA should help set up programmes to mitigate social impacts and monitor how these work.
9. Identify data sources: so that assessment can be judged/checked. Data sources should be declared; consequently, those interviewed should be warned, in case they might wish to withhold information that could threaten them (in such cases sources might be disguised).
10. Plan for gaps in data: SIAs always have gaps; where these can be identified, they should be declared and discussed with the commissioning body to see if the missing data makes safe/effective decision-making a problem. It may be that special efforts will have to be made to fill the data gaps. Of course, there may be gaps that are unknown, so those using SIA must not develop a sense of false security.

Source: partly based on a NEPA factsheet (January 2000) available at http://www.gsa.gov/pbs/pt/call-in/factshet/1098b/10_98b_4.htm

clause in NEPA (in Section 102) calls for federal agencies to make integrated use of the natural *and* social sciences to prepare an environmental impact statement (EIS). (An EIS is the end product of an impact assessment, the published results and recommendations which should also explore alternatives to the proposed development.)

Since 1970, the public and non-governmental organizations (NGOs) in developed countries have kept up pressure on authorities for EIA and SIA. In practice SIA has not had anywhere near the same level of support and official acceptance, especially legal support, as EIA (Burdge and Vanclay, 1996: 65). Between the 1970s and mid-1980s there was relatively little appli-

requiring SIA is Section 40 CFR 1508.14; Executive Orders No. 12898 and No. 12072 strengthen requirements and Executive Order No. 11988 calls for community involvement. In 1994 US Executive Order No. 12898 called for federal actions to address environmental justice in minority populations and low income groups, and to check the social effects of federal actions.

cation of SIA to programmes, policies or social change issues, and community responses to impacts were poorly understood. Before the late 1980s SIAs were mainly functionalist, community focused and applied at the project level; subsequently, interest has grown in using it to assess economic impacts, inter-group conflicts, political economy issues, impacts of new technology and healthcare (Burdge, 1995; Finsterbusch, 1985; Gale, 1984). Also, before the 1980s, many SIAs simply involved the application of what Dietz called 'traditional social analysis tools' (1987: 55). In 1973 and 1978 the US Council on Environmental Quality (CEQ) issued guidelines to improve the preparation of EISs, which stressed that all impacts on the human environment, including social, were to be considered. These 1978 CEQ guidelines in effect provided a legal foundation for SIA in the USA, although it was not specifically mandated (Burdge, 1995: 9; US Council on Environmental Quality, 1978).

During 1970 the US Department of the Interior had released an EIS for the Trans-Alaska Pipeline that was to run from Prudhoe Bay on the Arctic Sea to Valdez on Prince William Sound. Two NGOs, Friends of the Earth and the Environmental Defense Fund, went to Court against the consortium of US and Canadian companies seeking a permit for the pipeline and the US Department of the Interior, contending that the EIS had failed to deal adequately with the social and economic impacts that would affect indigenous peoples (Burdge, 1995: 4). After a delay of three years, an improved EIS was released, but this still addressed socio-economic impacts only poorly, to the extent that one of the Inuit tribal chiefs who was responsible for some of the land to be traversed by the pipeline commented that, although the impacts on the permafrost and wildlife had been studied reasonably thoroughly, there had been no attempt to assess the effect on the customs and ways of his people. (This exchange helped to raise the profile of SIA in North America.)

SIA in the USA received another boost in 1983 when the US Nuclear Regulatory Commission undertook an impact assessment before re-opening one of the Three Mile Island nuclear reactors that had come close to meltdown (in a populated area), the radioactive leak forcing an evacuation and causing much concern. A citizen's group's legal action forced the consideration of social and psychological impacts, otherwise the EIS would have been restricted to physical impacts (Llewellyn and Freudenburg, 1989; Sills *et al.*, 1982). Further progress was made in 1985 when the Northern Cheyenne Tribe fought a court action against the granting of a large federal coal exploitation lease because the EIA had included virtually no coverage of social, cultural or economic impacts. The tribe won its action, preventing the mining and provoking the judge to criticise the US Department of the Interior for an inadequate SIA (Freudenburg, 1986: 455).

Canada established an Environmental Assessment and Review Process (EARP) in 1973. This body, like the CEQ in the USA, has been influential in the development of SIA. Rather than just contract a social scientist or two to add the social dimension to an EIA, EARP put an emphasis on assessment aimed at helping those people affected by change to adjust.

SIA came to the forefront during the 1974–78 Berger Commission Inquiry. Justice Berger was appointed by the Government of Canada to examine the social, economic and environmental impacts of the proposed Mackenzie Valley Pipeline (Berger, 1977). This was to convey oil and natural gas from beneath the Beaufort Sea in the Arctic to British Columbia and Alberta in mid-Canada, crossing lands inhabited by some 30,000 native peoples. The Commission included in-depth hearings in local villages (in local languages), and granted funding to support the native peoples to make their case (Berger, 1983; Gamble, 1978; Gray and Gray, 1977). Mr Justice Berger's recommendation was that development be delayed for 10 years to allow settlement of native claims. The inquiry had considerable impact on Canadian policy-making, helped to establish the value of SIA and taught the lesson that it must genuinely involve local people.

Since the 1990s the Canadian Government has tended to seek to integrate SIA into EIA; the same could be said for Australia, but for Europe the position is still a little unclear. In Australia before the 1970s there was a failure to assess adequately the impacts on those Aboriginal peoples affected by developments. An attempt was made to rectify this during the Commonwealth Government-funded Ranger Uranium Mining Inquiry, and an SIA of the region affected by large-scale natural resources exploitation was undertaken (Australian Institute of Aboriginal Studies, 1984). Since the 1970s, SIA has been widely applied to developments affecting Aboriginal peoples in Australia. There have been similar uses for SIA in New Zealand, where Maori needs and perceptions were initially largely overlooked by assessors (Fookes, 1981a and 1981b) (*see* Chapter 8 for further discussion of SIA and indigenous peoples). In Australia, states like Queensland have been seeking actively to improve SIA practice since the mid-1980s (Dale and Lane, 1995).

During 1973, the Council of the American Sociological Association (ASA) formed a committee to develop standardized and systematic guidelines for sociological contributions to EISs – some have hailed the chair of this committee, C.P. Wolf, as the 'founder' of SIA (Dunlap and Catton, 1979; Freudenburg, 1986: 455; Wolf, 1975). The committee disbanded without making formal recommendations, though it did help prompt the ASA to establish an Environmental Sociology Section. In 1974 Wolf became convenor of the *ad hoc* Inter-agency Working Group on SIA and, in the same year, he organized a session on SIA at the annual meeting of the Environmental Design Research Association, which produced an influential publication (Wolf, 1974). During 1975 he edited a special issue of *Environment and Behavior* on SIA (Vol. 7, No. 6), and in 1976 established the 'Social Impact Assessment Newsletter'. In 1981 the International Association for Impact Assessment (IAIA) was founded, providing an important forum for the exchange of EIA, SIA, technology impact assessment, and hazard and risk assessment news, views and research findings. The IAIA now plays a central role in the promotion, improvement and regulation of impact assessment, including SIA, worldwide; it can reasonably be described as the area's main professional body.

Guides to SIA methods and procedures came thick and fast between the late 1960 and mid-1980s (e.g. Finsterbusch and Wolf, 1977; Finsterbusch, *et al.*, 1983); unfortunately, some were 'cookbooks' that did little to improve theory or methods. This 'blossoming' of North American SIA was related to a proliferation of highway, dam, pipeline, and other large construction projects and boomtowns associated with natural resource exploitation. The US Federal Highway Administration produced about one-third of the total, with the US Corps of Engineers probably the next most active in commissioning SIA, and the USDA Forest Service also making considerable use of it. In 1982 the First International Social Impact Assessment Conference was held in Vancouver, Canada, and by 1983 many US federal agencies had developed SIA procedures and regulations. By the early 1990s SIA was a common component of the policy-making process, for example being used to help decide the management of old-growth forests in the US Pacific northwest (Clark and Stankey, 1994; Stone, 1993).

Late-1970s recession and spending cutbacks slowed, and perhaps helped re-focus, the evolution of SIA (Llewellyn *et al.*, 1975). By the mid-1980s the Reagan administration had made funding less readily available and construction declined, reducing demand for impact assessments (Finsterbusch, 1995: 237). The trend was one of retrenchment, although a few new demands for SIA began to appear, notably for hazardous waste disposal or treatment, technology innovation, nuisance activity siting, tourism and aid to developing countries. A consequence of the retrenchment was that there was a shift to an increased amount of reflection and research on methods, approaches and theory, rather than the hurried and sometimes shoddy consultancy of the previous decade or so.

Some of the first international development planning guidelines to stress the importance of assessing social and socio-economic impacts were promoted by the United Nations Environment Programme in 1980. The US Agency for International Development (USAID), America's overseas aid agency, had issued guidelines for something similar to SIA in 1975: social soundness analysis (SSA). SSA has three components: assessing the compatibility of proposals with the local socio-cultural conditions (i.e. 'is it feasible, is it appropriate?'); establishing the likelihood that the development will diffuse to good effect (checking the spread effect); and checking the distribution of positive and negative impacts among various groups, locally and beyond ('Social Impact Assessment Newsletter' 1976, No. 46: p. 6). These aid-related assessments have often been feasibility studies, or retrospective social analyses, aimed at establishing whether cultural or institutional factors would hinder development, rather than predicting significant potential social impacts (Finsterbusch, 1995: 239) (*see* Chapter 7). SSA guidelines have been issued by various agencies (such as USAID, 1978). From the mid-1980s the World Bank, the Inter-American Development Bank, and increasingly other aid agencies, began to require EIA and SIA to check before funding development projects.

At the start of the new millennium, SIA has been evolving for more than

30 years, and seems likely to become more widely used as a tool by those seeking social development and sustainable development. SIA is likely to become better integrated with planning and policy making, and other impact assessment approaches (Bissett, 1996). SIA in the USA has tended to evolve into a relatively jargon-free management tool, part of the purpose of which is to inform citizens about proposals (Murdock *et al.*, 1986). However, it has been criticised for being 'atheoretical', descriptive and insufficiently explanatory (Muth and Lee, 1986), and that is still largely the case.

REFERENCES

Anon. (1993) Social impact assessment of investment/acquisition of technology projects in developing countries, with particular reference to the position of women. *Public Enterprise* **13(3–4)**, 239–56.

Australian Institute of Aboriginal Studies (1984) *Aborigines and Uranium*. Australian Government Publishing Service, Canberra.

Becker, H.A. (1997) *Social Impact Assessment: method and experience in Europe, North America and the developing world*. University College London Press, London.

Berger, T.R. (Mr Justice) (1977) *Northern Frontier, Northern Homeland: the report of the Mackenzie Valley Pipeline Inquiry* (2 vols). Government Supplies and Services Canada, Ottawa.

Berger, T.R. (1983) Energy resources development and human values. *Canadian Journal of Community and Mental Health* **1(1)**, 21–31.

Bissett, R. (1996) Social impact assessment and its future. *Mining and Environmental Management* **4(1)**, 9–11.

Buchan, D. and **Rivers, M.J.** (1990) Social impact assessment: development and application in New Zealand. *Impact Assessment Bulletin* **8(4)**, 97–105.

Burdge, R.J. (1994) *A Conceptual Approach to Social Impact Assessment: a collection of writings by Rabel J. Burdge and colleagues*. Social Ecology Press, Middleton (WI).

Burdge, R.J. (1995) *A Community Guide to Social Impact Assessment*. Social Ecology Press, Middleton (WI).

Burdge, R.J., Fricke, P., Finsterbusch, K., Freudenburg, W.R., Gramling, R., Holden, A., Llewellyn, L.G., Petterson, J.S., Thompson, J. and **Williams, G.** (1995) Guidelines and principles for social impact assessment: Interorganizational Committee on Guidelines and Principles for Social Impact Assessment. *Environmental Impact Assessment Review* **15(1)**, 11–43.

Burdge, R.J. and **Vanclay, F.** (1996) Social impact assessment: a contribution to the state of the art series. *Impact Assessment* **14(1)**, 59–86.

Clark, R.N. and **Stankey, G.H.** (1994) FEMAT's social assessment: framework, key concepts and lessons learned *Journal of Forestry* **92(4)**, 32–5.

Colson, E. (1971) *The Social Consequences of Resettlement: the impact of the Kariba Resettlement on the Gwembe Tonga*. Manchester University Press, Manchester.

Cottrell, W.F. (1951) Death by dieselization. *American Sociological Review* **16(3)**, 358–65.

Council on Environmental Quality (1978) *Regulations for Implementing Pre-Procedural Provisions of the National Environmental Policy Act (NEPA)*. CEQ, Washington (DC).

Culhane, P.J., Friesma, H.P. and **Beecher, J.A.** (1987) *Forecasts and Environmental*

Decisionmaking: the content and predictive accuracy of environmental impact statements. Westview, Boulder.

Dale, A.P. and **Lane, M.B.** (1995) Queensland's Social Impact Assessment Unit: its origins and prospects. *Queensland Planner* **35(3)**, 5–11.

Dietz, T. (1987) Theory and method in social impact assessment. *Sociological Inquiry* **57(1)**, 54–69.

Dunlap, R.E. and **Catton, W.R. jnr** (1979) Environmental sociology. *Annual Review of Sociology* **5**, 243–7.

Ellis, D. (1989) *Environments at Risk: case studies of impact assessment*. Springer, New York (NY).

Fernandes, A.J. (1990) Introducing social evaluation for improved project performance: a suggested checklist approach. *Project Appraisal* **5(1)**, 11–18.

Finsterbusch, K. (1985) The state of the art in social impact assessment. *Environment and Behavior* **17(2)**, 193–221.

Finsterbusch, K. (1995) In praise of SIA – a personal view of the field of social impact assessment: feasibility, justification, history, methods, issues. *Impact Assessment* **13(3)**, 229–52.

Finsterbusch, K., **Llewellyn, L.G.** and **Wolf, C.P.** (1983) *Social Impact Assessment Methods*. Sage, Beverly Hills (California).

Finsterbusch, K. and **Wolf, C.P.** (eds) (1977) *Methodology of Social Impact Assessment* (1st edn). Dowden, Hutchinson and Ross, Stroudsburg (Pennsylvania).

Fookes, T.W. (1981a) *Monitoring Social and Economic Impact: Huntley case study, final report series*. University of Waikato, Hamilton.

Fookes, T.W. (1981b) *Expectations and Related Findings, 1973–81*. University of Waikato, Hamilton.

Freudenburg, W.R. (1986) Social impact assessment. *Annual Review of Sociology* **12**, 451–78.

Gale, R.P. (1984) The evolution of social impact assessment: post-functionalist view. *Impact Assessment Bulletin* **3(2)**, 27–36.

Gamble, D.J. (1978) The Berger Inquiry: an impact assessment process. *Science* **199(3)**, 946–52.

Geisler, C.C. (1993) Rethinking SIA: why ex ante research isn't enough. *Society and Natural Resources* **6(4)**, 327–38.

Gismondi, M. (1997) Sociology and environmental impact assessment. *Canadian Journal of Sociology* **22(4)**, 457–79.

Gosling, L. and **Edwards, M.** (1995) *Toolkits: a practical guide to assessment, monitoring, review and evaluation* (Save the Children Fund Development Manual No. 5). Save the Children Fund, London.

Gray, J.A. and **Gray, P.J.** (1977) The Berger Report: its impact on northern pipelines and decision making in northern development. *Canadian Public Policy* **3(4)**, 509–14.

Green, E.C. (1986) *Practising Development Anthropology*. Westview, Boulder (CO).

Harrop, D.O. and **Nixon J.A.** (1999) *Environmental Assessment in Practice*. Routledge, London.

Holling, C.S. (ed.) (1978) *Adaptive Environmental Assessment and Management*. Wiley, Chichester.

Kirkpatrick, C. and **Lee, N.** (eds) (1997) *Sustainable Development in a Developing World: integrating socio-economic appraisal and environmental assessment*. Edward Elgar, Cheltenham.

Lee, N. (1996) Environmental assessment and socio-economic appraisal in development. *Project Appraisal* **11(4)**, 214–66.

Llewellyn, L.G. and **Freudenburg, W.R.** (1989) Legal requirements for social impact assessment: assessing the social science fallout from Three Mile Island. *Society and Natural Resources* **2(3)**, 193–208.

Llewellyn, L.G., Bunten, E., Goodman, C., Hare, G., Mach, R. and **Swisher, R.** (1975) The role of social impact assessment in highway planning. *Environment and Behavior* **7(3)**, 285–304.

Murdock, S.H., Leistritz, F.L. and **Hamm, R.R.** (1986) The state of socioeconomic impact analysis in the United States: an examination of existing evidence, limitations and opportunities for alternative futures. *Impact Assessment Bulletin* **4(3–4)**, 101–32.

Muth, R.M. and **Lee, R.G.** (1986) Social impact assessment in natural resource decision making: toward a structural paradigm. *Impact Assessment Bulletin* **4(3–4)**, 170–83.

O'Riordan, T. (1976) *Environmentalism.* Pion, London.

Rickson, R.E., Western, J.S. and **Burdge, R.J.** (1990) Social impact assessment: knowledge and development. *Environmental Impact Assessment* **10(1)**, 1–10.

Seebohm, K. (1997) Guiding principles for the practice of social assessment in the Australian water industry. *Impact Assessment* **15(3)**, 235–44.

Sharp, L. (1952) Steel axes for stone age Australians, in E. Spicer (ed.), *Human Problems in Technological Change.* Russell Sage, New York, 69–90.

Shields, M.A. (1975) Social impact studies: an expository analysis. *Environment and Behavior* **7(3)**, 265–84.

Sills, D.L., Wolf, C.P. and **Shelovski, V.B.** (eds) (1982) *Accident at Three Mile Island: the human dimensions.* Westview, Boulder (CO).

Stone, R. (1993) Spotted owl plan kindles debate on salvage logging. *Science* **261(5119)**, 287.

Tester, F.L. and **Mykes, W.** (eds) (1981) *Social Impact Assessment: theory, method and practice.* Detselig Enterprises, Ltd, Calgary (Canada).

Torgerson, D. (1980) *Industrialization and Assessment: social impact assessment as a social phenomenon.* York University Publications in Northern Studies, Toronto.

US Council on Environmental Quality (1978) *Regulations for Implementing the Procedural Provisions of the National Environmental Policy Act* (40CFR 1500–1501). CEQ, Washington (DC).

USAID (1978) *AID Handbook.* US Agency for International Development, Government Printing Office, Washington.

Wilson, E.O. (1998) *Consilience: the unity of knowledge.* Little, Brown and Co., Boston (MA).

Wolf, C.P. (1974) *Social Impact Assessment.* Dowden, Huchinson and Ross, Stroudsburg (PA).

Wolf, C.P. (1975) Report of the Committee on Environmental Sociology. *ASA Footnotes* No. 3 (August 1975), 3–22.

Further reading and resources

Introductions, guidebooks and handbooks

Armstrong, J. and **Harman, W.** (1979) *Strategies for Conducting Social Assessment.* Westview, Boulder (CO).

Asian Development Bank (1992) *Guidelines for Social Analysis of Development Projects*. Asian Development Bank, Manila.

Bauer, E.J. (1978) *Assessing the Social Effects of Public Works Projects*. Board of Engineers for Rivers and Harbors, US Corps of Engineers, Fort Belvoir (VA).

Becker, H.A. (1997) *Social Impact Assessment: method and experience in Europe, North America and the developing world*. University College London Press, London.

Branch, K., Hooper, D.A., Thompson, J. and **Creighton, J.C.** (1984) *Guide to Social Assessment: a framework for assessing social change* (1st edn 1981). Westview, Boulder (CO).

Bryan, C. and **Hendee, J.** (1983) *SIA in US Forest Service Decisions: background and proposed principles*. US Dept of Agriculture, Washington (DC).

Burdge, R.J. (1994a) *A Community Guide to Social Impact Assessment* (revised edn 1999). Social Ecology Press, Middleton (WI).

Burdge, R.J. (1994b) *A Conceptual Approach to Social Impact Assessment: a collection of writings by Rabel J. Burdge and colleagues*. Social Ecology Press, Middleton (WI).

Burkhardt, D.F. and **Ithelson, W.H.** (eds) (1978) *Environmental Assessment of Socioeconomic Systems*. Plenum, New York (NY).

Canter, L.W., Athinston, S.F. and **Leistritz, F.L.** (1985) *Impact of Growth: a guide for socio-economic impact assessment and planning*. Lewis Publishers, Chelsea (MI).

Christiansen, K. (1976) *Social Impacts of Land Development: an initial approach for estimating environmental impacts*. The Urban Institute, Washington.

Duncan, J. (1976) *Methodology and Guidelines for Assessing Social Impacts of Developments*. Duncan and Jones Inc., Berkeley (CA).

Dunning, J.H. (1978) *A Systematic Approach to SIA*. Westview, Boulder.

Finsterbusch, K., Llewellyn, L. and **Wolf, C.P.** (eds) (1983) *Social Impact Assessment Methods*. Sage, Beverly Hills (CA).

Finsterbusch, K. (1982) *Understanding Social Impacts: assessing the effects of public projects* (1st edn 1980). Sage, Beverly Hills (CA).

Finsterbusch, K. and **Wolf, C.P.** (1981) *Methodology of Social Impact Assessment* (1st edn 1977). Dowden, Hutchinson and Ross, Stroudsburg (PA).

Fitzsimmons, S.J., Stuart, L.I. and **Wolf, C.P.** (1977) *Social Assessment Manual: a guide to the preparation of the social well-being account for planning water resource projects*. Westview, Boulder (CO).

Francis, P. and **Jacobs, S.** (1999) Institutionalizing social analysis at the World Bank. *Environmental Impact Assessment Review* **19(3)**, 341–57.

Gosling, L. and **Edwards, M.** (1995) *Toolkits: a practical guide to assessment, monitoring, review and evaluation* (Development Manual No. 5). Save the Children Fund, London.

Halstead, J.M., Chase, R.A., Murdoch, S.H. and **Leistritz, F.L.** (1984) *Socioeconomic Impact Management: design and implementation*. Westview, Boulder (CO).

Harrop, D.O. and **Nixon, J.A.** (1999) *Environmental Assessment in Practice*. Routledge, London.

Integrated Resource Planning Committee (1977) *Social and Economic Impact Assessment Guidelines*. Co-published by the Integrated Resource Planning Committee and Government of British Columbia (Canada: bbatchelar@trafford.com).

Lang, R. and **Armour, A.** (1981) *The Assessment and Review of Social Impacts*. Federal Environmental Assessment Office, Ottawa.

Leistritz, F.L. and **Murdock, S.H.** (1981) *The Socioeconomic Impact of Resource Development: methods for assessment*. Westview, Boulder (CO).

McEvoy, J. III and **Dietz, T.J.** (eds) (1977) *Assessing Social Impacts*. Wiley, New York (NY).

Melser, P. (1983) *Assessing Social Impacts: a practical guide*. Ministry of Works and Development, Wellington.

Morris, P. (1977) *Guidelines for Social Impact Assessment Methodology*. Petro-Canada, Calgary (Canada).

National Research Council (1977) *Staffing and Management for Social, Economic, and Environmental Impact Assessments*. NRC Transportation Research Board, Washington.

Seebohm, K. (1997) Guiding principles for the practice of social assessment in the Australian water industry. *Impact Assessment* **15(3)**, 233–57.

Soderstrom, E.J. (1981) *Social Impact Assessment: experimental methods and approaches*. Praeger, New York (NY).

Taylor, C.N., Bryan, C.H. and **Goodrich, C.G.** (1995) *Social Assessment: theory, process and techniques* (Studies in Resource Management No. 7) (2nd edn; 1st edn 1990). Centre for Resource Management, Lincoln University (PO Box 56), Taylor Baines Associates, Christchurch (New Zealand).

Tester, F.J. and **Mykes, W.** (eds) (1981) *Social Impact Assessment: theory, method and practice*. Detselig Enterprises Ltd, Calgary (Canada).

Theys, J. (1978) *Environmental Assessment of Socioeconomic Systems*. Plenum, New York.

Togerson, D. (1980) *Social Impact Assessment: moving toward maturity*. York University, Toronto, Ontario.

Vanclay, F. and **Bronstein, D.A.** (eds) (1995) *Environmental and Social Impact Assessment*. Wiley, Chichester.

Vlachos, E., Buckley, W. and **Filstead, W.J.** (1975) *Social Impact Assessment: an overview* (IWRE Paper No. 75, p. 7). Institute for Water Resources, Fort Belvoir (VA).

Voland, M.E. and **Fleischman, W.A.** (eds) (1983) *Sociology and Social Impact Analysis in Federal Resource Management Agencies*. US Department of Agriculture, Forest Service, Washington (DC).

Waiten, M. (1981) *A Guide to Social Impact Assessment*. Research Branch, Corporate Policy, Indian and Northern Affairs, Ottawa KIA OHA.

Wildman, P.H. and **Baker, G.B.** (1985) *The Social Assessment Handbook: how to assess and evaluate the social impact of resource development on local communities*. Social Impacts Publications, Armidale (NSW).

Wilson, E.O. (1998) *Consilience: the unity of knowledge*. Little, Brown and Co., Boston (MA).

Wolf, C.P. (1975) SIA: the state of the art. *Environmental Interactions* **4(2)**, 144–67.

Wolf, C.P. (1976) SIA: the state of the art restated. *Sociological Practice* **1(1)**, 56–70.

Wolf, C.P. (1977) SIA: the state of the art updated. *Social Impact Assessment Newsletter* No. 20, 3–22.

Wolf, C.P. (ed.) (1974) *Social Impact Assessment: man–environment interactions*. Dowden, Hutchinson and Ross, Stroudsburg (PA).

World Bank (1998) *Integrating Social Concerns into Private Decision Making: a review of comparative practices in mining, oil and gas sectors* (World Bank Discussion Paper No. 384). World Bank, Washington.

Special issues

Special issue (1990) of *Environmental Impact Assessment Review* **10(1–2)** is devoted to social impact assessment.

Special issue (1995) of *Project Appraisal* **10(3)** is devoted to social impact assessment.

Bibliographies

Bowles, R.T. (1991) *Social Impact Assessment in Small Communities: an integrative review of selected literature.* Butterworths, Toronto.

Carley, M.J. (1984) *Social Impact Assessment: a cross-disciplinary guide to the literature.* Westview, Boulder (CO).

Carley, M.J. and **Bustelo, E.S.** (1984) *Social Impact Assessment and Monitoring: a guide to the literature* Westview, Boulder (reviews a large number of references).

Glickfeld, M., Whiney, T. and **Grigsby, T.E. III** (1977) *A Selective Analytical Bibliography for Social Impact Assessment.* Department of Civil Engineering, Stanford University, Palo Alto (CA).

Leistritz, F.L. and **Ekstrom, B.L.** (1986) *Social Impact Assessment and Management: an annotated bibliography.* Garland, New York (over 1000 references with notes).

Shields, M.A. (1974) *Social Impact Assessment: an annotated bibliography* (IWR paper No. 74–P6). US Army Engineer Institute for Water Resources, Fort Belvoir (VA).

Qualitative social research approaches

Bryman, A. and **Burgess, R.** (eds) (1999) *Qualitative Research* (four vols). Sage, London.

Flick, U. (1998) *An Introduction to Qualitative Research.* Sage, London.

Vanclay, F.M. (1989) *Social Impact Assessment Bibliography, a Database and Interrogation Program for DOS-based Personal Computers.* Centre for Rural Social Research, Charles Stuart University, Locked Bag 678, Wagga Wagga, NSW 2678 (Australia) (updated monthly: US$50 individuals, US$100 institutions; e-mail: fvanclay@csu.edu.au).

Journals

The following English-language journals often contain SIA articles.

Accounting, Auditing & Accountability Journal
Economy and Society
EIA Review
Environment and Behavior
Environment & Planning: Society & Space
Evaluation
Evaluation & Program Planning
Evaluation and Program Planning
Evaluation Review
Impact Assessment Bulletin (changed its title in 1994 to *Impact Assessment* and, in 1998, merged with *Project Appraisal* to form *Impact Assessment and Project Appraisal*, the journal of the International Association for Impact Assessment)
Journal of Risk Analysis
Project Appraisal (pre-1998)
Risk Analysis
Rural Sociology
Social Audit (Social Audit Ltd, London W1V 3DG)

Social Impact Assessment Newsletter (1976–82), often cited omitting the word *Newsletter*
Social Indicators Research
Society and Natural Resources
Social Indicators Research
Socio-Economic Planning Sciences
Sociological Review
Technological Forecasting and Social Change
The Futurist
Foresight: the Journal of Futures Studies, Strategic Thinking and Policy (Camford Publishing, UK)

Internet sources

Internet sources frequently change and material is seldom, if ever, subject to the same degree of 'peer review' as journal articles or published books; they should therefore be treated with a little caution.
Guidelines and Principles for Social Impact Assessment: prepared by the Inter-organizational Committee on Guidelines and Principles for Social Impact Assessment (May 1994) and available from http://www.gsa.jov/pbs/pt/call-in/siagide.htm
NEPA SIA call-in website, 1999: http://www.gsa.gov/pbs/pt/call-in/factshet/1098b/10_98b_7.htm
EIA Newsletter: contains some SIA articles; available from University of Manchester, Manchester MI3 9PL or http://www.artman.ac.uk/EIA/n116.htm
International Association for Impact Assessment (IAIA): http://IAIA.ext.Nodak.edu/IAIA
Australian EIA Network (1994) *Review of Commonwealth EIA – Social Impact Assessment* (updated 1997): reviews SIA in general and focuses on practice in Australia, New Zealand, Canada, the USA and the EU, at http://www.environment.gov.au/epg/eianet/eia/sia/sia.html
US National Environmental Policy Act (NEPA) 'call in' on SIA: http://www.gsa.gov/pbs/pt/call-in/factshet/1098b/1098bfact.htm
Information on SIA courses:
http://www.geography.unimelb.edu.au/12180298.htm
http://www.unimelb.edu.au/HB/subjects/121–004.html
http://www.topnz.ac.nz/info/courses/72297.html
SIA of technology: http://www.psu.edu/sts/courses/spr97/233/. . .ology.assessment/social.impact/index.html
Papers on specific aspects of SIA, cultural impact assessment, socioeconomic impacts etc. (charge for e-mail transmission, approx. C$10 per article at time of writing): Hardy Stevenson & Associates, http://home.echo-on.net/~hsa/tnt.htm
Accounting, Auditing & Accountability Journal (vol. 6 onwards), available from: http://www.mcb.co.uk/liblink/aaaj/jourhome.htm

Economic and social impacts of climate change – 'global warming' (IPCC Working Group III): http://www.ipcc.ch

Central Highlands Region Resource Use Planing Project (Queensland, Australia): information on Queensland SIA and review of other countries' SIA, at http://chris.tag.csiro.au/chrrupp/about/sia

2

THE VALUE OF SIA

The obvious values of SIA are:

- it can predict the likely negative (unwanted) impacts of a proposed development in time to allow these to be avoided or mitigated
- it helps to ensure that positive impacts (benefits and opportunities) are not missed or under-exploited
- it discloses the impacts of previous developments, so that any information already gleaned can be collected and fed into future planning, or used to assist current conflict mediation. SIA has other values too. One of these is as a research tool that can disclose how and why social change takes place and what the future pattern might be. However, it is not a perfect tool; one of its disadvantages is that it is difficult to repeat a study and get reasonably comparable results; another is that it can provide misleading or imprecise findings (Meidinger and Schnaiberg, 1980).

It is easy to be over-critical of SIA; it seeks to do a very difficult thing – predict social change – and, as Wildavsky noted (1996: *xxxv*), '. . . social change is one of the least understood subjects of all time'. It must also be stressed that SIA alone should not determine whether development proceeds; such decisions must be the responsibility of planners, decision-makers and, perhaps, the public. The role of SIA is to 'advise' and 'inform'; it should show the likely risks, benefits and development options available; also, like EIA, it must flag potentially irreversible and dangerous impacts.

In general, western society (*see* Glossary) has social control mechanisms that are weak – SIA has the potential to warn of what is needed sufficiently in advance for effective arrangements to be made. Through processes like SIA, planners and decision-makers can be better informed and perhaps made more accountable, thus improving their contributions. Recently, and not without some controversy, social scientists have claimed that, not only can they improve public involvement in ecosystem management, they can also make it possible to integrate social considerations with natural sciences in order to arrive at a better understanding of ecosystems than would otherwise be possible (Endter-Wada *et al.*, 1998; Force and Machlis, 1997). (Box 2.1 lists some of the arguments put forward in support of SIA.)

Whatever the arguments in its support, SIA cannot be justified if its costs outweigh the value achieved through it, nor if the results are too unreliable. Burdge (1995: 48–51), arguing the case for SIA, listed a number of 'myths' about it. These include:

- doing SIA adds to the cost of development
- doing SIA slows development
- SIA costs more than it is worth
- social impacts are usually obvious, so common sense should show them, making SIA unnecessary
- if impacts cannot accurately be measured, they should be ignored.

These points are often raised by critics, but seem largely unfounded.

Since the 1950s there have been calls for business, development planning and governments to carry out social audits, the aim being to obtain an oversight and review of social performance (Bauer and Fenn, 1973; Blum, 1958; Clark, 1977; Humble, 1973). Social auditing may be defined as periodic examination by independent experts to evaluate the performance of a body or business from the social point of view (looking at, for instance, the impacts of wages policy, products, research and development, employment practices and advertising). In the past these exercises have often been more like public opinion surveys than proper audits or assessments; in recent years, however, techniques and approaches have been much improved. Social auditing and social accounting are at present largely retrospective, whereas SIA seeks to be predictive. It should be noted that eco-auditing is spreading, and might lay a firmer foundation for the spread of social-auditing and SIA. There is a good

Box 2.1 Types of argument put forward in support of SIA

- Utilitarian – SIA can help ensure the greatest good for the greatest number, by increasing the chance of benefits and reducing the likelihood of avoidable costs. It can be used to focus and improve the provision of social services, make technological innovation more effective, and reduce the negative impacts of policies, programmes and projects.
- Justice – SIA helps show what will happen, or is happening, and thus aids judgement of a situation.
- Functionalism – SIA helps to ensure that a development works effectively.
- Democratic decision-making – In a democracy all parties, at least in theory, should share knowledge; SIA facilitates this sharing, helping to inform public and other groups.
- Ethical pluralism – To decide the best development path, all likely impacts need to be weighed.

Source: based on Finsterbusch, 1995: 234–5

deal of overlap between cost–benefit analysis (CBA) and SIA. CBA is, to some extent, predictive like SIA. CBA also has a strong methodological framework, prompting some to question whether SIA has much to offer that cannot be provided by CBA. In an effort to focus CBA on social issues, the field of social cost–benefit analysis (SCBA) has been developed. This still adopts a more economics-focused approach than does SIA.

THE VALUE OF SIA IN SOCIAL DEVELOPMENT

Social development has been defined as '. . . the incorporation of a people-oriented focus into general development efforts' (Marsden *et al.*, 1994: 10). One field in which SIA is likely to be of particular value is the formulation of sustainable development strategies (Hennings, 1996; Seley and Wolpert, 1985). Without supportive social development, sustainable development is unlikely.

Much of the evaluation of efforts to improve social development has been rather retrospective, adopting the approach of 'seeking to learn from experience' and tending to be introspective. Some social development practitioners are critical of SIA, probably through their misconception of what it is (Marsden and Oakley, 1990; Marsden *et al.*, 1998; ODA, 1993).

THE VALUE OF SIA IN POLICY-MAKING AND PLANNING

Policy analysis may be defined as 'analysing public policies to see what went wrong, to learn how to do better' (Wildavsky, 1996: *xxix*). But it has not been good at developing improved and appropriate practices. SIA has the potential to introduce forward-looking and objective assessment. SIA may also be valuable for mediation and conflict management (Manring *et al.*, 1990).

SIA is vulnerable to the criticism that it misses some impacts, is inaccurate and is often applied too late. It has also been attacked for being undertaken by 'outsiders' who do not adequately know the people with whom they are dealing. Some – perhaps most – of the faults of SIA are the result of misuse or careless application, rather than any fault with the concept itself. Burdge (1995: 5) observed that SIA can have a valuable catalytic and oversight role, to help make planning and administration more anticipatory and answerable to the public. It is possible that SIA will show better alternatives, perhaps cheaper and more effective than those that might otherwise be implemented. If it reduces impacts, it should cut development costs (including ongoing insurance charges) and can also suggest contingency measures.

So far, SIA has mainly been applied at project level, i.e. with a site-specific and limited time span focus. Until recently, widespread uncertainty, paucity of reliable data and lack of knowledge, meant that assessors found it easier to cope with small-scale and short-term issues (Wildavsky, 1996: *xxix*).

Increasingly, it is likely to be adopted for programmes and policies dealing with less site-specific and longer-term issues, such as global environmental change, technological innovation and financial policies. Long-term monitoring programmes may grow from SIA foundations. (The value of SIA in social policy-making is discussed in Chapter 4.)

The value of SIA in involving the public in decision-making

It has been argued that involving a community through SIA can help reduce the stress upon it caused by uncertainty (Wenner, 1988). If people feel less helpless, they may gain in confidence in other aspects of their lives. Also, SIA can enable people to feed valuable ideas and knowledge into the decision-making process (Burdge and Vanclay, 1996: 60); knowledge assessment – a subfield of SIA – has developed to enable them to do this. Environmental managers seeking to understand and control the use of natural resources need to be aware of social institutions, property rights, and peoples' capabilities, needs and aspirations; SIA can furnish this information (Berkes and Folke, 1998; Redclift, 1998).

SIA can inform and reassure people, making them less likely to oppose a development, although there may be situations where it has the opposite effect, triggering unwanted reactions such as land speculation, in-migration and resistance. Much depends on how well the SIA is conducted. The value of SIA as a means of empowerment has been widely discussed (see Chapter 4). It can provide people with an effective way to get their views heard – as shown by the Berger Inquiry and the Trans-Alaska Pipeline case discussed in Chapter 1. Without SIA government, large companies would probably behave in a much more one-sided manner. However, SIA is not a magic solution – a lot depends on how, and by whom, it is commissioned, undertaken and overseen. If any of areas are influenced too much by the developer there is a risk that unwanted findings will be played down, local people may be misled, and that less stringent rules and guidelines will be requested (Howitt, 1993).

The value of SIA in conflict management

SIA can be employed to reduce or resolve social, social-environmental and resource use conflicts (Finsterbusch, 1995: 246). To be effective in this, SIA must consider the potential for social conflict or, if that is already apparent, how it will progress. SIA can also be used to deal with perceived (but false) fears, which have the potential to cause conflict. However, Manring *et al.* (1990) voiced concern that SIA often adopted a social systems approach (see Chapter 3), which may not necessarily be able to identify potential conflicts.

Even when SIA is effective, the choices made after referring to it seldom disadvantage the rich and influential. Juslén (1995: 170), reporting on a 1993–94 study of the development and effectiveness of SIA in Finland, noted that in most cases the economically powerful proponent had a clear view of what was the best alternative, and this was usually the one chosen in spite of SIA. In Finland – and, it is fair to say, in many other countries too – SIA has, so far, often been relatively ineffective in influencing decision-making.

In organizations, when things go wrong, it may be difficult to establish fairly who is to blame; scapegoats or outsiders often suffer and the root cause, or causes, are missed. SIA can help identify where things have gone wrong.

THE VALUE OF SIA IN THE QUEST FOR SUSTAINABLE DEVELOPMENT

The value of EIA was stressed at the 1992 UN Conference on Environment and Development (the Rio 'Earth Summit') and in the publications this spawned, notably *Agenda 21*. Attempts to achieve sustainable development will founder if inadequate account is taken of prevailing social and political conditions. There have been attempts to better focus EIA on sustainable development (Htun, 1990), but less attention has been given to the (very considerable) potential of SIA. SIA suggests what social changes are likely and what measures may be needed to establish supportive social institutions crucial for promoting and sustaining sustainable development (Gagnon, 1995; Howitt, 1995). There is increasing interest in monitoring institutional change, applying SIA and, where possible, controlling development to improve governance and promote sustainable development (Vink, 1999). In 1999, the EU commissioned a consortium from the University of Manchester to carry out a sustainability impact assessment ('SIA') of ongoing World Trade Organisation negotiations (see http://europa.eu.int/comm/trade/2000_round/sia.htm).

SIA is now an important part of integrated environmental management, an approach that seeks to deal with all aspects of the environment (Burdge, 1994). Social institutions and attitudes determine how people use their environment. Social factors can cause people to degrade the environment, which may lead to negative social change, leading in turn to more environmental damage. It is therefore important to be able to understand and forecast social impacts. So, SIA has a crucial contribution to make to the drive for sustainable development.

Eco-audit and EIA have spread widely in the last 30 years, but there has been a tendency to neglect the assessment of social impacts. Certainly less has been spent on developing social auditing and SIA than on EIA (Glasson and Heaney, 1993), and it is, effectively, the poor relation of EIA.

The success of SIA in supporting sustainable development and in improving social development will depend largely on developing better methods and frameworks for its application, and on overcoming the institutional resistance that allows planners, decision-makers and powerful special interest groups (notably development promoters) to ignore or water down its recommendations. SIA is, unfortunately, sometimes used by consultancy companies seeking to make a living from it, rather than as an aid to improved decision-making, and by less-scrupulous planners and administrators who are keen to manipulate the public. What is needed is evaluation, together with control systems which ensure that SIA is consistently of a high standard and that its recommendations are acted upon correctly. There have been moves towards these controls in the field of EIA and eco-audit, where professional bodies are seeking to promote the accreditation of assessors and regular evaluation of assessment effectiveness, and to pressure planners and decision-makers into heeding assessment results.

Rakowski (1995) concluded from the evaluation of a developing country SIA that, 'even if SIA failed to identify impacts reliably, or was ignored by decision-makers' it still had the potential to yield a range of worthwhile subtle benefits (see Chapter 7).

REFERENCES

Bauer, R. and **Fenn, D.H. jnr** (1973) What is a corporate social audit? *Harvard Business Review* Jan–Feb **73(1)**, 37–48.

Berkes, F. and **Folke, C.** (eds) (1998) *Linking Social and Ecological Systems: management priorities and social mechanisms for building resilience*. Cambridge University Press, Cambridge.

Blum, F. (1958) Social audit of the enterprise. *Harvard Business Review* **36(2)**, 77–86.

Burdge, R.J. (1994) *A Conceptual Approach to Social Impact Assessment: a collection of writings by Rabel J. Burdge and colleagues*. Social Ecology Press, Middleton (WI).

Burdge, R.J. (1995) *A Community Guide to Social Impact Assessment*. Social Ecology Press, Middleton (WI).

Burdge, R.J. and **Vanclay, F.** (1996) Social impact assessment: a contribution to the state of the art series. *Impact Assessment* **14(1)**, 59–86.

Clark, A.C. (1977) *The Social Audit for Management*. Amacom, New York (NY).

Endter-Wada, J., Blahna, D. Krannich, R. and **Brunson, M.** (1988) A framework for understanding social science contributions to ecosystem management. *Ecological Applications* **8(3)**, 891–904.

Finsterbusch, K. (1995) In praise of SIA – a personal view of the field of social impact assessment: feasibility, justification, history, methods, issues. *Impact Assessment* **13(3)**, 229–52.

Force, J.E. and **Machlis, G.E.** (1997) The human ecosystem 2: social indicators in ecosystem management. *Society and Natural Resources* **10(4)**, 369–82.

Gagnon, C. (1995) Social impact assessment in Quebec: issues and perspectives for sustainable community development. *Impact Assessment* **13(3)**, 272–88.

Glasson, J. and **Heaney, D.** (1993) Socio-economic impacts: the poor relations in British environmental impact statements. *Journal of Environmental Planning and Management* **36(3)**, 335–43.

Hennings, W. (1996) Zukunftsfahiges Afrika? Folgen von Strukturanpassung und Transformation in Ghana. *Die Erde* **127(3)**, 221–33.

Howitt, R. (1993) Social impact assessment as 'applied peoples' geography'. *Australian Geographical Studies* **31(2)**, 127–40.

Howitt, R. (1995) SIA, sustainability and developmentalist narratives of resource regions. *Impact Assessment* **13(4)**, 387–402.

Htun, N. (1990) EIA and sustainable development. *Impact Assessment Bulletin* **8(1–2)**, 16–23.

Humble, J. (1973) *Social Responsibility Audit: a management tool for survival*. Foundation for Business Responsibilities, London.

Juslén, J. (1995) Social impact assessment: a look at Finnish experiences. *Project Appraisal* **10(3)**, 163–70.

Manring, N., West, P.C. and **Bidol, P.** (1990) Social impact assessment and environmental conflict management: potential for integration for integration and evaluation. *Environmental Impact Assessment Review* **10(3)**, 253–65.

Marsden, D. and **Oakley, P.** (eds) (1990) *Evaluating Social Development Projects* (Oxfam Development Guidelines No. 5). Oxfam, Oxford.

Marsden, D., Oakley, P. and **Pratt, B.** (eds) (1994) *Measuring the Process: guidelines for evaluating social development*. INTRAK, PO Box 563, Oxford.

Marsden, D., Pratt, B. and **Clayton, A.** (1998) *Outcomes and Impact: evaluating social change in social development*. INTRAK, PO Box 563, Oxford.

Meidinger, E. and **Schnaiberg, A.** (1980) SIA as evaluation research: claimants and claims. *Evaluation Review* **4(6)**, 507–35.

ODA (1993) *Social Development Handbook*. Overseas Development Administration, London.

Rakowski, C.A. (1995) Evaluating a social impact assessment: short-term and long-term outcomes in a developing country. *Society and Natural Resources* **8(6)**, 524–40.

Redclift, M. (1998) Across the social-ecological divide. *The Times Higher Education Supplement* **20 November 1998, 31.**

Seley, J.E. and **Wolpert, J.** (1985) The savings harm tableau for social impact assessment of retrenchment policies. *Economic Geography* **61(2)**, 158–71.

Vink, N. (1999) *The Challenge of Institutional Change: a practical guide for development consultants*. KIT Press, Amsterdam.

Wenner, L.N. (1988) Social impact assessment in retrospect: was it useful? *Impact Assessment Bulletin* **1(4)**, 11–24.

Wildavsky, A. (1996) *Speaking truth to Power: the art and craft of policy analysis* (2nd edn). Transaction Publishers, New Brunswick (NJ) (1st edn 1979 – Little, Brown & Co., Boston, MA).

3

SIA APPROACHES AND PROCESS

APPROACHES

Many disciplines contribute to SIA: notably sociology, anthropology, social psychology and social economics (Banks, 1990; Chase, 1990; Tester, 1983). In spite of the diversity of SIA approaches adopted as far as aims are concerned, it is possible to recognize some generic similarity between most.

By the start of the twentieth century, *laissez-faire* development had largely given way to 'modern' authoritarian control, increasingly guided by science. SIA (and EIA) in the early 1970s tended to adopt an empiricist and technocratic stance, perhaps seeking to show impact assessment as a 'hard', rather than 'soft', science (i.e. as reliable, sound and accurate). From the early 1980s, however, there has been a shift to a participatory rather than technocratic approach, although the latter still has the edge in practice. Nowadays, as well as the two opposite ends of the SIA approach spectrum – the participatory and the technocratic – there is also the more central 'integrative' approach. The likelihood is that a shift will increasingly take place towards the integrative approach, which combines elements of both technocratic and participatory SIA (in practice, however, things may not be so clear-cut). The integrative approach seems to hold considerable promise as a way of overcoming various methodological weaknesses, and of linking different impact assessment fields with SIA to achieve a more strategic oversight. Macfarlane (1999) studied ex-post audits and evaluated 23 mining-related SIAs, comparing technocratic, participatory and integrative methods to see which had been the most effective, and found that the integrative methods were the best.

There are two ways in which SIA can be adopted: either as an integral part of planning, decision-making and monitoring; or as a bolt-on extra (for EIA, the trend has been firmly towards the former) (Leistritz and Ekstrom, 1988).

It is widely argued that the more SIA is co-ordinated with the planning and decision-making processes (of SIA users), the greater is the probability of its serious utilization. Those involved in SIA (according to Freudenburg, 1986: 467) include:

1. the initiator of development or change (a company, government or NGO; it can also be due to an environmental shift)
2. a government or NGO concerned with public or vulnerable group welfare
3. the public, community or concerned individual(s).

An SIA may be conducted by any of these three groups, although it is increasingly likely to be initiated, and also perhaps overseen, by the second group. Clearly, SIA team composition has a great influence on the outcome. For a given situation one must select the best mix, asking the following questions.

- What proportion of assessors should be 'insiders' (i.e. local, involved people who are largely in control of development)?
- What proportion will be 'outsiders' (i.e. independent)?
- What level of experience should the assessors have?
- How good are their interpersonal skills?
- How neutral are the assessors?

The effectiveness of SIA is greatly affected by the law in force, by local circumstances, and by the ethics and professional rules of conduct prevailing among SIA practitioners. (For a simplified illustration of the relationships between SIA and the various stakeholders involved in development *see* Figure 3.1.) SIA can serve the needs of social development, but must be applied according to a systematic framework (Dunning, 1978). It has been argued that a framework for SIA should be derived with reference to development models, but as these are primarily economics-centred, they do not support a human-sensitive assessment well (Anon., 1993: 243).

Increasingly, it is argued that an SIA framework should focus on society and the individual; show who gets what; and try to promote sustainable development, human rights, social justice, and overall development (Anon., 1993: 246). To have any chance of fulfilling such ambitious aims, a framework will have to allow for adaptation to the unforeseen, extend the time-frame of assessment, and will need to be comprehensive in coverage. There are very different impacts during construction, throughout normal post-completion management (when operational change takes place), during project or programme closedown and following closedown. So, it is important to have a broad time-frame for SIA, because impacts can start virtually the moment a development is proposed; the intensity and type of impacts vary during development, and usually continue after development has ceased. For example, in South Wales, the Midlands and northern England (UK) coal mining impacts are still felt decades after the cessation of mining as communities established to service the industry adapt to pit closures (Gramling and Freudenburg, 1992). However, a large portion of SIA to date

FIGURE 3.1 The relationship between SIA and various stakeholders involved in development
Note: only the main stakeholders have been included

has been far too limited, spatially and in terms of time, and has focused predominantly on the implementation and construction phases of development.

Technocratic EIA and SIA often profess to use scientific methods to help achieve an ordered, deductive (iterative) and, hopefully, fairly objective approach to planning – the aim is strict neutrality and scientific evaluation. I use the words 'fairly' and 'scientific' because the assessment process inevitably involves subjective judgement by the assessors. Furthermore the sheer complexity, fickle nature of social issues, and the unpredictability of human responses to a given challenge means that assessors must draw on hindsight and professional judgement as much as science. The technocratic approach is seen by many to be one in which the assessor(s) are elitist experts (often outsiders) who decide what will be done and who are likely to promote their own views. Some social scientists have even objected to the technocratic approach as 'inappropriate reductionism'; however, their preferred alternative is often a participatory approach which, as Wildavsky has noted (*see* Chapter 2), can have grave shortcomings.

Non-technocratic SIA is widely seen as a way to analyse, understand and direct social change. Assessors adopting this approach accept that the SIA process is subject to political pressures (Craig, 1990: 39) and are likely to be willing to mediate in disputes and act on behalf of the public, not take a neutral stance. So, both technocratic and non-technocratic SIA are unlikely to be truly neutral, although assessors adopting the latter approach are likely to have a much more marked bias. The non-technocratic approach is usually to some degree participatory, seeking to incorporate local views and knowledge into decision-making and planning, and to inform or even involve locals. Roche (1999: 19) described this approach as 'People as active participants, rather than objects of impact assessment.' The participatory approach is therefore seen by many to be more democratic (although less objective or neutral). A crucial point, again stressed by Roche (1999: 29), is who decides what is a significant impact or what constitutes a valuable local view: the people affected by a development or the assessor(s) alone?

Division of SIA into technocratic, participatory and integrative is not the only possibility; Becker (1996: 17) preferred to simply classify SIA into 'analytical' and 'interpretative' approaches. Another classification of approach has been provided by Torgerson (1980: 139–42), who recognized the following types:

- empiricist (use of survey, 'objective' observation and experiment to forecast)
- theorist (a functionalist stance, with reliance on social theories to make predictions)
- ethnographic (the assessor tries to immerse him/herself in the potentially impacted community, so as to grasp its workings; as this takes time and can be a challenge, the approach may have limited value).

Yet another classification is possible. Craig (1990: 43) recognized the following, evolving, SIA models.

- Adversarial model: the key actors (proponent, government, local interest groups, NGOs etc.) each carry out an SIA, which may then be dealt with in a quasi-judicial manner. Conflict is accepted as part of a sort of arbitration process, rather than treated as something to be avoided.
- Straightforward research model: assessment is conducted according to guidelines set by a government or professional agency and SIA follows these, doing its best to conduct research.
- Collaborative model (some may call it a participatory model): communications are encouraged from the outset among all key actors, efforts are made to reach agreement on aims, terms of reference, methods, etc.; the assumption being that communication is possible and desirable.

Leistritz and Murdock (1981: 158–61) recognized a number of conceptual approaches to SIA, including the human ecologic and the functionalist. Those who support the former see humans as adapting to an ever-changing environment, which leads to constantly altering social institutions. Their view is that SIA should be used to see social institutions in an environmental framework. Those supporting a functionalist approach see humans as coming together to form social groups in order to more effectively perform 'essential' functions – such as survival, religion, community cohesion-building, etc. Consequently, they feel that SIA should seek to see how these functions vary.

Clearly, a number of different conceptual frameworks can shape the approach adopted for SIA, although all share the broad form and elements shown in Figure 3.2. Efforts should be made to select the most appropriate combination to create a framework for each situation. For example, one could develop an adaptive and interdisciplinary framework that would be especially useful where there is considerable uncertainty, as in developing-country situations. Alternatively, one might adopt an issues-oriented approach, which could integrate social assessment, social planning and social development, and seek to balance research and the need for action (Taylor *et al.*, 1995). A generalized SIA and impact management model is shown in Figure 3.3.

Since the late 1960s the systems analysis approach has been applied by those involved in many fields, including impact assessment (for a review *see* Palinkas *et al.*, 1985). Some treat SIA as a form of applied policy analysis that promotes interdisciplinary study and guides development. Alternatively, SIA may adopt an issues- or needs-centred approach, i.e. it aims to aid social impact management (Preister and Kent, 1981). This approach promotes public involvement in the assessment process and free circulation of results. Efforts are likely to be made to improve public input, to aid their understanding of

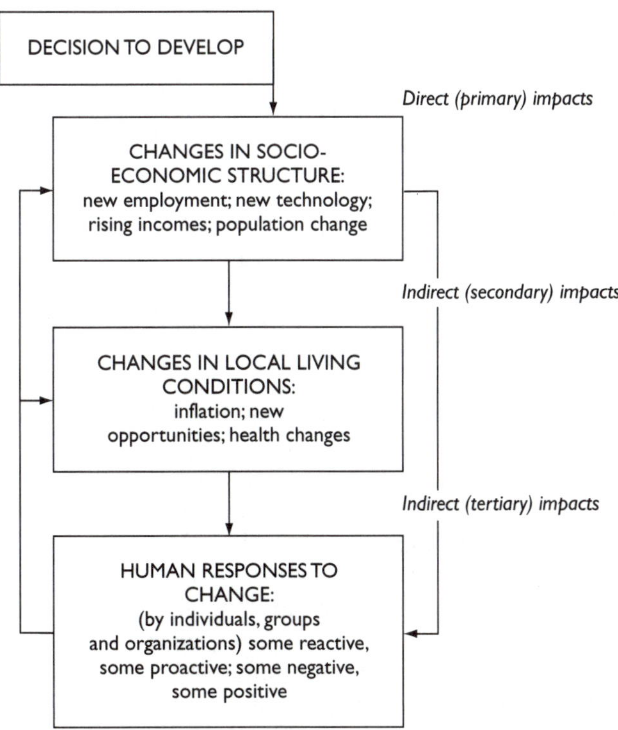

Figure 3.2 A conceptual framework for SIA
Source: redrawn, with modifications, from Kalinska (1981), Figure 2, p. 220

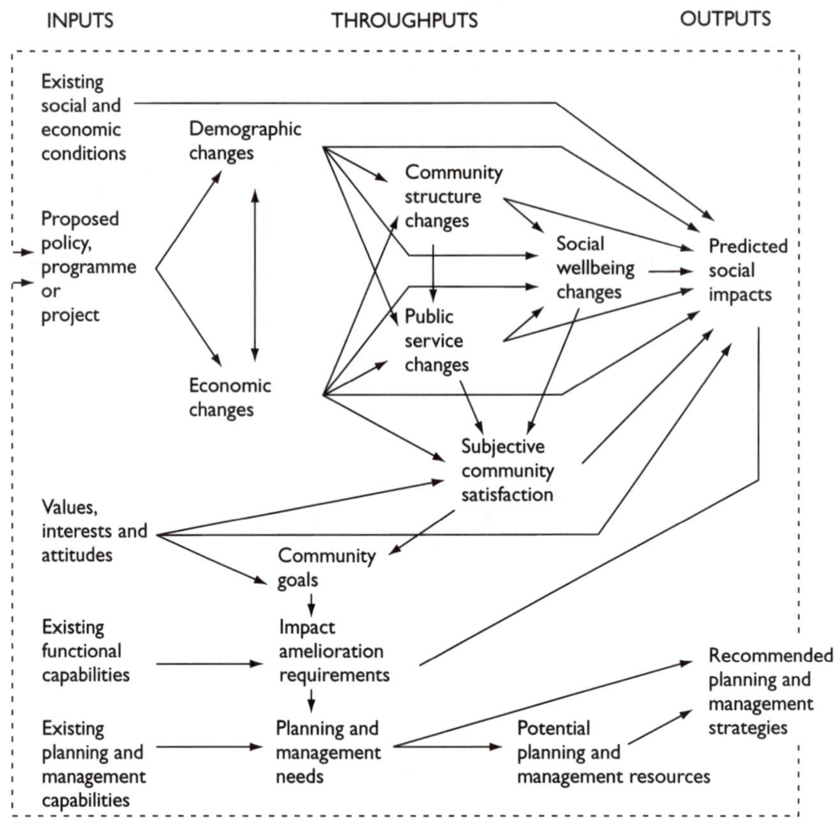

FIGURE 3.3 Generalized SIA and impact management model
Development (see left-hand side of the diagram: 'Proposed policy, programme or project') causes social impacts, which trigger feedbacks that affect the development activities and may also initiate impact management responses
Source: redrawn, with modifications, from Finsterbusch and Wolf (1981), Figure 1, p. 45

results and stimulate their interest. This involves identifying the interests and concerns of the public which then helps determine how the SIA is focused and what is studied. Catering for the 'people's choice' is likely to demand an approach that is also decentralized (micro-scale) (Preister and Kent, 1981). The issues-oriented approach can be flexible, adaptive and faster to apply than approaches that adopt a broader focus (Finsterbusch *et al.*, 1990: 42–44). Other possibilities are: to adopt a generic framework, which is sensitive to social change; or an interdisciplinary team framework, which supports an integrative and multidisciplinary approach to SIA (Armour, 1984: 23; Taylor and Bryan, 1990). Nowadays, the SIA goal often stated is to adopt a comprehensive and integrative approach, linking closely with EIA, technology assessment, planning, etc. In practice a compartmentalized, bolt-on, ready-made package of procedures (which is often insufficiently multidisciplinary) is often adopted, at worst consisting of a few consultants brought in for a short time to assess 'social issues'.

Burdge (1984 and 1995) recognized 'generic' and 'project-level' SIA. Supporters of the former argue that policy-makers and the public need to be sensitized to social change, so SIA's sensitivity to social impacts is more important than its ability to identify them accurately. Burdge felt that the project-level approach should emphasize the need to recognize and understand the changes that will be caused by a particular development, and not just encourage awareness that, with development, social change may take place (it is probably easier to make such an assessment the more restricted the scale of the study).

A commonly adopted approach has been 'comparative' SIA (Burdge, 1995: 22). Typically this takes the form of a study, where development is proposed or under way, using hindsight knowledge of similar cases to extrapolate and predict. Other possibilities are to use a 'systems modelling approach' – although this is less common in SIA than in EIA (Palinkas *et al.*, 1985) – or something like the Delphi technique (*see* Chapter 6) to identify and assess likely future scenarios.

SIA may adopt a group ecology approach (Flynn, 1985; Flynn and Flynn, 1982), which assumes that relationships among people in a community are structured, and that community residents form functional and interacting groups that can be identified and described. This involves the identification of functional groups and causal links between development and the local community. Through this, assessors try to identify the distribution of likely effects among the groups in the affected community.

Often the SIA focus is on the community because this is the level at which the costs and benefits of change are felt most acutely. The community also offers a manageable unit for SIA, so some assessors work with those active in community development hoping to find ways to explain the workings of communities and so to predict future scenarios (Bowles, 1981: 5–83). The community approach to economic development appeared in the 1940s, and has subsequently spread widely. However, the concept of community is still not well defined, and there has been bitter criticism of this approach; it seems to be something of a reaction to centralization, rigid control and perceived remoteness of the state, yet it is not clear whether the 'grass roots' (i.e. members of the community) work together for the common good. Many feel that, in practice, special interest groups are likely to get their own way more than might be the case with 'outside' central government control.

As already discussed, the dominant conceptual orientations of SIA are either political (the acceptance that the assessment is value-laden and seeks to empower locals), or technical (gather empirical data and give expert opinions as objectively as possible). These are different and may not easily be reconciled (Lane *et al.*, 1997: 303). Assessors usually adopt an anthropocentric stance, whereby SIA treats the environment as a source of 'resources' with utility for human needs. Faced with a decision between meeting immediate human needs and protection of environment, or biodiversity, this stance is likely to back the former (which may not, in the long term, give best social benefit or sustainable development).

SIA can be carried out at various scales: micro (fine-tuning, mainly concerned with specific projects and short-range planning – say five years ahead), meso (clusters of projects or programmes and looking perhaps 10 years or more ahead) and macro (questioning the basic cause of things, looking at general directions in which society changes, focusing over 10 years ahead and with much in common with futures studies (Becker, 1996: 18; Finsterbusch *et al.*, 1990: 9)). The macro-scale also implies focusing on what policy-makers deem to be required at national and international levels (for example, assessing political or legal system changes). The meso level is likely to involve assessment of impacts on collective behaviour (organizations, social movements). The micro level concentrates on the sources of impacts (working at the level of impacts on individuals) and suggests a framework for eliminating those that are negative; since many of the impacts are due to managerial decisions, this scale of SIA has to focus within the institution(s) involved, then suggest to the policy-makers how to reduce negative impacts. Public participation is more likely at the micro level because it is 'in their backyard' and, therefore, meaningful.

Most SIA has been conducted at project level, less at programme level and relatively little at policy level; effectively, much experience is of a short-term, site-specific focus. EIA and SIA are sometimes conducted on a regional scale (meso level), mainly focusing on economic indicators, employment data, demographic issues and so on (McDonald, 1990); economic assessment has often been conducted at this scale. Roche (1999) provided an interesting case study of programme impact assessment: an examination of the Bangladesh Rural Development Programme which affected 68,000 villages.

As with EIA there is a risk that the group commissioning an SIA will deliberately, or inadvertently, seek a 'cosmetic job' (i.e. will play down or hide unwanted impacts, and emphasize the beneficial impacts). For this reason, SIA should use transparent methods and approaches that are easy to follow, ideally with firm regulations imposed by an independent body or government. As already mentioned, it is likely that assessors will ultimately have to be accredited by a professional or government body. Whatever the approach adopted, SIA should seek to ensure that:

- it is never used to justify decisions already made;
- it is integrated into the planning process at the earliest possible stage, so it can be used to choose between, and to formulate, alternatives;
- it does not impose unsuitable changes – e.g. changes suitable for the USA on the EU, or changes suitable for the EU on developing countries; SIA will need to determine what is suitable;
- it should go beyond impact identification to recommend actions, measures and ongoing monitoring.

These aims are fine in theory but, in practice, SIA reflects western (especially North American) liberal, democratic attitudes and regimes where public access to decision-making has become the norm. SIA is a complex process, prone to be mis-applied, poorly conducted, under-supported and at least partly ignored. In addition, satisfactory interdisciplinary or multidisciplinary approaches can be difficult to achieve (Rickson *et al.*, 1990).

PROCESS

If the SIA process is effective, dispassionate and thorough, it should identify and help to counter attempts to manipulate development to serve special interest groups. Like EIA, SIA can encourage decision-makers and planners to 'look before they leap' (*see* Box 3.1). It is common for the SIA process to be divided into at least eight steps or stages:

1. scoping
2. formulation of alternatives
3. profiling
4. projection
5. assessment
6. evaluation
7. mitigation (if needed)
8. ongoing monitoring.

(*See* Box 3.2 for more details of these steps, and also Figure 6.1.)

Project and programme development has phases which are, typically, as follows: (a) initiation or construction; (b) stable, ongoing management; (c) adjustment(s); (d) closedown; (e) replacement or rehabilitation. Ideally, SIA should be repeated for each of these, and because the impacts are likely to differ in type and intensity at each phase, assessment methods will probably

BOX 3.1 CHARACTERISTICS OF THE SIA PROCESS

- A systematic effort to identify, analyse and evaluate the social impacts of a proposed project or other change affecting individuals and social groups within a community, or on an entire community, in advance of the decision-making process, in order that the information derived from the SIA can actually influence decisions.
- A means for developing alternatives to the proposed course of action, and of determining the full range of consequences for each alternative.
- A means of increasing knowledge on the part of the developer and the impacted community/communities.
- A means of raising consciousness and the level of understanding of the community, and a way of placing the affected people in a better position to understand the broader implications of the proposals.
- The SIA should include within it a process to mitigate or avoid the impacts likely to occur if development goes ahead.

Source (with modifications): Burdge and Robertson, 1990

Box 3.2 Typical stages in the SIA process

(*See also* Chapter 6, Box 6.1.)

1. **Scoping:** the assessor(s) identify the potentially impacted people(s)/society(ies) and their concerns, in an attempt to determine the type, scale and focus of assessment. Identification of the actors. The limits of assessment and terms of reference are decided with reference to available expertise, funding and time available. Methods are decided, key informants identified, sources of data suggested. Decision made on what indicators to study. Community needs and aspirations are determined.[1]
2. **Formulation of alternatives:** develop reasonable alternatives to the proposal, based on the needs of the community(ies)/society(ies) and their attitudes, etc. A wide range of techniques may be used at this stage: public meetings, questionnaires, advisory groups, public data sources and so on.[2]
3. **Profiling:** determination of what is likely to be impacted. Describe the social units affected. Identify the indicators to measure. Establish the current social condition; a 'social profile' (*see* Glossary) is likely to be drawn up – this provides a measure of the social characteristics of an area prior to the start of a proposed development. As in EIA, establishment of baseline data (*see* Glossary) is necessary – i.e. determining what the current conditions and trends are (what would happen if the proposed development did not take place) – and social profiling helps to do this. Methods are tested and data collected.
4. **Projection:** using information gathered, the assessor(s) makes projections of what is likely to happen and who is affected – without the proposed development proceeding, if it proceeds or if alternatives are adopted. Identify indicators to study; identify cause–effect linkages and feedbacks (*see* Glossary). The scenarios identified can suggest avoidance and mitigation measures, and help to develop ongoing monitoring.
5. **Assessment:** the assessor(s) tries to determine the magnitude of impacts, what effect likely changes will have, what impacts are most significant and how people will react. Determine potential for avoidance or mitigation.
6. **Evaluation:** an analysis of trade-offs. What are the net benefits? Who benefits? Who loses out? Is the overall impact acceptable? Advisory groups and community discussions may help (feedback from affected people is sought). The preferable development alternative(s) are identified. At this stage the evaluation may be presented as a public document or report to decision-makers, often as part of, or alongside, an environmental impact statement (EIS).
7. **Mitigation:** measures to counter unwanted impacts are identified.
8. **Monitoring:** measurement of actual impacts (which can be compared with predicted impacts) via observation. Lessons learnt can be fed back into policy-making and planning. Develop plan for ongoing monitoring to warn of any need for further action.
9. **Ex-post audit:** without this check on the effectiveness and cost of SIA, methods are likely to be slow to improve, and sceptics may not be convinced of its value.

Source: various, including Burdge and Robertson, 1990

[1] Some would add an extra stage here, before Step 1: 'problem identification'.
[2] Some would add an extra stage here, before Step 3: 'SWOT analysis' (see Chapter 6 for a discussion of SWOT analysis).

need to vary from phase to phase. Carley (1986) asked whether SIA should make as much effort to look ahead at later phases, or be restricted more to observing and acting as watchdog? There is a tendency for decision-makers to conduct EIA and SIA only after phase (b); yet, social impacts start on the day a development is proposed.

For physical developments, early phases often entail vegetation clearance, earth movement, river flow modification and so on, along with the arrival of a team of construction workers (perhaps with relatives and camp followers). For media developments, healthcare innovations, tax changes and legislative changes there will be little or no physical disruption, at least at first, but social and economic impacts soon occur and a complex cascade of further social, economic and physical impacts may be triggered. Impacts may be propagated at any phase, merely by the introduction of new information or the circulation of rumours.

What is often forgotten is that, even when a project, programme or policy is well established, any shift in management, social or environmental conditions can trigger impacts. As soon as closedown of an established activity is announced, there are likely to be impacts, as employees and the local community fear job losses or the risk of pollution from abandoned facilities. Communities that have adapted to a development that, in due course, ceases can seldom return to their original activity and may find it difficult to develop an alternative. For example, fishermen may become oil field workers, sell their boats and lose the skills of fishing; should the oil become exhausted, the ex-fishermen are unlikely to return to their old livelihood. Where a settlement owes its identity and pride to a single company or group of companies there can be serious loss of community cohesion and confidence if there is recession and closure.

Finsterbusch (1985: 194) noted that a series of related questions are addressed in SIA (this holds true for SIA that is focused on projects, programmes, policies and technological innovation).

- Problem identification: 'What is the problem?'
- Policy development: 'What should be done?'
- Impact assessment: 'Which alternative is best?'
- Response: 'Avoidance, mitigation or adaptation?'

SIA should help shape monitoring, which may take different forms (*see* Carley, 1986):

- to give feedback on the success of any action taken
- periodic inspection for a stated purpose
- periodic checks to see if things comply with a permit or licence that states demands
- experimental monitoring to check a society or environment, and to recognize unexpected impacts
- repetitive monitoring of specific things to detect change
- performance monitoring to check if a target has been met

- monitoring to determine whether a development has been a success/remains a success
- monitoring for cumulative impacts (*see* Chapter 5 for a discussion of cumulative impacts).

For strategic planning, ongoing monitoring is vital (Bankes and Thompson, 1980). Programme evaluation and monitoring (performance auditing) generally implies an evaluation by a team of government, independent or company assessors – in practice the focus tends to be mainly on whether goals have been met within projected costs. For effective evaluation or monitoring, there is a need for a clear conceptual framework and supportive institutions.

The legal framework

Legislation, in the form of the 1969 US National Environmental Policy Act (discussed in Chapter 1), helped establish SIA. Several court cases were initiated in North America in the decade following 1970, when local people, ethnic groups or non-governmental agencies felt the required degree of multidisciplinary impact assessment, i.e. covering social as effectively as physical impacts, was absent. There is still a need for more legislation in most countries to support SIA (Boggs, 1994). (For further discussion of SIA and the law *see* Chapter 4.)

References

Anon. (1993) Social impact assessment of investment/acquisition of technology projects in developing countries, with particular reference to the position of women. *Public Enterprise* **13(3–4)**, 239–56.

Armour, A. (1984) Teaching SIA in times of transition. *Impact Assessment Bulletin* **3(2)**, 19–26.

Banks, E.P. (1990) Ethnography: an essential tool for impact prediction. *Impact Assessment Bulletin* **8(4)**, 19–30.

Bankes, N. and **Thompson, A.R.** (1980) *Monitoring for Impact Assessment and Management*. Westwater Research Centre, Vancouver.

Becker, H.A. (1996) *Social Impact Assessment: method and experience in Europe, North America and the developing world*. University College London Press, London.

Boggs, J.P. (1994) Planning and the law of social impact assessment. *Human Organization* **53(2)**, 167–74.

Bowles, R.T. (1981) *Social Impact Assessment in Small Communities*. Butterworths, Toronto.

Burdge, R.J. (1984) Teaching social impact assessment at the college level. *Environmental Impact Assessment Review* **3(2)**, 48–55.

Burdge, R.J. (1995) *A Community Guide to Social Impact Assessment*. Social Ecology Press, Middleton (WI).

Burdge, R.J. and **Robertson, R.A.** (1990) Social impact assessment and the public involvement process. *Environmental Impact Assessment Review* **10(1)**, 81–90.

Carley, M.J. (1986) From assessment to monitoring: making our activities relevant to the policy process. *Impact Assessment Bulletin* **4(3–4)**, 286–303.

Chase, A.K. (1990) Anthropology and impact assessment: development pressures and indigenous interests in Australia. *Environmental Impact Assessment Review* **10(1–2)**, 11–25.

Craig, D. (1990) Social impact assessment: politically oriented approaches and applications. *Environmental Impact Assessment Review* **10(1–2)**, 37–54.

Dunning, J.H. (1978) *A Systematic Approach to SIA*. Westview, Boulder (CO).

Finsterbusch, K. (1985) State of the art in social impact assessment. *Environment and Behavior* **17(2)**, 193–221.

Finsterbusch, K., Ingersol, J. and **Llewellyn, L.** (eds) (1990) *Methods for Social Analysis in Developing Countries*. Westview, Boulder (CO).

Finsterbusch, K. and **Wolf, C.P.** (eds) (1981) *Methodology of Social Impact Assessment* (2nd edn). Dowden, Hutchinson and Ross, Stroudsburg (PA) (1st edn 1977).

Flynn, J. (1985) A group ecology method for social impact assessment. *Social Impact Assessment* Nos 99–104, 12–25.

Flynn, J. and **Flynn, C.B.** (1982) The group ecology method: a new conceptual design for social impact assessment. *Impact Assessment Bulletin* **1(4)**, 11–19.

Freudenburg, W.R. (1986) Social impact assessment. *Annual Review of Sociology* **12**, 451–78.

Gramling, R. and **Freudenburg, W.R.** (1992) Opportunity–threat, development, and adaption: toward a comprehensive framework for social impact assessment. *Rural Sociology* **57(2)**, 216–34.

Kalinska, B.M. (1981) An approach to social impact assessment research in the Athabasca Oil Sands region, in F.J. Tester and W. Mykes (eds), *Social Impact Assessment: theory, methods and practice*. Detselig Enterprises, Calgary (Canada), 207–31.

Lane, M.B., Ross, H. and **Dale, A.P.** (1997) Social impact research: integrating the technical, political, and planning paradigms. *Human Organization* **56(3)**, 302–10.

Leistritz, L.F. and **Ekstrom, B.** (1988) Integrating social impact assessment into the planning process. *Impact Assessment Bulletin* **6(2)**, 17–20.

Leistritz, F.L. and **Murdock, S.H.** (1981) *The Socioeconomic Impact of Resource Development: Methods of Assessment*. Westview, Boulder (CO).

McDonald, G.T. (1990) Regional economic and social impact assessment. *Environmental Impact Assessment Review* **10(1–2)**, 25–36.

Macfarlane, M. (1999) An Evaluation of Social Impact Assessment Methodologies in the Mining Industry. PhD thesis: University of Bath, Bath (UK).

Palinkas, L.A., Harris, B.M. and **Petterson, J.S.** (eds) (1985) *A Systems Approach to Social Impact Assessment: two Alaskan case-studies*. Westview, Boulder (CO).

Preister K. and **Kent, J.** (1981) The issue-centred approach to social impacts: from assessment to management. *Social Impact Assessment* Nos 71–72, 3–13.

Rickson, R.E., Burdge, R.J., Hundloe, T. and **McDonald, G.T.** (1990) Institutional constraints to adoption of social impact assessment as a decision-making and planning tool. *Environmental Impact Assessment Review* **10(3)**, 233–43.

Roche, C. (1999) *Impact Assessment for Development Agencies: learning to value change*. Oxfam (with Novib), Oxford.

Taylor, C.N. and **Bryan, C.H.** (1990) A New Zealand issues-oriented approach to social impact assessment, in K. Finsterbusch, J. Ingersoll and L. Llewellyn (eds) (1990) *Methods for Social Analysis in Developing Countries*. Westview, Boulder (CO), 37–54.

Taylor, C.N., Goodrich, C. and **Bryan, C.H.** (1995) Issues-oriented approach to social assessment and project appraisal. *Project Appraisal* **10(3)**, 142–54.

Tester, F.J. (1983) Psychoanalysis and social impact assessment. *Impact Assessment Bulletin* **2(2)**, 148–59.

Torgerson, D. (1980) *Industrialization and Assessment: social impact assessment as a social phenomenon*. York University Publications in Northern Studies, Toronto.

4

INTEGRATING SIA

This chapter explores how SIA might better be integrated with other impact assessments, and with the diversity of fields involved in planning, implementation and management. Without better integrated, more strategic SIA, it is difficult, if not impossible, to understand and then plan and manage a wide range of things (community change, socio-economic-environmental interactions and the institutions that shape resource use, for instance).

It has been argued for a long time that mainstream SIA is too isolated from other impact assessment fields. Without good exchange of information between the various forms of impact assessment these, and SIA will be less effective, and sustainable development more difficult to achieve (Fischer, 1999). There is interest in more integrative approaches which allow SIA, EIA and other impact assessments to better contribute to planning, programme and policy decision-making (the latter widely referred to as the 'strategic level'). Application at the local (usually project) level tends to give a snapshot view, which is of limited value for problem avoidance, the pursuit of sustainable development, or the negotiation of complex and ongoing issues such as world trade agreements, EU long-term regional development, national policies, programmes of expenditure or research, etc. (Annema *et al.*, 1999; Ravetz, 1998; Tassey, 1999).

While there has long been a demand for SIA to be better integrated with other assessment and monitoring, there have been few clear proposals of how to go about it (Armour, 1988; Bond, 1995; Gold, 1978; Leistritz and Chase, 1982). There have also been attempts to side-step SIA by mixing more sociology and anthropology into EIA (Gismondi, 1997).

From the early 1970s to the 1980s SIA was usually added on to EIA, its findings being a relatively minor part of an EIS. Such SIA has often been carried out half-heartedly, as an afterthought, with limited support, expertise and time for completion, and mainly to satisfy legal requirements and calm public concern. Poor-quality SIA soon led to protests, legal actions, inquiries and, gradually, to improved practice, increased funding and a better methodology.

Risk and hazard assessment have long been demanded by insurance companies, investors and public safety bodies; EIA has been embraced by planners and environmental managers since the mid-1970s. However, SIA has had a weaker legal backing, has been less well funded and has generally enjoyed a lower profile, demand for it being limited mainly to large resource developments and highway building in the 1970s and 1980s. In part this was a result of history, environmental impacts attracting attention first and then the social problems associated with large-scale developments. It was also affected by the pecking order among academics, planners and decision-makers, whereby social studies have been less respected than physical sciences and economics. The slower spread of SIA probably also reflects the greater difficulty of predicting and assessing accurately the significance and likelihood of social and cultural impacts. Another factor has been the comparatively recent entry of those trained or educated in social studies into influential positions in planning and decision-making concerned with natural resource development, environmental management and technology innovation.

Integrating SIA with planning and policy-making

Planning, one can argue, is the first step in administering policy; it is essentially a problem-solving process with several discernible stages: need/problem identification; need/problem definition; alternatives identification; best alternative selection; implementation (Armour, 1990: 6). Planning, according to Burdge (1995), consists of three main stages:

1. the policy stage – during which the broad goals and the means of achieving them are defined
2. the programme stage – during which the means to attain the goals are operationalized
3. the project stage – the actual implementation of activities designed to achieve the goals established by (1) using means decided in (2).

Policies (according to Smith, 1993: 50) may be stated, implied, perceived or acted upon, and have five components:

1. an object, or set of objectives
2. a desired course of events
3. a selected line of action (or inaction)
4. a declaration of intent
5. an implementation of intent.

A policy is thus a pattern of purposive, or goal-oriented, choices and actions rather than separate discrete decisions (Smith, 1993: 50). Policy-making involves two decisions: to act; or to decide between alternatives in relation to a pre-defined goal or objective(s) (Burdge, 1995: 31).

Smith (1993: 62–64) recognized three routes to represent interests within the policy process: lobbying decision-makers; public participation; and dispute resolution. Lobbying can be defined as 'stimulation and transmission of a communication by someone other than a citizen acting on his or her own behalf, directed at a policy-maker, planner or other decision-maker'. It is a powerful way of influencing policy and planning and may take the form of trying to influence public opinion through things like manipulating the media, or advertising. SIA practitioners must be aware and take care that public involvement in decision-making does not actually favour lobby groups. Alternatively, a lobby group may seek to sway decision-makers by bribery of various kinds, gentle briefing or lobbying by pressure groups, etc. In western-style democracies, lobby groups are often shadowy intermediaries between the public and decision-making, and it is difficult for SIA to predict the effect they may have.

There have been repeated calls for impact assessment, including SIA, to be better integrated with planning in order to be more effective (Armour, 1990; Burdge, 1987; Leistritz and Ekstrom, 1988; Rohe, 1982). Similarly, calls have been made for SIA to be better integrated with policy-making (Finsterbusch, 1984; Freudenburg and Keating, 1985; Finsterbusch and VanWicklin, 1989; Wolf, 1980) and with management. Integration has been defined as a philosophy of management expressed as a requirement for a high degree of co-ordination of all involved (Armour, 1990: 9; Rossini and Porter, 1983). To achieve effective integration and consistent application of SIA requires changes in administrative, legal and institutional practices in order to develop suitable frameworks (Burdge, 1994: 248; Gramling and Freudenburg, 1992).

SIA is now widely accepted as part of the development planning process. However, in practice it presents challenges because of the difficulties involved in predicting accurately the behaviour of social systems, and because of the sheer range of impact assessment 'subsets' focusing on socio-political assessment, socio-economic assessment, cultural impact assessment, socio-environmental assessment, socio-health assessment, demographic assessment and others.

There is currently some debate as to whether SIA is a planning and policy-making tool, a technical/scientific process aimed at gathering empirical data and providing expert opinion on social impacts, or a means of making much more fundamental changes to the development approach (something value-laden, essentially a political process seeking participation and the empowerment of local people) (Dale and Lane, 1994; Howitt, 1989; Lane *et al.*, 1997: 303). In the latter guise it may make planners think before they act, and help to ensure that they are more accountable to the public – strengthening the precautionary principle and supporting the quest for sustainable development. Boggs (1994: 167) went as far as to argue that SIA can provide a 'mandate for social knowledge use'. However, some feel that SIA is little more than the use of established applied social science to assess development that has already been initiated by other disciplines and to show the likely adverse or positive effects, rather than something involved in the intimate shaping of choices and sequencing of activities.

The role of SIA as a planning tool is, according to Burdge (1995: 31), to 'support judgement' (*see also* Burdge, 1990). As a policy tool SIA is seen to offer a means of evaluating and enhancing selection between available policy options with respect to pre-defined objectives. It may also help make policy by identifying alternatives (Finsterbusch, 1984: 37; Juslén, 1995; Wolf, 1980). Doubtless there are situations where SIA practitioners are just validating or part-modifying already-shaped decisions – hardly a planning activity. Without adequate legislative support, that is a risk.

Some countries have been using SIA to support planning for three decades or more. New Zealand began in the early 1970s (under the Environmental Protection and Enhancement Procedures of 1973, intensifying consideration of social issues after the 1977 Town and Country Planning Act). In 1989 New Zealand's Resource Management Bill required further consideration of social issues by planners; a Social Impact Assessment Working Group had been set up in 1984 to develop and promote SIA, and by the late 1980s various newsletters and associations were active. SIA has also contributed to the planning process in New Zealand; for example, helping officials explore the best ways to ensure that Maori communities are not excluded from healthcare system improvements (Association for Social Assessment, 1994). As discussed earlier, in both EIA and SIA there has been debate about whether the aim should be mainly to provide an objective, 'technocratic' planning tool, or a politicized process which assumes that public participation is essential for successful development, and facilitates it.

Public involvement is not, however, straightforward, and there are different degrees of participation:

- extract information of use to SIA from people
- influence or educate people
- control people
- keep people informed, within limits
- consult and heed people
- ensure that the public play an active role in the SIA process.

'Public' is a vague term; an authority may not wish to involve or inform all groups in society; although, in western democracies, there is at least some attempt to do so. There may be situations where it is in the national interest to over-rule local people's wishes and vice versa. Smith (1993: 66) identified four prerequisites for effective public participation:

1. the legal right and opportunity to participate
2. access to information
3. resource provision
4. the 'representativeness' of the participants.

Most participation has been project- or issues-related.

Lane *et al.* (1997: 303) argued that planning was to large degree a political process and that SIA has largely disregarded this; they proposed a number of research methodologies to counter this, in order to promote better integration. Among these proposals were the improvement of links between technical and political SIA, and a more participatory approach that involves all affected groups in the assessment and planning process (Lane *et al.*, 1997). Others have advocated the use of strategic perspectives analysis (SPA), a flexible participatory process that can be used both to conduct SIA and to integrate it into socio-political development planning (Dale, 1993; Dale and Lane, 1994; Lane *et al.*, 1997: 304). Briefly, SPA is used as a procedural framework for identifying stakeholders and exploring their interests; it then determines what, if any, planning procedures are appropriate. There have been proposals for using SPA as a route to participatory SIA, as way to integrate sustainable development objectives into structural adjustment (*see* Glossary) programmes (Abaza, 1998) and, presumably, as a way of integrating them with other types of programme.

SIA has the potential to allow planners to prepare for events before they might happen, rather than having to react to developments. Together with EIA and other impact assessment fields, SIA supports the 'precautionary principle', and can also show how crucial social institutions might change and possibly endanger or assist sustainable development efforts. Dale and Lane (1994: 254) suggested that SIA may be useful for assessing the cultural perspectives or values of interest groups that need to be accounted for in development. As a means of improving participation in policy-making, SIA can inform stakeholders about how they are likely to be affected by various alternatives. SIA can also show decision-makers how various groups are likely to be affected and how they may react.

Simply making social impact information available, either before decision-making, or as the result of a retrospective SIA, does little to aid policy formulation, because it has little effect on outcome. It is preferable that SIA practitioners should be actively involved in the advance planning of development. In practice this is often not the case – rather the SIA is conducted by consultants and is wholly or partly ignored by planners and decision-makers (Burdge, 1995: 18).

Integrating SIA with management

While there has been application of SIA to socio-economic impact management (Halstead *et al.*, 1984), it has to be admitted that, in spite of much advocacy for proactive SIA, and for it to be integrated with planning and management, there is a lack of tried and tested procedures for actually achieving these goals (Dale and Lane, 1994: 256).

Integrating SIA with social policy

Social policy assessment focuses on monitoring and predicting the outcomes of policy proposals or decisions (Boothroyd, 1998). While social research and social evaluation research are well established, much of it is retrospective (unlike SIA). According to the concept of pareto optimality, a social policy is desirable if everyone is made better off, or someone is better off without anyone else becoming worse off as a consequence. SIA is of value to those concerned with social policy because it can be a powerful tool for evaluating major socio-economic changes and the effectiveness of policies in attaining goals (Weston, 1982; Wildman, 1990). SIA also has the potential to help protect social policy against uncertainty by permitting assessment in advance of the likely effects of change in policy. However, SIA practitioners have sometimes been criticized for 'taking the side of the involved people'; while this may add a vital and often overlooked perspective, there are situations where central government has to concentrate scarce funds rather than equitably spread them too thinly to really achieve much, and in such cases local needs may have to come after regional, national or global well-being.

SIA can be the basis for a rational problem-solving process, facilitating decision-making by determining the range of social costs and social benefits likely to be generated by development alternatives (Burdge, 1995). SIA may be used to examine how ideological changes affect social welfare; for example, Xing (1999) conducted retrospective assessments of China between the period of Mao and the appearance of economic mobilization.

That SIA often performs poorly may be less to do with scientific inadequacy or clumsy practitioners, than with 'external institutional circumstances of practice' (Boggs, 1994: 172; Rickson *et al.*, 1990). Similar conclusions were reached by Dale *et al.* (1997) in an attempt to explain why in Queensland, Australia, the use of SIA lagged behind EIA even though there was supportive legislation. They found that there were difficulties caused by technocratic discipline-bias in planning opposing social studies, lack of adequate SIA expertise and poor appreciation of the value of SIA; they also found that there was a need to 'institutionalize' it better (i.e. improve the institutional arrangements that support it).

Integrating SIA with other impact assessments

Risk and hazard assessment

There has been surprisingly little written on the use of SIA by risk and hazard assessment, although the need for integration has been noted (Bond, 1995; Freudenburg, 1984). If people's reactions and perceptions are unexplored, risk and hazard assessment will have limited application. Since 1970 most EIA handbooks and guidelines have stressed the desirability of considering socio-economic and cultural impacts; but, it is only since the mid-1980s that this has been done on a regular basis, and only from the mid-1990s that efforts have been as serious as those to assess physical impacts.

Schwing and Albers (1980) present a number of studies of the social aspects of risk assessment. Risk assessment focuses mainly on the chances of an event occurring, on its costs and on the perceptions it generates. The key question is usually: 'Is the 'actual' predicted risk acceptable?' Risk assessors also tend to concentrate more on the implications of predictions for insurance, business, investors and planers. SIA goes further into exploring the social impacts of each predicted event and is more likely to inform or involve the public. The literature on risk assessment, especially technology assessment, is full of warnings that past predictions have been far from accurate and comprehensive. For example, who predicted the social impacts of motor cars, even in the 1900s when they were already spreading? (Responses to natural disasters are discussed in Chapter 13.)

Technology assessment

As modern technology spreads and has major impacts on people, the importance of technology assessment (TA) grows, and with it the need to better study the social issues involved and the social impacts generated. It has been argued that this is best achieved through closer integration of TA and SIA (Van den Ende *et al.*, 1998). TA must often consider the needs of the population that may be exposed to an innovation; for example, in healthcare, consideration of community values and equity issues are vital before decisions are made to adopt costly new treatments or equipment (Tugwell *et al.*, 1995).

Strategic environmental assessment

Strategic environmental assessment (SEA) seeks to assess impacts at local (project-tier) level, up to regional (programme-tier) level, and even to national (policy-tier) or international (international agreements-tier) levels (DeBoer and Sadler, 1996; European Commission, 1994; Goodland and Tillman, 1995; Kirkpatrick and Lee, 1999; Lee and Kirkpatrick, 1996; Lee and Kirkpatrick, 2000; Lee and Walsh, 1992; Partidario, 1997; Tal and Vellinga, 1998; Therivel and Partidario, 1996; Toth and Hizsnyik, 1998; Wood and Djeddour, 1992) (some definitions of SEA are given in Box 4.1). A number of countries now have, or are developing, SEA legislation; The Netherlands, for example, established a statutory system in 1987, New Zealand in 1991 and Australia in the 1990s; the UK, EU and various agencies (such as the World Bank) are moving towards adopting it (Owen Harrop and Ashley Nixon, 1999: 149–69). SEA is seen as a way of considering sustainable development opportunities and threats in a proactive way. It can be used to assess a wide variety of things, including: long-term research programmes; national transport policies; development and aid policies; ongoing trade agreement impacts; and the effects of global warming (Kessler and vanDorp, 1996;

Shepherd and Ortolano, 1996). The process has also been used for evaluating draft plans for water and irrigation development (Hedo and Bina, 1999).

High hopes have been voiced for SEA as a means of pursuing sustainable development and as a way of dealing more effectively with cumulative and indirect impacts (SIA currently has difficulty in doing this) (Abaza, 1996; Kirkpatrick and Lee, 1997; Lee and Kirkpatrick, 2000). It is difficult to assess cumulative impacts at the project level because of interactions with other projects, with regional developments, and national and global influences – all of which are beyond the view of project-level (micro) SIA. This has long been realized; even in the first century BC it was observed by a Roman statesman that: '. . . amid a multitude of projects no plan is devised'. If SIA is to be linked with EIA and other types of impact assessment, and with planning and decision-making, SEA may have potential as a starting point for what might better be termed 'integrated strategic assessment' (ISA) (Fischer, 1999).

SEA methodologies are still in a relatively early stage of evolution, but according to Therivel *et al.* (1992: 29) they are already encouraging the co-ordination of various policies and programmes, and are likely to ensure that planning decisions are made in a more open and rational way, promoting equity and participation. To stand any chance of achieving sustainable development there must be appropriate and stable institutions that support it, whatever the strategic approach; it must therefore include SIA to help ensure that such institutions are developed. Without a proactive approach to planning and policy-making, which includes SIA with other fields of impact assessment, the pursuit of sustainable development will be difficult, because social institutions and human behaviour must be understood and monitored, and changes predicted.

Integrated and strategic approaches might stand a better chance of identifying cumulative impacts and avoiding a snapshot view, than does mainstream SIA. However, these approaches must still overcome the sheer complexity and difficulties faced by policy-makers and development planners. It may be that discrete and parallel SIA, EIA, TA, hazard assess-

Box 4.1 Some definitions of strategic environmental assessment (SEA)

- Formalized, systematic and comprehensive process that evaluates the environmental effects of policies, plans, and programmes (Fischer, 1999: 146).
- A systematic and comprehensive process of evaluating the environmental impacts of a policy, plan or programme and its alternatives, leading to the preparation of a written report; the findings are used to ensure publicly accountable decision-making (based on Therivel *et al.* 1992: 20).
- The consideration of the environmental impacts of programmes, policies and plans, as well as projects.

Sources: various (paraphrased)

ment and so on would be better left independent, but carefully co-ordinated. Horton and Memon (1997) warned against having excessive expectations for SEA.

Cultural impact assessment

Burdge and Vanclay (1996: 59) suggested that 'Cultural impacts involve changes to the norms, values, and beliefs of individuals that guide and rationalize their cognition of themselves and society.' Within SIA and project appraisal, cultural impact assessment comprises a more or less discrete sub-field, although much of it has taken the form of an ex-post review of cultural change (Cochrane, 1979; Schoeffel, 1995; Stea and Buge, 1983). Culture is not easy to define (*see* Glossary); King (1998 and 2000) suggest that it consists of ways in which people live, work, play and organize to meet their needs. Alternatively, one could define it as the norms, values and beliefs that guide and rationalize a community's perception of itself. Cultural impacts are changes to the norms, values and beliefs of individuals that guide and rationalize their cognition of themselves and their society (Burdge and Vanclay, 1996: 59). Often it is expressed spatially through culturally significant sites: sacred groves, wells, springs, holy sites, buildings, old battlefields, Aboriginal songlines, etc. These places may seem unremarkable and of little value to the culturally ill-informed but can have very important religious, historic or folkloric significance (Dickens and Hill, 1978).

Archaeological sites can be culturally important in that they may support national identity, they provide a sense of tradition, and can sometimes yield tourism earnings (Bourdillon *et al.*, 1995; Ralston and Thomas, 1993). Cultures often develop and sustain myths (as a way for people to make sense of events). Myths are not just folk memories, they are still developing and will continue to do so; and because some myths have great impact on society and economy, they should be of concern to SIA (Balsamo, 1996).

Cultural traits may exercise strong control over resource use; for example: taboos, traditions, gender roles, religious beliefs and superstition may ensure that a fishery is not over-fished or that another resource is not over-exploited. Cultural traits and fashion determine what people wish to consume; a food or other commodity may be in demand by one group of people while shunned by another culture. So, a development may alter a given culture; a multicultural society may experience a range of impacts from the same change because each culture has a different vulnerability or reaction; and understanding of culture is important for planners and administrators.

Cultural impacts may result in the loss of unique and valuable knowledge, skills or perspectives. New ideas, fashions and beliefs can soon cause the abandonment of old ways, yet some cultural traits are robust and resistant to change. Some, such as ethnobotanists, seek out cultural information – perhaps as a form of cultural 'rescue dig' – to prevent its total loss, but sometimes to enable commerce to develop this knowledge for profit. The value of such traditional (or indigenous) knowledge cannot be over-stressed. For example, without traditional knowledge from Ecuadorian Indians, quinine may never have become available to Europeans, and untreatable malaria would have had a massive impact on the history of tropical development. (For a fascinating account of Amazonian ethnobotany, *see* Davis, 1997.) In the UK, until the 1970s, shipbuilding skills were to be found in north-east England; more southerly towns, such as Swindon, could build heavy locomotives, and potteries and engineering workshops were scattered across the Midlands. Since 1945 many of these skills and their associated cultural traits have declined or been lost (e.g. the brass bands associated with mining or heavy industry works have suffered).

Gilder (1995) tried to conceptualize culture as a lifestyle, and then operationalize it using the 'social resource unit' to try and assess the impacts of a proposed golf course on one of the few remaining relatively undisturbed Hawaiian communities. Few modern communities are undisturbed, or socio-culturally uniform, so cultural impact assessment may be getting more complex. Cultural impacts of economic change, of technological innovation, of social change, of resettlement of peoples can be enormous. Indigenous peoples have suffered cultural impacts worldwide, especially after AD 1600, through contact with Europeans, and since the 1940s through the spread of mainstream global culture (*see* Chapter 8).

Cultural impact assessment has received less attention than mainstream SIA (Canter, 1977; Cochrane, 1979; Edelstein and Klee, 1995; Gloria, 1990; Schoeffel, 1995; Wolf, 1978). In the USA some impetus for SIA to cover cultural issues was given by 1980 amendments to the National Historic Preservation Act (1966) which expressed concern that 'intangible elements of . . . cultural heritage . . .' should receive protection in the same way as archaeological and architectural material, and by the publication of a draft report by the Association of American Anthropologists entitled 'Cultural Conservation: the protection of cultural heritage in the United States'. The result has been that North American cultural impact assessment has focused mainly on archaeological and architectural features, neglecting lifestyles, intercultural perceptions, folklife, community values, landholding practices and so on (Howell, 1983; King, 1998 and 2000; Loomis, 1982). As discussed in Chapter 8, traditional knowledge and culture, which can be exploited by drug companies, crop breeders and the like, has attracted attention.

Studies and attempts to predict cultural impacts are often sectoral in focus, because this is a good way to cope with their complexity. For example, Tan *et al.* (1987) reviewed the cultural impact of American TV in the Philippines, Hughes (1986) tried to assess how industrial pollution would affect New Zealand Maoris, the impact of technology innovation on the family has been explored by Carlson (1989), and cultural impacts have also been explored by those interested in tourism development (such as Ahmed, 1986). There have been calls for more ethnographic studies and participant observation to be incorporated into SIA (Howell, 1983), and for integrating quality of life and social impact studies (Olsen *et al.*, 1985). Proctor (1998) argued for more effort to assess the cultural dimensions of global environmental change, i.e. what role culture has in such change and what cultural impacts global change may have.

SIA AND ETHICS

How are SIA practitioners beholden to their employers? What should be their terms of reference? Are they responsible to the public and impacted people, or to their academic discipline? The most common ethical conflict is probably the conflict between academic truth and real-world (commercial or political) expediency. For example, there may be temptation or pressure to tone down or distort findings to suit the commissioning body or avoid official embarrassment. A good example would be those scientists in the UK making early warnings about bovine spongiform encephalopathy (BSE or 'mad cow disease'; *see* Glossary), some of whom faced media ridicule and pressures from various bodies, their peers and employers.

Roche (1999: 187–9) examined the ethics of impact assessment undertaken by NGOs active in development aid. Cernea (1991) observed that many of those conducting SIA are anthropologists, a field that professes to have ethical responsibility towards the interests of those studied, rather than wider development. EIA and eco-audit have begun to move towards accreditation by a professional body that would develop and enforce a code of ethics which, if not followed, could mean an inquiry, financial penalties or the assessor being struck off (i.e. being stripped of their accreditation in order to prevent their practising); it is likely that SIA will follow suit.

SIA AND THE LAW

Without legal requirements for SIA, its development in the USA would doubtless have been much slower (Llewellyn and Freudenburg, 1989; Meidinger and Freudenburg, 1983). The US National Environmental Policy Act (NEPA), passed by Congress in 1970, required impact assessment to include consideration of socio-economic as well as physical impacts. (NEPA's factsheet on SIA and the law is available from http://www.gsa.gov/pbs/pt/call-in/ factshet/1098b/10_98b_2.htm.)

However, it took a number of court actions to establish the need for more than a superficial SIA; notably the drawn-out, often conflicting, conclusions of litigation over the restarting of the Three Mile Island nuclear facility (Llewellyn and Freudenburg, 1989). As SIA concepts and methods come before courts and undergo legal scrutiny, standards should improve, and the public and planning authorities will get a clearer idea of what is expected.

It is important for SIA to be supported by law if it is to be effective. The law can ensure that SIA is applied and that the process is regulated fairly (Canadian Institute of Resources Law, 1993). Since the 1980s there has been considerable development of environmental law, which has given more support to EIA than to SIA. There is, however, a downside of support from the law: when legislation determines, at least in part, the focus of SIA, it may be difficult to reconcile legal requirements with a professional approach and priorities. Boggs (1994: 171) observed that 'The discipline of SIA . . . must be distinguished from the actual practice of SIA which is defined and utilized by agencies.' There seems to have been a gradual shift since NEPA to SIA assessing the needs of not only the commissioning client, but also those of the ultimate client: the democratic polity at large (Boggs, 1994: 172).

In some states, SIA practice seems to have failed to keep up with legislative opportunities; for example, Dale *et al.* (1997) felt that, in Queensland, in spite of good legal support for SIA, progress had been slow because only relatively recently have social impacts been seen to be worthy of serious exploration (strange, given the degree to which social impacts can determine election results).

SIA AND PARTICIPATION

Social psychologists, social anthropologists, market researchers and behavioural sociologists have spent a great deal of time exploring participation issues and have generated a huge literature on participatory research, planning and policy-making. One of the more active fields has been that of participatory rural appraisal (PRA), which seeks to establish what farmers and villagers would benefit from and what they are capable of doing successfully. For perhaps the last 15 years, the participatory approach has been popular with many development agencies and NGOs. Recently, however, there have been some signs of disillusionment and a shift towards integrative approaches (Cooke and Kothari, 2000).

From the outset it should be made clear that 'participation' is a vague term, and one that can be interpreted in a wide variety of ways. Various benefits are claimed for it, among which are that it can: inform people of what is being done; brief them after it has been done; try to involve them fully in decision-making from an early stage; diligently feed public opinion into the development process; and even empower people to offer their views and participate (Holland and Blackburn, 1998). Critics note that it can be a means to get away with ignoring public opinion by giving the impression that people are involved, or a way of sifting public opinion to play down those aspects that developers do not welcome; there may also be situations where public opinion may need to be over-ruled for the wider good of a nation or the world. One must be cautious as to what is meant by the term 'public': is it community participation (implying a more localized group), or is it national, or global population? For whatever group or population, is it participation for all, or just selected segments? Some are sceptical of the real value of participation, dismissing it as 'theology in search of a method' (meaning that they are worried about objectivity and the capacity to effectively conduct participatory SIA). A more cynical view is not uncommon, with administrators saying things akin to 'we believe in participation – as soon as we've made our decision we will consult and inform the public'. It is also fair to say that it is usually the richer, better-educated and more influential members of society that participate, while the weaker remain marginalized and unheard.

In the 1970s, decision-makers and SIA practitioners typically treated the public as a passive patient or even an adversary; social impacts were assessed by outside 'experts', who sometimes had little local knowledge (and occasionally little other experience), and the results were presented as an often inaccessible and unintelligible report made available to a restricted group of decision-makers. Alternatively, results would be 'published' or discussed at a public hearing by a skilled presenter who was able to shrug off awkward questions (Connor, 1998). Nowadays, in a growing number of countries the public is more likely to be treated as an active partner in the development process (Connor, 1997; Creighton, 1981). Interchange of information between planners and the public can have huge benefits: it can gather data, reduce unrest and opposition (although sometimes the opposite may happen), facilitate conciliation, identify useful modifications to developments, bestow legitimacy on decisions made; improve the accountability of officials, and better safeguard people's interests.

Burdge and Robertson (1990) argued forcefully that public involvement must be an integral part of SIA. If people lack knowledge, their perceptions of a proposed development are questionable, and in all probability, opinions will change considerably once they gain a better grasp of a situation (for instance, support for nuclear power generation may turn after a few years to opposition). Participation may speed up the process and help managers cope with such changes. Some of the impetus for increasing public participation may reflect the ongoing shift in the West from representative democracy to participatory democracy, i.e. citizens increasingly expect to be consulted by their governments and public servants (Daneke *et al.*, 1983: 12). Unfortunately, participation often fails to develop in a really helpful and creative manner and, as Daneke *et al.* (1983: 4) pointed out, no matter how good participation is, planners still have to make the right decisions and implement them successfully. The public may want something, but decision-makers may need to decide otherwise. SIA and decision-makers should be considering sustainable development, which means looking after the interests of future generations; public and community interests are likely to favour present-day benefits and may resist trade-offs to provide for the future. So, public support for something may not mean a wise decision. This all has to be weighed against the situation where planners and administrators feel that they 'know best' and try hard to impose their views.

Public or community participation, no matter how carefully undertaken, is not a substitute for thorough SIA. Typically, some form of attitude survey is used to assess public views. There are, however, problems with this approach: it is difficult to ensure that it is representative; and a decision must be made as to how to include the views identified in the SIA final statement (this may require exploration of how social impacts are socially constructed) (Burningham, 1995). SIA should not judge, rather it should report what the impacts will be and advise on the best course of action (Burdge and Vanclay, 1996: 75).

It is widely argued that SIA should consider impacts from the point of view of the impacted group(s). In the cases where development will affect indigenous groups, care should be taken not to over-stress Eurocentric, western concepts of what constitutes development, or utilitarian rules (i.e. 'acting for the common good'), and to ensure the adequate consideration of spiritual beliefs, customs and so on (Burdge, 1994: 229; Lane *et al.*, 1997: 304; Suprapto, 1990). Participation becomes more challenging where a society is composed of a number of social, ethnic, gender or age groups that differ in interests, needs, skills and ability to articulate their opinions (this is probably true of most situations).

Although it may not immediately be apparent from the literature, not many countries go beyond informing the public to actually allow them some say in decision-making; Rickson *et al.* (1990: 235) noted that participatory democracy '. . . is atypical in the global political scene'. Left- or right-wing authoritarian governments are unlikely to welcome SIA approaches that encourage popular participation and empowerment (*see* Glossary). Planners and policy-makers may only target some of the groups in a community or society, and this gives a distorted form of participation. There is a risk if decision-making is delegated to locals that there will be corruption and perhaps tribalism (in developed and developing countries). If participation is handled poorly it can lead to frustration, alienation and opposition.

When should participation take place? Ideally at the earliest data-gathering stage – as well as part-way through assessment to enable people to make an input to final recommendations – and at the close, when SIA is acted upon. US law usually requires a public hearing within 45 days of the publication of a draft EIS. Common techniques used for 'participation' are listed in Box 4.2. These vary in their effectiveness and some do not facilitate dialogue. Public hearings, for example, can be a good way to collect information or foster consensus, but they are also widely used by decision-makers to control participation (as mentioned earlier, they can be manipulated skilfully: the public is allowed to air its frustration and fears, antagonism is defused, yet decisions are little altered, indeed they are legitimized). Other problems with public hearings are as follows.

- They can be very unrepresentative, tending to elicit input from those who might be hurt by a development rather than those who might be helped, and so emphasizing the negative and perhaps branding those concerned as troublemakers.
- Uninterested, but possibly impacted, people (often a large percentage of the total population) fail to make an input.

- To aid mass participation at a meeting, the information released to the people may be over-simplified and distorted.
- Some special interest groups may avoid participation so as to retain their status as opponents.
- A NIMBY ('not in my back yard') reaction may be encountered, perhaps orchestrated by only a few people, and possibly even by outsiders; these views may not represent the good of the community as a whole (which is what public involvement should be seeking to protect).

Participation can be seen as a learning process: the assessors have to learn how to encourage and support participation, and the participants in many situations (if not all) must be informed, even educated, before they have the confidence or ability to pass on useful information to developers or become usefully involved in other ways (Webler *et al.*, 1995). Several approaches have been developed which combine evaluation, education and participation; one of these is the so-called 'fishbowl technique' (Daneke *et al.*, 1983: 18–20). This appeared in the 1970s and consists of several rounds of interaction with the public; brochures are issued to inform them about SIA aims and to invite feedback, which is then incorporated into a second brochure (and, if need be, the process is repeated). These methods can help inform and guide, but hopefully not manipulate, responsible citizen action. Another approach is to

Box 4.2 Techniques used in SIA for public participation

- key informants
- advisory groups
- community forum
- Delphi technique
- nominal group exercise
- questionnaire survey
- jury panel
- citizen committee
- public hearing
- workshop, mail or telephone survey (these can be two-way)
- referendum
- workshop
- 'drop-in shop'
- 'phone-in'
- newsletter
- public display of information

Note: some of the above simply collect information; some are consultative; some are concerned with empowerment; some require involvement in policy formulation or planning.
Source: several sources, including Smith (1993: 67) and Milbrath (in Daneke *et al.*, 1983: 89)

use an ombudsman and a spokesperson to act as intermediaries and, if necessary, mediators. Focus groups have become a popular means of involving people in decision-making (Kruger, 1994; Morgan, 1993; Morgan and Spanish, 1984) (*see* Chapter 6). Care must be exercised when using focus groups to ensure that decision-makers do not manipulate them, or try to claim they are not responsible for policies because 'the people decided what they wanted'. Like SIA in general, participation is constrained by time and logistics, especially funding; ideally it should be simple, transparent and cost-effective.

SIA AND EMPOWERMENT

A question that has been asked by a number of social scientists and NGOs is: 'Can SIA empower communities?' (Gagnon *et al.*, 1993; Smith, 1993: 72). A second question ought to follow: 'Should SIA empower communities, or is it better it remains neutral?' The answer to the first is that SIA does not necessarily empower people, and may do the opposite. Howitt (1989: 159) makes the point that where SIA is neutral and advising decision-makers, it is essentially empowering them. In Australia, Canada and the USA, SIA has been hailed as an important means of survival for indigenous peoples facing encroachment by the state or commercial interests (Howitt, 1989: 154). An early and influential example is the Canadian Mackenzie Valley Pipeline case (the Berger Inquiry), where SIA was seen as a catalyst for equitable development (*see* Chapter 8). The 1975 Ranger Uranium Environmental Inquiry (Australia) is often cited as another, although somewhat different, example of the role of SIA as a means of empowerment (Howitt, 1989: 155–7; *see also* Howitt, 1993).

It should be remembered that there are countries where to be caught with a book on participation or empowerment could result in harassment by security forces and even imprisonment. Not all countries are yet willing to embrace participation and empowerment, and many elected, as well as undemocratically appointed, officials feel that their election provides a mandate to act on behalf of the people.

SIA AND REGIONAL PLANNING

Development planning has often adopted a regional approach. Generally, regional planners favour an integrated approach, which means that SIA can be included (Illo, 1988; McDonald, 1990; Makin and Gillman, 1987).

SIA and Gender

Gender assessment has spread since the start of the UN Decade for Women (1971–81). Verloo and Roggeband (1996) argued that developments are seldom gender-neutral, and so gender impact assessment is needed to assess the potential effects of new policies, plans or programmes on gender relations. They noted (1996: 17) that nowhere in the 1994 Interorganizational Committee on Guidelines for Social Impact Assessment is there any recommendation for gender assessment. Gender assessments have been conducted (Freeman and Frey, 1991; Feldstein and Jiggens, 1994; Gurung, 1995; ICPE, 1993; Miyata, 1995; Thomas-Slayter *et al.*), and Rao *et al.* (1996) examined the social impact of leprosy, noting that for women there is a marked delay in diagnosis and also in seeking treatment. It would be interesting to see similar assessments for other diseases in order to establish whether there are gender differences. There may be a marked divergence between the sexes as to how they respond to developments (Stout-Wiegand and Trent, 1983), and male and female are also likely to differ in their vulnerability to impacts (Moen, 1981).

References

Abaza, H. (1996) Integration of sustainable objectives in structural adjustment programmes using SEA. *Project Appraisal* **11(3)**, 217–28.

Abaza, H. (1998) Integration of sustainability objectives in structural adjustment programmes through the use of strategic environmental assessment, in C.H. Kirkpatrick and N. Lee (eds) *Sustainable Development in a Developing World: integrating socio-economic appraisal and environmental assessment*. Edward Elgar, Cheltenham, 25–45.

Ahmed, S.A. (1986) Perceptions of the socioeconomic and cultural impact of tourism in Sri Lanka. *Canadian Journal of Development Studies* **7(2)**, 239–55.

Annema, J.A., Van Wee, B., Van Hoek, T. and **Van den Waard, J.** (1999) Evaluation of Dutch public investment plans. *Environmental Impact Assessment Review* **19(3)**, 305–17.

Armour, A. (1988) Methodological problems in social impact monitoring. *Environmental Impact Assessment Review* **8(3)**, 249–65.

Armour, A. (1990) Integrating impact assessment into the planning process. *Impact Assessment Bulletin* **8(1–2)**, 3–14.

Association for Social Assessment (1994) Social assessment and Maori policy development. *Social Impact Assessment Newsletter* No. 35, 10–11.

Balsamo, A. (1996) Myths of information: the cultural impact of new information technologies. *Technology Assessment & Strategic Management* **8(5)**, 341–8.

Boggs, J.P. (1994) Planning and the law of social impact assessment (comment). *Human Organization* **53(2)**, 167–74.

Bond, A. (1995) Integrating SIA into EIA. *Environmental Assessment* **3(2)**, 125–30.

Boothroyd, P. (1998) *Social Policy Assessment Research: the establishment, the underground. A state-of-the-art report*. International Development Research Centre (IDRC), Ottawa.

Bourdillon, N., Braithwaite, R., Hopkins, D. and **France, R.** (1995) Archaeological and other material and cultural assets, in **P. Morris**. and **R. Therivel** (eds) (1995) *Methods of Environmental Impact Assessment*. University College London Press, London, 96–119.

Burdge, R.J. (1987) The social impact assessment model and the planning process. *Environmental Impact Assessment Review* **7(4)**, 141–50.

Burdge, R.J. (1990) Utilizing social impact assessment variables in the planning model. *Impact Assessment Bulletin* **8(1–2)**, 85–99.

Burdge, R.J. (1994) *A Conceptual Approach to Social Impact Assessment: a collection of writings by Rabel J. Burdge and colleagues*. Social Ecology Press, Middleton (Wisconsin).

Burdge, R.J. (1995) *A Community Guide to Social Impact Assessment*. Social Ecology Press, Middleton (WI).

Burdge, R.J. and **Robertson, R.A.** (1990) Social impact assessment and the public involvement process. *Environmental Impact Assessment Review* **10(1–2)**, 81–90.

Burdge, R.J. and **Vanclay, F.** (1996) Social impact assessment: a contribution to the state of the art series. *Impact Assessment* **14(1)**, 59–86.

Burningham, K. (1995) Attitudes, accounts and impact assessment. *Sociological Review* **43(1)**, 100–22.

Canadian Institute of Resources Law (1993) *Fairness in Environmental and Social Impact Assessment Processes: proceedings of a seminar convened by the Canadian Institute of Resources Law, University of Calgary and the Federal Environmental Assessment Review Office, Vancouver, British Columbia, 1–3 February 1993*. The Banff Centre, Vancouver.

Canter, L.W. (1977) Prediction and assessment of impacts on the cultural environment, in L.W. Canter (ed.), *Environmental Impact Assessment*. McGraw-Hill, New York (NY), 153–61.

Carlson, P.A. (1989) Technology on the home front: social impact assessment and domestic culture. *Impact Assessment Bulletin* **7(1)**, 1–4.

Cernea, M.M. (1991) *Putting People First, Sociological Variables in Rural Development*. The World Bank, Washington (DC).

Cochrane, G. (1979) *The Cultural Appraisal of Development Projects*. Praeger, New York (NY).

Connor, D.M. (1998) Participative social impact assessment and management cross-cultural application. *Impact Assessment and Project Appraisal* **16(1)**, 65–9.

Connor, D.M. (ed.) (1997) *Constructive Citizen Participation: a resource book* (6th edn). Development Press, Victoria, British Columbia, Canada.

Cooke, B. and **Kothari, U. (eds)** (2000) *Participation, the New Tyranny*. Zed, London.

Creighton, J.L. (1981) *The Public Involvement Manual*. ABT Books, Cambridge (MA).

Dale, A.P. (1993) An Assessment of Planning for Government Funded Land Use Development Projects in Australian Aboriginal Communities. PhD thesis, Griffith University, Brisbane.

Dale, A.P. and **Lane, M.B.** (1994) Strategic perspectives analysis: a procedure for participatory and political social impact assessment, *Society and Natural Resources* **7(3)**, 253–67.

Dale, A.P., Chapman, P. and **McDonald, M.L.** (1997) Social impact assessment in Queensland: why practice lags behind legislative opportunity. *Impact Assessment* **15(2)**, 159–80.

Daneke, G.A., Garcia, M.W. and **Priscoli, J.D.** (eds) (1983) *Public Involvement and Social Impact Assessment*. Westview, Boulder (CO).

Davis, W. (1997) *One River: science, adventure and hallucinogenics in the Amazon Basin*. Simon and Schuster, London.

DeBoer, J. and **Sadler, B.** (eds) (1996) *Strategic Environmental Assessment: environmental assessment of policies* (VROM, Series No. 54). Ministry of Housing, Spatial Planning and the Environment (VROM), The Hague.

Dickens, R.S. Jnr and **Hill, C.E.** (eds) (1978) *Cultural Resources: planning and development*. Westview, Boulder (CO).

Edelstein, M.P. and **Klee, D.A.** (1995) Cultural relativity of impact assessment: Native Hawaiian opposition to geothermal energy development. *Society and Natural Resources* **8(1)**, 19–34.

European Commission (1994) *Strategic Environmental Assessment: existing methodology*. European Commission (DG-XI), Brussels.

Feldstein, H. and **Jiggens, J.** (eds) (1994) *Tools for the Field: gender analysis in farming systems research and evaluation*. Kumarian Press, West Hartford (CT).

Finsterbusch, K. (1984) Social impact assessment as a policy science methodology. *Impact Assessment Bulletin* **3(2)**, 37–43.

Finsterbusch, K. and **VanWicklin, W.A.** (1989) Project problems and shortfalls: the need for social impact assessment in AID projects, in S.S. Nagel and R.V. Bartlett (eds), *Policy Through Impact Assessment: institutionalized analysis*. Greenwood Press, New York (NY), 73–84.

Fischer, T.B. (1999) Comprehensive analysis of environmental and socioeconomic impacts in SEA for transport related policies, plans and programmes. *Environmental Impact Assessment Review* **19(3)**, 275–303.

Freeman, D. and **Frey, R.S.** (1991) A modest proposal for assessing social impacts of natural resource policies. *Journal of Environmental Systems* **20(4)**, 375–404.

Freudenburg, W.R. (1984) Probabalistic risk assessment and social impact assessment: the need for cross-fertilization. *Impact Assessment Bulletin* **3(2)**, 44–7.

Freudenburg, W.R. and **Keating, K.M.** (1985) Applying sociology to policy: social science and the environmental impact statement. *Rural Sociology* **50(4)**, 578–605.

Gagnon, C., **Hirsch, P.** and **Howitt, R.** (1993) Can SIA empower communities? *Environmental Impact Assessment Review* **13(4)**, 229–53.

Gilder, N.M. (1995) A social impact assessment approach using the reference group as the standard of impact analysis. The case of Hana: Hawaiians and the proposed golf course. *Environmental Impact Assessment Review* **15(2)**, 179–96.

Gismondi, M. (1997) Sociology and environmental impact assessment. *Canadian Journal of Sociology* **22(4)**, 457–79.

Gloria, H.K. (1990) Environmental impact study: a cultural assessment of the ethnolinguistic groups in Mt Apo National Park (Philippines). *Tambara: Ateneo de Davao University Journal* **7(1)**, 83–100.

Gold, R.L. (1978) Linking social with other impact assessments, in R.K. Jain and B.L Hutchings (eds), *Environmental Impact Analysis: emerging issues in planning*. University of Illinois Press, Urbana (IL), 105–16.

Goodland, R.J. and **Tillman, G.** (1995) *Strategic Environmental Assessment – Strengthening the Environmental Assessment Process*. The World Bank, Washington (DC).

Gramling, R. and **Freudenburg, W.R.** (1992) Opportunity–threat, development, and adaption: toward a comprehensive framework for social impact assessment. *Rural Sociology* **57(2)**, 216–34.

Gurung, D. (1995) *Tourism and Gender: impact and implications of tourism on Nepalese women* (ICIMOD Paper No. M6195/3). International Centre for Integrated Mountain Development, Kathmandu (Nepal).

Halstead, J.M., Chase, R.A., Murdock, S.H. and **Leistritz, F.L.** (1984) *Socioeconomic Impact Management: design and implementation*. Westview, Boulder (CO).

Hedo, D. and **Bina, O.** (1999) Strategic environmental assessment of hydrological and irrigation plans in Castilla y Leon, Spain. *Environmental Impact Assessment Review* **19(3)**, 259–73.

Holland, J. and **Blackburn, J.** (1998) *Whose Voice? Participatory Research and Policy Change*. Intermediate Technology Publications, London.

Horton, S. and **Memon, A.** (1997) SEA: the uneven development of the environment? *Environmental Impact Assessment Review* **17(3)**, 163–75.

Howell, B.J. (1983) Implications of the Cultural Conservation Report for social impact assessment. *Human Organization* **42(4)**, 346–50.

Howitt, R. (1989) Social impact assessment: lessons from the Australian experience. *Australian Geographer* **20(2)**, 153–66.

Howitt, R. (1993) Social impact assessment as 'applied peoples' geography'. *Australian Geographical Studies* **31(2)**, 127–40.

Hughes, H.R. (1986) Assessing cultural impacts: industrial effluents and the New Zealand Maori. *Environmental Impact Assessment Review* **6(3)**, 285–300.

ICPE (1993) Social impact assessment of investment/acquisition of technology projects in developing countries, with particular reference to the position of women. *Public Enterprise* **13(3–4)**, p. 239.

Illo, J.F.I. (1988) *Irrigation in the Philippines: impact on women and their households. Women's roles and gender differences in development: cases for planners, Asia* 2. The Population Council, Bangkok.

Juslén, J. (1995) Social impact assessment: a look at Finnish experiences. *Project Appraisal* **10(3)**, 163–70.

Kessler, J.J. and **vanDorp, M.** (1996) Structural adjustment and the environment: the need for an analytical methodology. *Ecological Economics* **27(3)**, 267–81.

King, T.F. (1998) How the archaeologists stole culture: a gap in American environmental impact assessment practice and how to fill it. *Environmental Impact Assessment Review* **18(2)**, 117–33.

King, T.F. (2000) What should be the 'cultural resources' element of an EIA? *Environmental Impact Assessment Review* **20(1)**, 5–30.

Kirkpatrick, C.H. and **Lee, N.** (1999) Special issue: integrated appraisal and decision-making. *Environmental Impact Assessment Review* **19(3)**, 227–32.

Kirkpatrick, C.H. and **Lee, N.** (eds) (1997) *Sustainable Development in a Developing World: integrating socio-economic appraisal and environmental assessment*. Edward Elgar, Cheltenham.

Kruger, R.A. (1994) *Focus Groups: a practical guide for applied research* (2nd edn). Sage, Thousand Oaks (CA).

Lane, M.B., Ross, H. and **Dale, A.P.** (1997) Social impact research: integrating the technical, political, and planning paradigms. *Human Organization* **56(3)**, 302–10.

Lee, N. and **Kirkpatrick, C.** (eds) (1996) *Project Appraisal* **11(4)** – special issue on environmental assessment and socio-economic appraisal in development.

Lee, N. and **Kirkpatrick, C.** (eds) (2000) *Integrated Appraisal and Sustainable Development in a Developing World*. Edward Elgar, Cheltenham.

Lee, N. and **Walsh, F.** (1992) Strategic environmental assessment: an overview. *Project Appraisal* **7(3)**, 126–37.

Leistritz, F.L. and **Chase, R.A.** (1982) Socioeconomic monitoring systems: a review and recommendations. *Journal of Environmental Management* **19(4)**, 333–49.

Leistritz, F.L. and **Ekstrom, B.** (1988) Integrating social impact assessment into the planning process. *Impact Assessment Bulletin* **6(2)**, 17–20.

Llewellyn, L.G. and **Freudenburg, W.R.** (1989) The legal requirements for social impact assessment: assessing the social science fallout from Three Mile Island. *Society and Natural Resources* **2(3)**, 193–208.

Loomis, O. (1982) Cultural Conservation: the protection of cultural heritage in the United States (mimeo). Publication details unknown.

McDonald, G.T. (1990) Regional economic and social impact assessment. *Environmental Impact Assessment Review* **10(1–2)**, 25–36.

Makin, K. and **Gillman, C.** (1987) *Regional Social Impact Review – East Cape.* State Services Commission, Social Impact Unit, Wellington.

Meidinger, E.E. and **Freudenburg, W.R.** (1983) The legal status of social impact assessment: recent developments. *Environmental Sociology* **34(1)**, 30–3.

Miyata, K. (1995) The social impact of electronic media: a gender difference perspective (in Japanese). *Journal of Mass Communication Studies* **49(1)**, 59–71.

Moen, E. (1981) Women in energy boom towns. *Psychology of Women Quarterly* **6(1)**, 99–112.

Morgan, D.L. (ed.) (1993) *Successful Focus Groups*. Sage, Newbury Park (CA).

Morgan, D.L. and **Spanish, M.T.** (1984) Focus groups: a new tool for qualitative research. *Qualitative Sociology* **7(3)**, 253–70.

Olsen, M.E., Canan, P. and **Hennessy, M.** (1985) A value-based community assessment process – integrating quality of life and social impact studies. *Sociological Methods and Research* **13(3)**, 325–61.

Owen Harrop, D. and **Ashley Nixon, J.** (1999) *Environmental Assessment in Practice.* Routledge, London.

Partidario, M. do R. (1997) Strategic environmental management: key issues emerging from recent practice. *Environmental Impact Assessment Review* **13(3)**, 145–61.

Proctor, J.D. (1998) The meaning of global environmental change: retheorizing culture in human dimensions research. *Global Environmental Change: Human and Policy Dimensions* **8(3)**, 227–48.

Ralston, I. and **Thomas, R.** (eds) (1993) *Environmental Assessment and Archaeology* (Occasional Paper No. 5). Institute of Field Archaeologists, Birmingham (UK).

Rao, S., Garole, V., Waluwalkar, S., Khat, S. and **Karandikar, N.** (1996) Gender differentiation in the social impact of leprosy. *Leprosy Review* **62(3)**, 190–199.

Ravetz, J. (1998) Integrated assessment models: from global to local. *Impact Assessment and Project Assessment* **16(2)**, 147–54.

Rickson, R.E., Burdge, R.J., Hundlow, T. and **McDonald, G.T.** (1990) Institutional constraints to adoption of social impact assessment as a decision-making and planning tool. *Environmental Impact Assessment Review* **10(1–2)**, 233–43.

Roche, C. (1999) *Impact Assessment for Development Agencies: learning to value change.* Oxfam (with Novib), Oxford.

Rohe, W.M. (1982) Social impact analysis and the planning process in the United States: a review and critique. *Town Planning Review* **53(4)**, 367–82.

Rossini, F.A. and **Porter, A.L.** (eds) (1983) *Integrated Impact Assessment.* Westview, Boulder.

Schoeffel, P. (1995) Cultural and institutional issues in the appraisal of projects in developing countries: South Pacific water resources. *Project Appraisal* **10(3)**, 155–61.

Schwing, R.C. and **Albers, W.A. Jnr** (eds) (1980) *Societal Risk Assessment: how safe is safe enough?* Plenum Press, New York (NY).

Shepherd, A. and **Ortolano, L.** (1996) Strategic environmental assessment for sustainable urban development. *Environmental Impact Assessment Review* **16(4–6)**, 321–35.

Smith, L.G. (1993) Impact Assessment and Sustainable Resource Management. Longman, Harlow.

Stea, D. and **Buge, C.** (1983) Cultural impact assessment: two cases in Native American communities. *Environmental Impact Assessment Review* **1(4)**, 397–412.

Stout-Wiegand, N. and **Trent, R.B.** (1983) Sex differences in attitudes toward new energy resource development. *Rural Sociology* **48(4)**, 637–46.

Suprapto, R.A. (1990) Social impact assessment and planning: the Indonesian experience. *Impact Assessment Bulletin* **8(1–2)**, 25–8.

Tal, R.S.J. and **Vellinga, P.** (1998) The European Forum on Integrated Environmental Assessment. *Environmental Modeling and Assessment* **3(2)**, 181–91.

Tan, A.S., Tan, G.K., and **Tan, A.S.** (1987) American TV in the Philippines: a test of cultural impact. *Journalism Quarterly* **64(1)**, 65–70.

Tassey, G. (1999) Lessons learned about the methodology of economic impact studies: the NIST experiences. *Evaluation and Program Planning* **22(1)**, 113–19.

Therivel, R. and **Partidario, M. do R.** (eds) (1996) *The Practice of Strategic Environmental Assessment*. Earthscan, London.

Therivel, R., Wilson, E., Thompson, S., Heany, D. and **Pritchard, D.** (1992) *Strategic Environmental Assessment*. Earthscan, London.

Thomas-Slayter, B., Esser, A.L. and **Shields, M.D.** (1993) *Tools for gender analysis: a guide to field methods for bringing gender into sustainable resource management*. Clark University, Worcester.

Toth, F.L. and **Hizsnyik, E.** (1998) Integrated environmental assessment methods: evaluation and applications. *Environmental Modeling and Assessment* **3(2)**, 193–207.

Tugwell, P., SitthiAmorn, C., O'Connor, A., Hatcher Roberts, J., Bergevin, Y. and **Wolfson, M.** (1995) Technology assessment: old, new, and needs-based. *International Journal of Technology Assessment in Health Care* **11(4)**, 650–62.

Van den Ende, J., Mulder, K., Knot, M., Moors, E. and **Vergragt, P.** (1998) Traditional and modern technology assessment: towards a total research methodology and learning strategy for social impact assessment. *Technological Forecasting and Social Change* **58(1)**, 5–22.

Verloo, M. and **Roggeband, C.** (1996) Gender and impact assessment: the development of a new instrument in The Netherlands. *Impact Assessment* **14(1)**, 3–20.

Webler, T., Kastenholz, H. and **Renn, O.** (1995) Public participation in impact assessment: a social learning perspective. *Environmental Impact Assessment Review* **15(5)**, 443–63.

Weston, H. (1982) *Social Impact Assessment and its Relationship to Social Policy*. Kinhill, Melbourne.

Wildman, P. (1990) Methodological and social policy issues in social impact assessment. *Environmental Impact Assessment Review* **10(1–2)**, 69–79.

Wolf, C.P. (1978) The cultural impact statement, in R.S. Dickins jnr and C.E. Hill (eds), *Cultural Resources: planning and management*. Westview, Boulder (CO), 178–93.

Wolf, C.P. (1980) Getting social impact assessment into the policy arena. *Environmental Impact Assessment Review* **1(1)**, 27–36.

Wood, C. and **Djeddour, M.** (1992) Strategic environmental assessment: EIA of policies, plans and programmes. *Impact Assessment Bulletin* **10(1)**, 3–21.

Xing, L. (1999) The transformation of ideology from Mao to Deng: impact on China's social welfare outcome. *International Journal of Social Welfare* **8(2)**, 86–96.

5

CHALLENGES FACED BY SIA

> 'SIA . . . cannot be regarded as a science in the conventional sense of the word . . .' (Torgerson, 1980: 35)

SIA has made considerable progress since the 1970s, but the methodology, techniques and approach need improvement, and there are many constraints on its effective practice (Wolf, 1981). There is still debate as to whether SIA should be treated separately from, or integrated with, other impact assessments, although the latter view seems to be gaining support. SIA has attracted less support and funds than EIA (Glasson and Heaney, 1993) and, when they are undertaken, SIAs are often partly or wholly ignored by decision-makers (Juslén, 1995). In many countries there are ambiguities about SIAs' legal status (Kirkpatrick and Lee, 1997). In short, there are many challenges facing SIA. (Some of the weaknesses of SIA are listed in Box 5.1.)

Torgerson (1980: 4–6) argued that SIA is a social phenomenon, and that those involved in carrying it out are involved in social activities with social consequences; to be effective, assessors must be aware of the social context. Put crudely, an assessor is more of an 'actor' than an impartial and objective outside observer. Thus, even if applied in a technocratic fashion, SIA is not uninvolved or value-free. It should also be stressed that some social impacts are much more difficult to assess than others. Torgerson (1980: 137) was critical of any approach to SIA that sought to compare costs with benefits, as early efforts generally did; it is better, he argued, to ascertain the full nature and extent of probable impacts.

Improving the theoretical foundations of SIA

Dietz (1987) noted that cost–benefit and risk assessments are guided by efficiency notions derived from welfare economics; and that systems analysis rests on systems theory. However, SIA has generally been carried out on an

Box 5.1 Some of the weaknesses of SIA

- Lack of standardization of approach.
- Poorly funded compared with EIA.
- Often given too little time for adequate assessment.
- Often allowed only one opportunity for assessment (giving a spatially and temporally limited 'snapshot' view).
- Difficulties in ensuring repeated, reliable results because the theoretical basis has been poor.
- SIA deals with the more complex/changeable factors of EIA, so is likely to be less accurate and slower.
- Social science traditions involved in SIA tend to be critical and discursive, rather than predictive and explanatory. Thus, it is difficult to get a solid supportive theoretical framework.
- SIA has mainly been applied at corporation, federal government or regional authority level, and has often focused a great deal on economic costs and too little on how local people will be affected by development.
- Often, SIA has access to only a poor database, so projections are hindered.
- The social sciences involved tend to have different, even contradictory language, units of measurement, interpretation of indices, etc. Also, the various social impacts must be assessed using a wide range of different units, so comparison of results is a problem.
- SIA is often conducted by consultants who are poorly trained in social science (some SIAs have been conducted by non-social scientists, sometimes by graduate students), or have too restricted an expertise (as with EIA, accreditation may resolve this).
- SIA has been too infrequently subjected to appraisal to see how it performed and what went wrong; consequently there is a failure to learn as much as might have been possible from hindsight.
- Hindsight is often denied a wide enough audience because it is confined to 'grey literature' (reports of restricted circulation that are seldom peer reviewed).
- SIA is treated more as an approval mechanism to determine whether a development should proceed, and what conditions should be applied. There is a failure to use SIA for ensuring effective monitoring, mitigation of problems and management.
- Legislation fails to oversee the SIA process adequately and may allow authorities simply to ignore findings.
- SIA is less likely to deliver clear, concise, relatively straightforward recommendations than EIA, because social issues can be complex and difficult to address.

Sources: Burdge and Vanclay (1996: 66–70); Burningham (1995); Little and Krannich (1988)

ad hoc basis (frequently in a biased way), often in grudging response to laws or regulations. Geisler (1993: 332) developed the arguments of Rees (1988), stressing that unless SIA '. . . is replicated like an experiment over time, it will be conducted on a reactive, project-by-project, short-term basis of limited value to sustainable development'. Laws, regulations, terms of reference and guidelines tend to differ; consequently there have been calls for a better theoretical framework for SIA to help improve its practice and ensure that the right questions are asked.

There are challenges to overcome in order to arrive at a better theoretical foundation, as outlined below.

1. If humans are to be assured a reasonable, and sustainable, livelihood it is vital that developers understand and relate to both socio-economic and ecological workings. Unfortunately, social scientists have been relatively slow to develop an interest in environmental issues (Freudenburg and Keating, 1992). Dunlap and Catton (1979) reviewed the reasons why sociologists delayed exploring environmental issues, noting (1979: 260) that it was largely the development of SIA that prompted the American Sociological Association to establish an Ad Hoc Committee on Environmental Sociology, charged with establishing guidelines for sociological contributions to EISs.
2. Many, possibly most, social science theories are 'theories in name only . . . being more akin to perspectives or world views than to theories of physical science' (Little and Krannich, 1988: 23). So, there are difficulties with finding a theoretical base from the social sciences, and the complexity and holistic nature of SIA makes it daunting. Little and Krannich (1988: 24) concluded that, rather than pursue a futile hunt for a single unifying theory for SIA, effort should be made to use available theories as guides for the SIA process. As a model for this, they advocated the use of local communities as the primary unit of analysis and called for a conceptual framework to order this.

One 'learning difficulty' faced by SIA is that the literature focuses heavily on the USA, and on 'snapshot' applications (*see* Chapter 3). There are surprisingly few comparisons or syntheses of information on SIAs; one has been conducted by Deng and Altenhoefel (1997), who examined 74 SIAs conducted by the US Army Corps of Engineers, the US Forest Service and the Federal Highway Administration. Their study found that: there was too much emphasis on economic, and too little on cultural, social and psychological impacts; and that the US Government had a contradictory role, as both development promoter and protector of public interests. SIA, it seems, was weakened by being used to try to help resolve that contradiction.

There is a need to draw from studies of attitude, perception and the psychology of social impacts to help improve SIA (Albrecht and Thompson, 1988; Latane, 1981; Meissen and Cipriani, 1984). One problem is that it is difficult to assign consistent, accurate and universal values to psychological factors – which makes the objective comparison of situations difficult. Something like noise impact can be recorded as decibels of noise in a given time, but factors such as severe psychological stress have to be recorded in a more subjective way (though they are nevertheless of great importance).

METHODOLOGICAL CHALLENGES

There has been growing interest in improving SIA methodology (Morvaridi, 1997). Two questions are often asked about SIA: 'What constitutes a necessary and adequate assessment?' and 'How can SIA avoid giving only a "snapshot" view and become more ongoing?' A better assessment approach might be to use SIA to link pre-development assessment, impact assessment during implementation and ongoing monitoring (Geisler, 1993: 329). Torgerson (1980: 140) considered the first question, urging SIA to combine theoretical approaches with empiricism; he also observed that, while many claim assessors are seeking to promote the welfare of the whole community, in reality they are more likely to be meeting the wishes of certain powerful and persuasive special interest groups.

SIA would better assist development planners if it could reliably identify 'social capital', the abilities, traditions and attitudes which help ensure that a group of people will support each other, respond to challenges in a constructive manner and innovate. In many situations, social capital has been damaged or lost, is being eroded, or is at risk; it is important to try and develop SIA to detect threats to social capital and, if possible, to advise on the prevention of damage to such an important key to sustainable development.

Most guidebooks to SIA stress the importance of measuring attitudes, values and behaviour. In practice, assessing people's present attitudes and perceptions often presents real challenges – even for social psychologists (who should be given the task). Yet, SIA must go beyond that to establish likely future attitudes, and predicting these is tremendously difficult. Assessing present or future attitudes is beset by difficulties; for example, how are they to be measured, scaled, compared in an objective way? Should consideration of attitudes be done once as part of a pre-development SIA, or repeated to establish how they change as time progresses? Attitudes affect perceptions and people's interpretation of events, and so play a crucial part in determining actions and responses. For example, once people develop mistrust in a developer or an authority, this can be very difficult to overcome and SIA might help ensure that such a situation is prevented or defused. To determine reliably the attitude of people to, say, a nuclear power station, an atomic waste repository or a conservation area may be a goal of SIA, but such a simplistic 'attitude survey' is probably not a good enough foundation from which to predict future behaviour. Attitudes may not be well formed, and the linkages between attitude and behaviour are complex; put crudely, there is often a big difference between what people say or feel and what they actually do.

Environmental management has developed a working concept: best practicable environmental option (BPEO), whereby efforts are made to assess an optimum way forward for a development. BPEO may not be the most beneficial way environmentally, nor the most cost-effective, but it is the best that can reasonably be achieved in practice. It might be worth SIA promoting a similar concept to planners and the public best practicable social option (BPSO).

SIA has to contend with communities in which various groups may be very differently affected, possibly at different times. There is thus a need to develop a precise, probably multiple-focus, SIA. One of the steps of SIA is to identify stakeholders and target groups. This may be difficult if a community is changing rapidly, if there are seasonal residents or tourists, new arrivals and so on. Social impacts can be difficult to predict, even when successive developments have virtually identical pre-development conditions and involve very similar changes, because other factors may shift; for example, even the same society may react very differently to identical repeated challenges. Also, differing external influences may be felt. Given this unpredictability, SIA should adopt an adaptive, flexible approach.

Better assessment of indirect and cumulative impacts has long been a goal of EIA (Bain *et al.*, 1986; Carley, 1984). A proposal or action can cause physical or social impacts (first-order or direct impacts), these in turn may each trigger one or more (indirect or second-order) social or physical impacts, which in their turn may form a chain of causation (*see* Figure 5.1). With each successive step, accurate prediction becomes more of a challenge, even if there is no crossover from physical to social or vice versa, and ignoring the possibility of positive or negative feedbacks. To make matters worse, unrelated chains of causation may combine at some point (in time or space) to cause difficult-to-predict cumulative impacts.

Even with project-focused SIA, cumulative impacts pose a challenge, but when SIA is applied to programmes and policies, or longer-term projects, cumulative impacts are more likely to be encountered and are very difficult to predict. To counter this weakness, Geisler (1993: 330) argued that SIA should start with sound aims, but should also be flexible and adaptive so that it can respond to new developments. Other possibilities are to make use of strategic approaches to assessment (*see* the discussion of SEA in Chapter 4), or to predict scenarios, rather than attempt precise forecasting (*see* Figure 6.3).

INSTITUTIONAL CONSTRAINTS

One of the most obvious, and quite widespread, problems faced by SIA is the failure of established administrations to take it seriously. Burdge (1994: 229–38) reviewed the institutional constraints that hinder the effective adoption of SIA by national and local decision-makers. He defined institutional constraints as patterns of behaviour, values and beliefs that have been established, including patterns of prestige, power, governance and economics. Finsterbusch (1995) stressed the likelihood of the intrusion of 'politics' into the effective practice of SIA, noting that 'Politics is the main reason why SIAs are often not conducted when they are needed, why SIAs are sometimes not done well, and why they are sometimes purposely biased.' He also bemoaned 'the impact of "bureaucratization"', which is supposed to standardize by

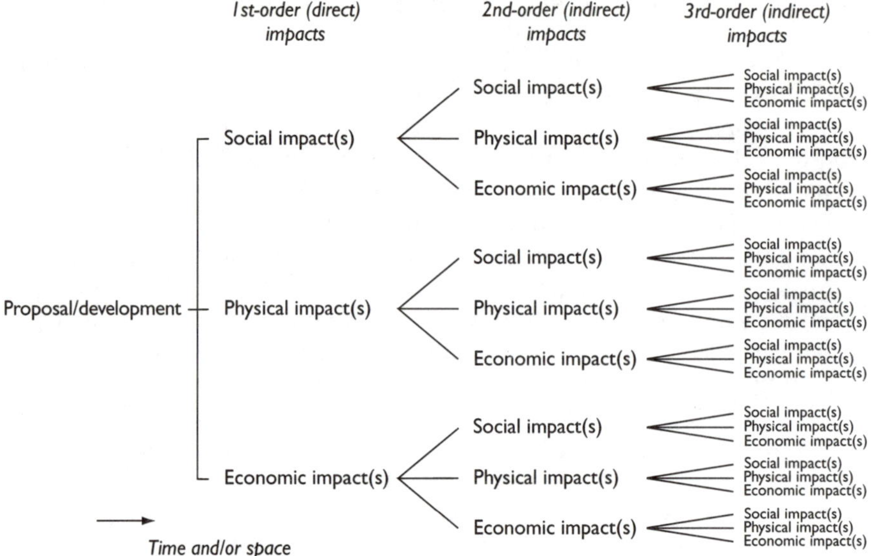

FIGURE 5.1 Direct and indirect impacts (as far as 3rd order)
In practice it can be difficult to trace impacts beyond 5th order, even using network diagrams; often, the approaches adopted identify only 1st order – which may give a false sense of security to SIA users. There can be cumulative impacts, whereby different chains of causation come together to cause a problem (or benefit); these are often very difficult to identify. This is a gross simplification – in reality complex positive and negative feedbacks, and indirect impacts, conspire to make prediction a challenge. As an impact propagates down the 'chain of causation' (moving towards the right-hand side of the diagram) there are indirect impacts and possibly feedbacks (not shown).

taking the formula that works best and to routinize by developing workable procedures for implementing it, and institutionalizing these procedures as practices, guidelines and regulations. Finsterbusch (1995: 247) observed that 'bureaucratic processes are efficient *if* the activity being analysed is a relatively standard event. . . . But relatively inflexible procedures can become dysfunctional for all nonstandard cases.' SIA often deals with the non-standard and unexpected; yet, without bureaucratic regulations, SIA would probably be more often avoided, and assessment in practice should be flexible and professional.

There are clearly theoretical, methodological and institutional weaknesses and contradictions; and there are other factors to consider too. Burdge and Vanclay (1996: 63) stressed that the 'effectiveness of SIA rests on the integrity of the SIA practitioners'.

Professional constraints

There have been calls for improved professional standards since the 1980s (Williams and Freudenburg, 1988). A set of guidelines was published in the 1990s by the Interorganizational Committee on Guidelines and Principles for SIA in various journals, including *Environmental Impact Assessment Review* **15(1)**: 11–43. There is a trend in eco-auditing and EIA towards professional accreditation and monitoring of practitioners. Whether voluntary or compulsory, such moves would help improve the practice of SIA, spread established international standards (improving quality and consistency), and help shape the development of future assessments and professional ethics. Accredited practitioners would be monitored by a professional body and would have their accreditation withdrawn if they mispractised. In time, those commissioning SIA would tend to avoid non-accredited practitioners for a number of reasons.

Paying for SIA

There is still some resistance to using SIA on the part of administrators, economists and others who are not convinced that it is cost-effective, and who may also be afraid that it will lead to delays or even the abandonment of development. More specifically, some fear that SIA gives opposition groups the support necessary for them to mobilize against a development. Finsterbusch (1995) felt that SIA was generally relatively inexpensive, yet could provide vital information for effective decision-making and the avoidance or management of negative developments. Even when costly, SIA can provide a worthwhile input to sustainable development efforts (Scott, 1999).

The cost of SIA depends on the size and diversity of the population under study, the complexity of the proposed development (and its alternatives), the approach and methods selected and whether similar assessments have already been conducted elsewhere. In practice, those commissioning SIAs usually specify a budget and time-scale and the SIA is tailored to this in the scoping stage. As with EIA there are two extremes – 'quick and dirty' or slow and thorough – although choice of technique and the skill of the assessors can speed assessment and improve accuracy.

Corporate SIA

Business is increasingly turning to green, environmentally friendly approaches, and more and more companies profess to support the goal of sustainable development. To aid the pursuit such goals, there is growing employment of environmental managers, environmental advisers and use of the eco-audit, EIA, and hazard and risk assessment (Preston, 1983). Realization that the sustainability and avoidance of environmental problems is difficult without understanding and managing social institutions and socio-economic change has been slower to develop. The study and management of these key issues will draw heavily on SIA, so corporate interest should increase (Michalenko, 1981). Also, there should be a shift from current usage, which is mainly to rely on SIA to improve public relations, assist in the acquisition of funds, operating licences, and planning permission, and to satisfy watchdogs (mainly concerned NGOs). The shift will be towards the use of SIA for more integrated forward planning, for research purposes (to help monitor and understand developments), and as a way of extending eco-audit to consider more than physical impacts. SIA will probably become an important part of corporate environmental management.

The influence of impact assessment has been noted by a number of researchers and practitioners. For example, SIA may trigger local fears, suspicion and worries; it may prompt land speculation, out- or in-migration, or changes in real estate prices. People may become familiar with participation and empowerment during SIA, and may continue to seek these. Impact assessment is often a form of advocacy (which can be defined as the pursuit of change in policy or practice for the benefit of specific individuals or groups). Advocacy can take the form of lobbying, public campaigning, capacity building, public education, etc. In effect, advocacy is arguing for something, and this generally falls short of providing a workable strategy for achieving goals. For effective (beneficial) advocacy, it is crucial that those involved understand the relationships between various stakeholders, and how these might shift during the evolution of a policy, programme or project – SIA may help in this (Roche, 1999: 92, 263–6).

REFERENCES

Albrecht, S.L. and **Thompson, J.G.** (1988) The place of attitudes and perceptions in social impact assessment. *Society and Natural Resources* **1(1)**, 69–80.

Bain, M.B., Irving, J.S., Olsen, R,D., Still, E.A. and **Witmer, G.W.** (1986) *Cumulative Impact Assessment: evaluating the cumulative effects of multiple human developments.* US Department of Energy, Washington (DC).

Burdge, R.J. (1994) *A Conceptual Approach to Social Impact Assessment: a collection of writings by Rabel J. Burdge and colleagues*. Social Ecology Press, Middleton (WI).

Burdge, R.J. and **Vanclay, F.** (1996) Social Impact Assessment: a contribution to the state of the art series. *Impact Assessment* **14(1)**, 59–86.

Burningham, K. (1995) Attitudes, accounts and impact assessment. *The Sociological Review* (new series) 43, 101–22.

Carley, M.J. (1984) *Cumulative Socio-economic Monitoring*. Northern Economic Planning Branch, Indian and Northern Affairs Canada, Ottawa.

Deng, F. and **Altenhoefel, J.** (1997) Social impact assessments conducted by federal agencies. *Impact Assessment* **15(3)**, 209–32.

Dietz, T. (1987) Theory and method in social impact assessment. *Sociological Inquiry* **57(1)**, 54–69.

Dunlap, R.E. and **Catton, W.R. jnr** (1979) Environmental sociology. *Annual Review of Sociology* **5,** 243–73.

Finsterbusch, K. (1995) In praise of SIA – a personal review of the field of social impact assessment: feasibility, justification, history, methods, issues. *Impact Assessment* **13(3)**, 229–52.

Freudenburg, W.R. and **Keating, K.M.** (1992) Increasing the impact of sociology on social impact assessment: toward ending the inattention. *American Sociologist* **17(2)**, 71–80.

Geisler, C.G. (1993) Rethinking SIA: why ex-ante research isn't enough. *Society and Natural Resources* **6(4)**, 327–38.

Glasson, J. and **Heaney, D.** (1993) Socio-economic impacts: the poor relations in British EISs. *Journal of Environmental Planning and Management* **36(3)**, 335–43.

Juslén, J. (1995) Social impact assessment: a look at Finnish experiences. *Project Appraisal* **10(3)**, 163–70.

Kirkpatrick, C. and **Lee, N.** (1997) *Sustainable Development in a Developing World: integrating socio-economic and environmental management*. Edward Elgar, Cheltenham.

Latane, B. (1981) The psychology of social impact. *American Psychologist* **36(4)**, 343–56.

Little, R.L. and **Krannich, R.S.** (1988) A model for assessing the social impacts of natural utilization on resource-dependent communities. *Impact Assessment Bulletin* **6(2)**, 21–35.

Meissen, G.J. and **Cipriani, J.A.** (1984) Community psychology and social impact assessment: an action model. *American Journal of Community Psychology* **12(3)**, 393–86.

Michalenko, G. (1981) Social assessment of corporations, in F.J. Tester and W. Mykes (eds), *Social Impact Assessment: theory, method and practice*. Detselig Enterprises Ltd, Calgary (Canada), 168–79.

Morvaridi, B. (1997) *Environmental and Social Impact Assessment: methodological issues* (DPPC Discussion Paper Series 2 No. 1). Development and Project Planning Centre, University of Bradford, Bradford (UK).

Preston, L.E. (1983) Business and society: managing corporate social impact. *California Management Review* **25(3)**, 168–71.

Rees, W.E. (1988) A role for environmental assessment in achieving sustainable development. *Environmental Impact Assessment Review* **8(4)**, 273–91.

Roche, C. (1999) *Impact Assessment: learning to value change*. Oxfam (with Novib), Oxford.

Scott, D. (1999) Is public participation in the pipeline? A social impact assessment of marine waste disposal in southern Kwazulu-Natal. *Water Science and Technology* **39(10–11)**, 47–54.

Torgerson, D. (1980) *Industrialization and Assessment: social impact assessment as a social phenomenon*. York University Publications in Northern Studies, Toronto.

Williams, G. and **Freudenburg, W.** (1988) The Guidelines Project: professional standards for SIA. An idea whose time has come? *SIA Newsletter* **12(3–4)**, 16–21.

Wolf, C.P. (1981) Getting social impact assessment into the policy arena. *Environmental Impact Assessment Review* **1(1)**, 27–36.

6

THE TOOLS OF SIA: METHODS AND TECHNIQUES

> 'Society is the means whereby cultural ends become realized' (Erickson, 1979: 210)

To be effective SIA demands as good a set of baseline data as possible, without this it is difficult, if not impossible, to establish the current situation from which likely changes caused by different development options (including no development) can be judged. It is also helpful to have information on past changes to help show what might happen in the future (this is known as 'backcasting'). Finally, information is needed on current and likely future changes. The life sciences often use control groups or control studies to provide a reference against which an experiment can be compared. This may be possible for SIA; for example, a 'standard' group of people can be studied in parallel with the target group being assessed.

'Methods' and 'techniques' are terms frequently used but seldom clearly defined: a methodology is a general manner of approaching something, a technique is a specific application of a tool or approach (Wildman, 1990). Methodology is like a plan of battle, and techniques the types of weapon used. To further complicate things, some refer to 'tools', which is too vague a term to really pin down, although the expression overlaps a good deal with 'techniques'. However good the methodology adopted for SIA, the assessors involved must have a good level of experience and should be motivated to carry out a sound assessment; often, this has not been the case. Clearly, the right method(s) must be selected to suit the situation(s). Another point worth stressing is that SIA should be conducted in an iterative fashion, so that depth and detail is added as the assessment proceeds (Finsterbusch and Wolf, 1981: *xiii*) (*see* Figures 6.1 and 6.2).

There are broadly two types of techniques: conceptual or theoretical, which seek to discover how and why things happen (it should not be forgotten that SIA can be a research approach); and methodological or practical,

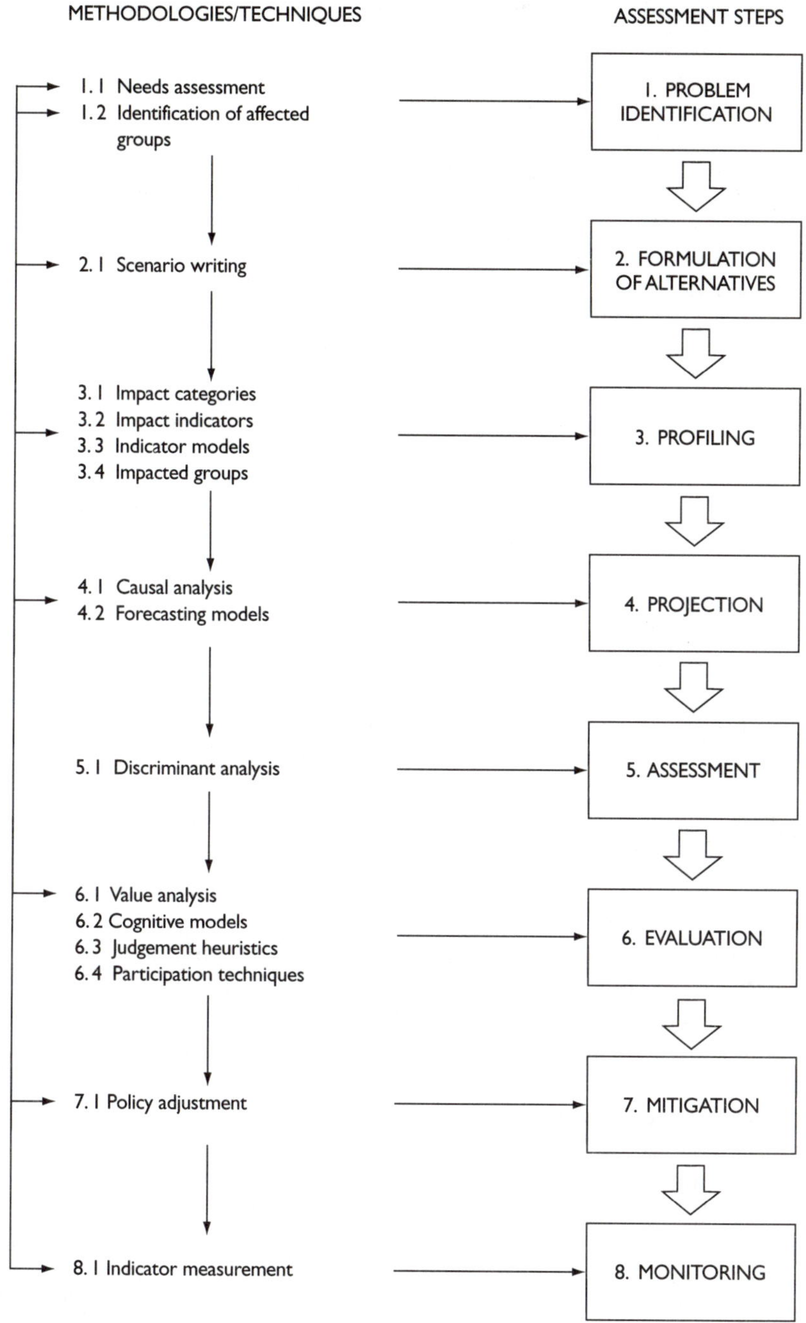

FIGURE 6.1 SIA assessment steps (stages) related to methodologies/techniques
Source: adapted by the author from various sources

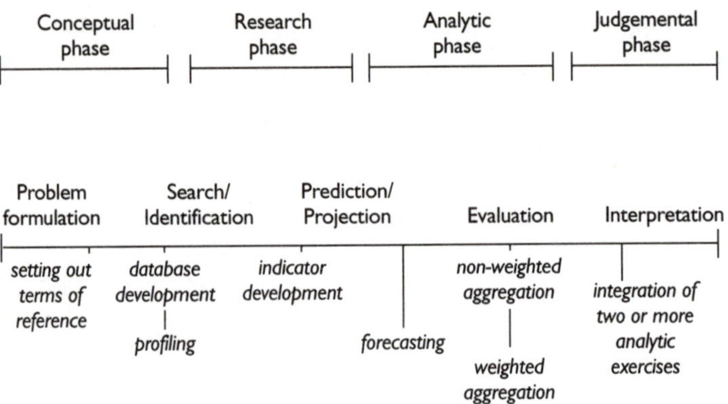

FIGURE 6.2 Phases and activities in SIA
Source: redrawn, with minor modifications, from Carley and Wathey (1981), Figure 1, p. 16

which aim to be of applied value. SIA methods and techniques must show how companies, government or NGO projects, programmes and policies will function and evolve; how various groups of people might behave over time; or how technology, economics, politics and environment are likely to develop – each a very tall order. While some progress has been made, there are still problems meeting such goals (Armour, 1988). There is also the question of whether to seek to incorporate the perceptions of local people in development planning; if the decision is to do so, then SIA must involve some element of attitude studies (Albrecht and Thompson, 1988; Burningham, 1995).

SIA uses a range of techniques, many developed by other disciplines (Cox, 1995); often, these have to be modified, or at least fine-tuned, in order to work properly. SIA can call upon well-established and expanding fields of evaluation research, mainly focused on determining how projects, programmes and policies have performed, or are performing, in economic or social terms. Many of the larger aid agencies and international bodies – such as the World Bank, UNDP and OECD – have evaluation departments to carry out such tasks, and some have produced handbooks or guidelines (*see*, for example, Cracknell, 1983; Freeman *et al.*, 1979; Gardner, 1978; Rossi and Freeman, 1982). SIA may make use of such published methods, but in the main adopts a more future-oriented anticipatory approach, picking methods to suit specific needs.

Planners and decision-makers generally seek objective advice based on accurate, reliable quantitative data. In practice, SIA is under pressure to obtain baseline data and make assessments fast, cheaply and, as far as possible, of a quantitative nature. In order to do this, use is often made of secondary sources (e.g. census tables, official statistics and published university research findings). There is a need for information on the culture(s) involved, and to get this assessors tend to rely on narrative accounts and interviews. There is also the question of independent, objective assessment; often assessors have to go some way towards appeasing those who commissioned the assessment. Whether consultants or academics, it is difficult to avoid being influenced by any of the various interests involved. In some cases the assessors appear to be independent but actually support the proposals (a kind of 'cosmetic' SIA).

Social and cultural reality is often complex and subject to changes that can be unpredictable and sudden; SIA must also often cope with factors that are 'unmeasurable' or that must be assessed in non-quantitative ways, or that are so little understood that useful measurement is unlikely. SIA often has to make use of qualitative data and approaches that physical scientists view as subjective, this makes it difficult to achieve the degree of objectivity some clients seek, and so they mistrust it. Also, social units are less rigid and fixed than those used in the sciences. Gold (1978) made the point that data analysed quantitatively is often seen as objective, whereas qualitative analysis is often seen as subjective. Yet, carefully collated qualitative data can be valuable, while quantitative data may be poorly gathered or may measure something of limited value. SIA should use good qualitative and quantitative data, seek to ensure that its use is transparent and, as far as possible, use as many lines of corroborative evidence as possible.

SIA essentially deals in informed judgement and it may not be possible to repeat successive assessments to give consistent results; whereas, in science, application of a given methodology should give results that are broadly comparable. Indeed, an assessment inevitably reflects the conceptual stance of the assessor(s). What works well for a particular team, perhaps with adequate time to conduct studies, may fail with other assessors, especially in real-world situations where assessment must be done in a hurry.

Although indirect and cumulative impacts are inevitable, few 'mainstream' SIA techniques at present really search them out; and, when identified, these are often not really seriously considered. That is a real problem, because if those commissioning the SIA are unaware of the risk of indirect and cumulative impacts they are probably given a false sense of security.

The techniques and data required for SIA depend on the method adopted and the step in the assessment undertaken; these steps are listed in Box 6.1, but can be summarized as follows:

1. description of the setting
2. identification of areas of concern
3. forecasting/prediction of impacts and review of alternative development options
4. assessment/evaluation of the implications of identified impacts.

The techniques for Steps 1 and 2 are mainly concerned with characterization and establishing trends; those for Step 3, more with projection and prediction; and those for Step 4 with evaluation of significance and testing the reliability of assessment (Canter, 1977).

A considerable portion of SIA could be said to be 'backcasting' (that is, drawing on hindsight experience from the site in question and similar situations elsewhere to project future impacts). For developments like resettlement, highway or dam construction, structural adjustment policies and tourism there is a good body of information to work from, and quite straightforward desk research can go some way towards providing a satisfactory SIA. It is important that SIA results are published and circulated to ensure the continued improvement of hindsight experience. Also, as far as possible, common units of measurement, similar approaches and transparent techniques should be used. The forecasting methods used by SIA are mainly 'borrowed' from EIA, social studies, market research, social psychology and futures research (Henshel, 1976; Johnston, 1970).

Methods and techniques suitable for SIA at one point in the development process – say, during project construction – may not be appropriate at another. As policies, programmes and projects evolve, different impacts are generated, and the social groups and cultures involved are likely to have altered. So, a given SIA should be repeated over time, and it must not be assumed that the approach and techniques that worked the last time will again be appropriate; there must be a reappraisal of the technique(s) to use for each assessment (Geisler, 1993). This fine-tuning is one of the tasks of the scoping stage of an SIA.

Social theory can inform SIA of what questions to ask, how to ask them, what social indicators to monitor, and how to interpret the answers (Land, 1970). It is also important to note that SIA is a learning process; each SIA has the potential to increase knowledge as it progresses, and to contribute to the future improvement of other assessments.

One may divide socio-economic forecasting methods into 'extrapolative' and 'normative' (*see* Glossary). The former makes predictions on the basis of the past, using approaches such as the Delphi technique, scenario prediction, brainstorming and various forms of modelling. The latter is more goal-oriented and normative (a process that ranks or selects 'what ought to be' according to prescribed goals or evaluative criteria) in approach, using techniques such as contextual mapping, decision theory and various matrix methods.

Whatever methods or techniques are used, it is important to keep in view the point that SIA seeks to compare the situation, assuming no development takes place, with what is likely if there is development (Finsterbusch, 1985: 202). A situation may be static, improving or degrading, or may be prone to cyclic or random change; development can sometimes improve things, even if it is not especially successful. To be able to make such judgements, SIA must gather sufficient baseline data. This may be relatively easy where there are published sources of information (e.g. a census, published articles, established monitoring systems and so on). When such secondary data is not available in adequate amounts, the assessor must turn to primary data (research in the form of brainstorming, modelling, surveys, interviews, and the like), and this can be slow and costly. There has been a tendency for all impact assessment (EIA, SIA etc.) to emphasize negative impacts and fail to register likely positive (beneficial) impacts and opportunities.

SIA DATA

What social, socio-economic, cultural or psychological variables should SIA examine (Bauer, 1967; Sheldon and Freeman, 1970)? What are deemed to be useful, reliable social or socio-economic indicators (Force and Machlis, 1997)? A social indicator acts as a surrogate for states and characteristics that may not be directly measurable (deVries: *see* reference to website below). The choice of indicator in any given case depends on the results of scoping, and there may have to be adjustments as assessment proceeds. Data may be gathered by monitoring a single variable for which crucial threshold values are known; or a composite indicator (index) may be used, obtained by the statistical manipulation of several key variables (e.g. a 'physical quality of life index' based on measurements of income, health, life expectancy, educational attainment and so on, a 'human freedom index', or a sustainable development index) (Baster, 1972; Diener, 1997; Rossi and Gilmartin, 1980; Vogel, 1997).

Indicators may be internal and subjective (e.g. job satisfaction), or external and more objective (e.g. income level, or employment status). There is seldom such a thing as a single, reliable indicator – the assessor must usually seek a number, and indeed would be strongly advised to select the best mix of indicators, so that different lines of evidence can be seen to point to a conclusion (Carley, 1981 and 1984; Cochran, 1979; Fox, 1974; Schonfield and Shaw, 1972). This cross-checking of results using different indicators and methods is important.

A review of a range of social indicators is provided by Roche (1999: 41–55) and, in 1998, deVries (*see* http://www.nzaia.org.nz/wkshps/1998/Wkshp98.htm) outlined social indicators in assessment and policy development. Accurate and detailed data is of less use to planners and decision-makers than relevant and reliable data (Macfarlane, 1999: 64). Gramling (1992) argued that employment data can provide a useful, flexible source of data for SIA. Macfarlane (1999) tabulated the typical characteristics of data used by technocratic and participatory approaches to SIA (Table 6.1; *see also* the discussion of technocratic, participatory and integrated approaches to SIA in Chapter 3).

TABLE 6.1 Data characteristics of technocratic and participatory SIA

	Technocratic	**Participatory**
Nature of data	value-free	value-laden
Source of data	expert(s)	community
Type of data	quantitative	qualitative
Slope of data	nomothetic	ideographic

Source: Macfarlane (1999: 64, Table 4.2)

Finding the right mix of social indicators which enable the assessor to cross-check and be sure of results is not easy. Wildavsky (1996: 31–2) was sceptical of many of the social indicators used to measure social processes. He argued that great care was needed in their selection and use: '. . . a fast train is worse than a slow one if it takes you to the wrong station' (1996: 32).

SIA may focus on various levels; for example, individual well-being, social interactions and community well-being. For many communities, SIA will have to measure the needs, responses, attitudes and so on of more than one group. Minority cultural groups may value things such as kinship, tradition and cultural cohesion, more than, say, economic progress, improved communications, social freedom and industrial development, which are favoured by society as a whole. The tools adopted for SIA depend on the approach selected (*see* Chapter 3); for example, if a local group focus is wanted, then techniques for community-managed impact assessment would be appropriate.

Generally, the following are the key variables.

- Population characteristics: collect data on structure and organization of potentially affected people; obtain details of the ethnic, social and economic groups; gather information on employment, wealth and poverty; check whether there is any seasonality of livelihood; explore the likely impacts of possible development alternatives.
- Community and institutional structure: gather data on how communities are organized and on likely responses to change.
- Political and social resources: gather data on relationships, stability of communities and attitudes; identify stakeholders; explore how power is exercised.
- Individual and family factors: collect data on the daily lives of people; collect information on attitudes to risk, change, proposed development and alternatives; establish what is feared and what is valued.
- Community resources: examine how people use their environment: livelihood data, cultural data and information on access to facilities.

Much of the aforementioned information can be found at http://www.gsa.gov/pbs/pt/call-in/factshet/1098b/10_98b_4.htm.

There will be many, if not most, cases where an SIA fails to obtain adequate data. Assessors must, therefore, determine how good their data is, decide whether it is practical to collect more and, in any statements issued, identify the gaps honestly and clearly, so as to indicate how reliable the picture is.

Impact identification

Identifying potential impacts can be easier than measuring them. However, the assessor can draw upon a huge range of sources and use a wide variety of techniques to identify and then assess impacts: desk study of literature; interviews; brainstorming discussions by experts and so on. An impact may affect individuals, families, specific age groups, cultures or gender groups, neighbourhoods, regions and communities.

There are various ways in which impacts can be classified; a useful approach is that adopted by Shields (1975), who divided them according to their effects (the impact may be physical, social, cultural or economic).

- Demographic impacts: rates of urban growth, rural depopulation, mortality changes, birth rate changes, etc. These are relatively easy to measure and predictions are generally quite reliable, although there can be sudden changes caused by human or natural disasters (Leistritz and Murdock, 1981: 63–103).
- Economic impacts: employment, taxation, property price changes, inflation, supply and demand patterns. These can often be expressed in relatively consistent monetary units.
- Impacts on social values and attitudes: (a) community cohesion – changes within a given area to the ties between individuals and groups, or altered sense of belonging or local pride, etc.; (b) lifestyle – changes to accepted values and day-to-day behaviour (perceptual and behavioural qualities).

A number of disciplines are likely to have data and techniques on variables relating to those categories; lifestyles, for example, are of interest to market research and advertising organizations. Demographic change is often monitored by national census and social service organizations; forecasting from mortality data is relatively reliable, but for fertility and migration, prediction is more difficult (Becker, 1990). Economic change is generally measured by governments, regional authorities, economists and the larger banks.

Deciding what are, or will become, critical socio-economic factors is difficult and must be undertaken by appropriately skilled social scientists (as should be the case with any decision to weight selected variables). Other problems are posed by sudden unexpected and dramatic change, such as that caused by technological innovation, natural disaster, fashion changes, fiscal changes or social unrest (especially warfare).

Once scoping has given a reasonable indication of the type of impact and where it might be felt (*see* Box 6.1) efforts can be made to gather appropriate data to confirm or disprove its validity and, ideally, predict its magnitude. As soon as it is clear where to focus, the assessor should conduct baseline studies (much of this is done in the profiling stage of SIA, *see* Box 6.1). The baseline studies should give an indication of the current, past and probable future situation, so that the effect of proposed development can be factored in to see what changes it might cause. (It is possible that a development could stabilize or improve conditions, rather than cause problems – indeed that should be the aim of all developments.) Baseline studies are a vital step before impact projections can be made. With time and cost constraints, and the sheer complexity of the task, baseline studies often rely on secondary data gathered by desk research, and expert opinion survey. It should be stressed that SIA assessors must bear in mind that 'correlation is not necessarily causation'; too often, symptoms are read as causes or spurious correlations are taken as proof of cause–effect. For example, rising unemployment may be blamed for increasing crime rates, yet causal links may not have been proved. In the same way, social indicator trends may be an unreliable means of forecasting: things may suddenly shift and even reverse.

The quest for quantitative, rather than qualitative, data may cost more and slow down SIA to little real advantage (Lawrence, 1993; Patton, 1987). Both quantitative and qualitative measurements are valuable and may be mutually supportive. There are, of course, situations where non-quantifiable factors such as psychological trauma, stress, degradation of aesthetic features and deterioration of community cohesion have somehow to be quantified and accorded value. Law courts, compensation boards, governments and the like ultimately have to decide on a compensation sum for such impacts. In EIA complex weighting techniques have been tried, but have been criticized for furnishing 'pseudo-quantification' at the cost of loss of transparency of technique (it can be difficult for the EIA user to see whether there has been careless or skilful distortion of data).

There is a real risk that an SIA will allocate too much importance to 'measurable' (i.e. quantifiable) variables and not enough to less easily measured, but crucial, variables. This seems to have been the case with economic impacts which, being easier to quantify than social impacts, may come to dominate SIAs (Leistritz and Murdock, 1981). Many, including Dietz (1987), have warned of the risk of hiding value judgements in a less than transparent evaluative process. There have been cases where SIA has embarked on statistically dubious combinations of incommensurable variables to obtain single 'summary' values, or the production of weighted selected variables. The question of whether to weight selected SIA variables or treat them as being all of the same importance should be judged carefully, and it must be made clear to those viewing the SIA results.

Methods

Methods and techniques for SIA began to be developed in the 1970s (*see* Becker, 1997; Finsterbusch and Wolf, 1981; Leistritz and Murdock, 1981; Llewellyn *et al.*, 1983; Rickson *et al.*, 1990; Soderstrom, 1981; Wolf, 1983). Although subsequently, and particularly since the mid-1980s, those conducting SIA have reviewed their methodologies, assessments are still often conducted in an *ad hoc* manner. There will almost certainly never be an accepted standardized overall methodology (Wildman, 1990). Finsterbusch (1985: 199) felt that, although there were methodological differences, in general these were 'variations on the same theme'. Publication of *Guidelines and Principles for Social Impact Assessment* (Inter-organizational Committee on Guidelines and Principles, 1994) has helped to improve standardization (Finsterbusch, 1995), and the more methods are standardized, rather than *ad hoc*, the easier it is to make comparisons between different SIAs. Improved comparability of results helps future assessments and the disclosure of cumulative impacts.

The goal of many SIAs is the projection of likely socio-economic impacts generated by developments already well into the planning stage or even under way. This leaves little time for in-depth research, and is a particular problem where new and unknown technology is involved, and where people's reactions are uncertain. A range of techniques for assessing current, and projecting future, perspectives and attitudes has been developed by the social sciences, psychology and market research (Burningham, 1995; Dale and Lane, 1994; Meissen and Cipriani, 1984). Nevertheless, even simple assessments of the number of people likely to be affected by a relatively straightforward development can be problematic: a few years ago planners suggested that the Three Gorges Dam in China would dislocate about 1.5 million; more recent projections suggest that the figure is more likely to be over 3 million. Even something as relatively 'easy' as determining how many people may migrate to or from an area presents a challenge because assessment must take account of shifting attitudes and opportunities.

A commonly adopted SIA methodology starts by trying to describe the current situation and then attempts to project future conditions, as they would be with and without the proposed development. This is the sort of process published by the Inter-organizational Committee on Guidelines and Principles (which has 10 generic steps). Most professionals would now add that SIA should go on to help establish monitoring and management regimes (*see* Box 6.1 and also Box 3.2).

Although each case is unique, when an SIA is relatively simple, straightforward and can relate to a reasonable amount of hindsight experience, it is possible for the assessors to make progress quickly and cheaply, relying a good deal on desk research and using available data sources. All SIA starts with the use of available information to assist scoping, but for complex, large and novel applications, specialist expert study will be needed. It is important that methods help ensure the approach is systematic so that as little as possible is missed and there is no undue bias. In the real world, available time, funding, expertise and official commitment to SIA determine how thorough assessment can be.

Some assessment is little more than the use of common sense; for example, by checking the characteristics of the workforce likely to be recruited for a development, a good deal of information on likely impacts is gathered, showing whether they will move on after construction or settle, whether they will come into conflict with locals, what diseases they might transmit to the development area and so on.

TECHNIQUES

A wide range of forecasting techniques is outlined in brief in this section. They are but a fraction of what is need for SIA, for once an impact or scenario

Box 6.1 A general methodology for SIA

(*See also* Chapter 3, Box 3.2.)

Steps	Analytical operations/activity
1. Scoping	Set level(s) of assessment (policy/programme project); establish TOR; boundaries of study; time-frame for completion/repetition of assessment; budget; team, etc. Public participation is increasingly seen as a vital component needed to provide data and to ensure that people are involved in decision-making.
2. Problem identification	Formulate goals; identify impacted social groups/stakeholders; establish their concerns; carry out a needs assessment; determine what to evaluate and how.
3. Establish alternatives	Identify 'reasonable' alternatives and gather information about them, having examined the concerns disclosed by Step 2. During evaluation (Step 7) likely direct, and if possible indirect and cumulative, impacts can be factored in.
4. Profiling	Determine who is affected; 'tune' measurement techniques; take measurements and compile social profile. This is the step that describes the social units affected by the proposed development.
5. Projection	Try to establish what effect the impacts will have; assess what will happen with or without development.*
6. Assessment	Present significant impacts; relate to development alternatives. Assess how those impacted will respond (this is often a step that is neglected).
7. Evaluation	Re-check the impacted group's concerns and needs; study trade-offs and try to rank development alternatives. Seek to identify the best option. It is at this stage that attempts to establish indirect and cumulative impacts are most likely to be effective.
8. Mitigation	Identify possible mitigation/avoidance/adaptation measures and assess their likely impacts. SIA can be an important tool for mediation.
9. Monitoring	Establish/advise on ongoing monitoring; decide when and how to conduct next SIA; check how accurate this SIA has been.
10. Management	Devise management plan; adjust procedures, review objectives, etc.

Note: the ten steps listed here are based on, but do not quite match those proposed by the Inter-organizational Committee on Guidelines and Principles (1994), or NEPA (1999), *see* http://www.gsa.gov/pbs/pt/call-in/factshet/1098b/10_98_5.htm. Step 4 published in these guidelines is a 'scoping' step, preceded by: 'develop public involvement', 'information gathering to identify and consider alternatives' and 'define baseline conditions'. Otherwise there is broad overlap with the steps listed above, although NEPA suggests that, before developing a mitigation plan, there should be an effort to identify new alternatives in light of unexpected developments since starting the SIA.

TOR = terms of reference.

* Even without development the situation may be one of decline or improvement, no change, cyclic change, random change or predictable change.

Sources: Finsterbusch (1985: 200–1); Inter-organizational Committee on Guidelines and Principles (1994); Wolf (1983)

has been identified, the assessor has to determine the reliability of the prediction, its implications and significance. The forecasting techniques can be divided roughly into extrapolative and normative. The former group includes conjecture, brainstorming, the Delphi technique, trend analysis, correlation and regression statistical techniques, simulations, gaming, and scenario prediction. Normative techniques include modelling, decision theory, matrix methods and network methods.

SIA, like EIA, uses a wide range of techniques – some it has developed, many others are borrowed from other fields, including sociology, psychology, anthropology, risk assessment, economics, market research, management studies, ecological modelling, structural analysis (*see* Glossary) and systems analysis (Henshel, 1982; Muth and Lee, 1986; Peters, 1986). As with EIA, a valuable characteristic of a technique is that it should help improve objectivity of assessment and reduce the risk that variables are missed or double-counted. The bulk of techniques are used to help understand situations and to predict future events. Others are employed to calculate the significance of identified impacts, to present results (in an impact statement or report) and to help choose between available development options.

SIA usually has to be carried out to a tight deadline, so data collection and processing has to be rushed. These quick and dirty techniques may suffice for practical SIA, but are unlikely to have much value for researchers wanting accurate data. Many of the techniques used by SIA must be modified for a given assessment situation. There is constant evolution of new and improved techniques, and it is desirable that they be applied by specialists. Some techniques have generated mountains of literature. So, it is impossible and undesirable to give more than a brief overview here. One point that should be emphasized, however, is that some SIAs expend too much effort on identification of impacts and not enough on the next stage: careful assessment and evaluation. With growing improvements in computing facilities, increasing bodies of personal data available on databases and rapidly evolving modelling, expert systems and statistical analysis programs, some of the challenges facing SIA are diminishing – notably, preparation time is being reduced and accuracy increased.

SIA is more likely to predict future scenarios or employ conjecture than to make accurate forecasts (a scenario can be defined as a narrative description of the potential course of development) (*see* Figure 6.3). As Finsterbusch (1985: 207) noted, a scenario can be derived from little more than guesswork, so as much as possible should be done to check its plausibility. Also, it is important to ensure that the way a scenario is derived is clear, and to invite independent experts to carry out checks on a SIA team's results. Finsterbusch (1995: 245) went further, calling for outside expert checks at several points in the SIA process, especially where an assessment was not routine but broke new ground or was particularly difficult.

Brainstorming

Some would hesitate to recognize this as a real primary data gathering method because it is based more on speculation than research. Brainstorming is a quick initial step for generating ideas and suggestions (rather than research data). An appropriate group is encouraged to discuss an issue, often using a flipchart or blackboard on which a discussion leader can quickly note points with minimal disruption to proceedings before attention shifts to something else.

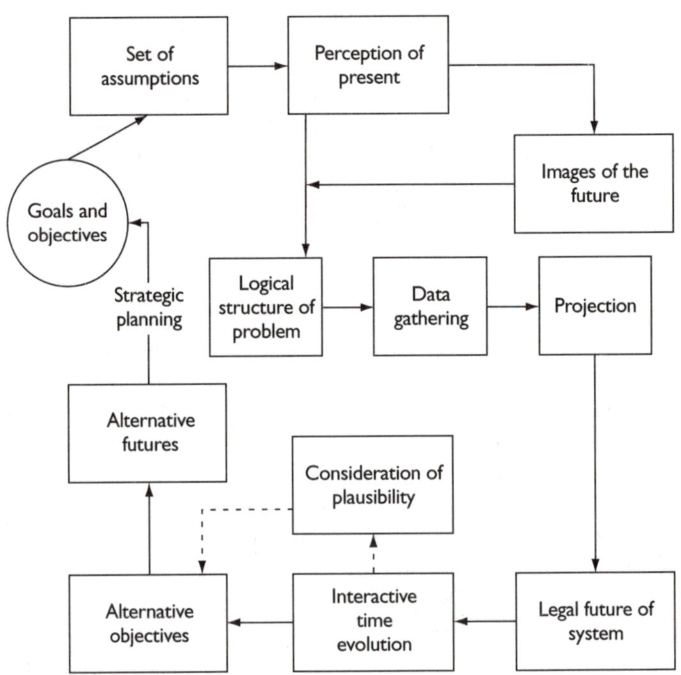

Figure 6.3 Steps in scenario generation
Source: Vlachos (1981), Figure 1, p. 168

Desk study

Desk study is an important source of ideas and data. However, in the past (and as is sometimes still the case) there has been too much dependence on this source for EIA and SIA. Desk studies explore available secondary sources for relevant information. Nowadays, this is much faster and more effective, thanks to online literature searching and data retrieval; however, limited information may be available in developing countries, and for new technologies and problems.

Checklists and matrices

Checklists and matrix techniques are frequently used and help to ensure a systematic approach. Checklists can be compiled from desk studies of similar developments that have already been undertaken (i.e. they can draw on hindsight knowledge). Matrices are sometimes valuable at the presentation of results (EIS) stage, because they can be used to present clearly the pattern of impacts. More sophisticated forms of matrices can show interrelationships that may hint at, or even expose, chains of causation (i.e. indirect impacts); they can be used to highlight clusters of impacts associated with some activity, impacted feature, or group of people. Matrices are a good way to present the results of SIA to the public in a simple visual manner. Matrices suitable for SIA include the Leopold matrix (used for EIA) (Barrow, 1997: 138), and similar forms can be borrowed from social accounting and other disciplines (King, 1981).

While some matrix approaches are quick and simple (and cheap), most have the disadvantage that they only show first-order (direct) impacts. If those commissioning the SIA or the public are unaware of the failure to display indirect and cumulative impacts, they are likely to be given a false sense of security.

Network analysis

Network analysis has advantages over techniques like matrices, because it can follow chains of causation and thus offer hope of identifying some of the indirect impacts. Widely used for EIA, network techniques are also used in SIA (Griffiths, 1980).

Systems analysis

This is a large and specialist field which allows the modelling of past, current or future scenarios. Widely used, some may argue that systems analysis is as much an approach as a technique. Natural regions are often used for systems analysis (for example, river basins). As computer models improve, the approach depends more and more on good-quality data for reliable results; when this is not available, critics may use the phrase 'garbage in garbage out' (GIGO).

The Delphi technique

This is one way of blending expert opinion through several iterative interviews, so as to reach agreement on likely future scenarios (*see* Box 6.2). Where an adequate run of reliable data is available it should be possible to make reasonably accurate extrapolations to produce future projections; fiscal impact assessment (*see* Glossary), for example, may provide projections of likely changes in costs and revenues for governments or international agencies (Becker, 1988; Hill and Fowles, 1975; Leistritz and Murdock, 1981: 125).

Value tree analysis

This can be used to gather information on the values held by social groups (through interviews), and then to arrange and display it in a hierarchical structure so that the most socially compatible option can be distinguished (Peters, 1996). Tree diagrams are multipurpose tools for simplifying and prioritizing problems and objectives. They can guide design and evaluation and show the underlying causes of events, or they can be used to rank and measure things in relation to each other. Similar techniques (forerunners) are used in the life sciences.

Box 6.2 The Delphi technique

Finsterbusch (1985: 207) described the Delphi technique as a 'technique for maximizing the reliability of the subjective judgements of a group of experts'.

The technique uses a planned programme of consecutive, iterative, individual interrogations (these can be carried out by questionnaire or even by e-mail) interspersed with information feedback. Each expert is advised of the answers of other experts (without knowing who gave the answers) and has earlier responses available so that he/she has an opportunity to review and amend. The technique allows relatively objective determination of 'consensus' from a panel of evaluators about a given question. It is a way of reaching a conclusion where there is a wide diversity of disciplines (i.e. it supports a holistic approach); it reduces the risk of 'senior' figures intimidating others into adopting their viewpoint. It can be relatively fast and is suited to situations with high degrees of uncertainty – incomplete data or knowledge. It is also systematic (reducing the risks of something being overlooked) – a guide sheet is used to ensure that all experts consider the same issues; this helps to make comparisons consistent.

There is a risk that there may be more than one conclusion if two or more groupings of view appear during the assessment. Also, one may question whether experts or the sort of people selected for participation really do hold views representative of society at large. The technique is attractive to some assessors because they can side-step some responsibility for decision-making by claiming that the 'experts', or whoever took part, made the decision.

Sources: Ament (1970); Helmer (1968); Leistritz and Murdock (1981: 179–80); Linstone (1985); Miller and Cuff (1986); Pill (1971); Yong *et al.* (1989

Flow charts

Often a first step in constructing a model is to draw up a flow chart. This is a diagram that shows the causal relationships between relevant variables (Finsterbusch and Wolf, 1981: 51). Different-shaped boxes can be drawn to represent various social interactions (beneficial, negative, etc.), and the lines connecting boxes can indicate strong or weak links, feedbacks, degree of probability, etc. Flow charts are best treated as hypothetical simplifications of reality, which should be verified by further empirical research.

Surveys and interviews

It is only possible in this section to give very light coverage of the huge field of surveys and interviews.

There are two broad types of survey: quantitative and qualitative. Relevant techniques have been developed by psychology, sociology, human geography, market research and planning. Lack of time and funds generally means that assessors have to sample from the total population or carry out a spatially limited study: a survey. The choice of sample, size of sample and the way in which it is interpreted are important. Surveys may be carried out by directly involving the individuals sampled by means of personal interview, mail or telephone questionnaire; alternatively, secondary sources may be used (for example, employment data) (Buzzard, 1990; Fink and Kosecoff, 1998; Gramling, 1992; Sapsford, 1999). Surveys may be random, repeated to check whether change has taken place, seasonal to explore variations during each year, repeated at longer intervals, or conducted in several other ways. Surveys and interviews may be conducted using matched pairs (of villages, social groups or individuals). Alternatively, there may be 'snowballing': an initial exploration used to select further in-depth studies.

There are many forms of interview, ranging from simple and unstructured, to semi-structured, to structured (i.e. varying in the degree to which pre-agreed questions are asked) (Roche, 1999: 66–74). For some interviews the assessor seeks to be passive, and merely prompts and records; for others, assessors are actively involved. There is also a technique which bears some similarity to interviews: narrative research (the use of sources like life stories, statements, autobiographies, etc.) (Arksey, 1999; Atkinson, 1998; Kvale, 1996).

Structured interviews and surveys collect data from a selected subset of the whole group on which the research is focusing. For example: interviewees may be extracted in a more or less random manner from some list, such as a telephone directory; or they may be households that fall on the grid-lines of a map; or people whose house or telephone number coincides with a random number table. Alternatively, interviewees may be selected on the basis of some known activity: those who return a product guarantee slip after a purchase; those listed in an electoral roll with a given characteristic; those stopped when visiting a particular locality; all of these are much more 'selected' than the samples drawn by random selection.

The actual collection of interview or survey data can take various forms: through questionnaires, telephone interviews, suggestion boxes, etc. Sources may be recorded or they may remain anonymous (clearly, those in the latter group are more likely to speak their minds). Surveys are usually necessitated when there is no readily available source of data, like a census or employment statistics. The survey process may take a variety of forms, but these typically share the same process (Gardner, 1978; Leistritz and Murdock, 1981: 163; Moser and Kalton, 1979):

- selection of type of survey (random, stratified, etc.)
- sample design
- sample frame selection
- sample selection
- questionnaire or interview design
- questionnaire or interview pre-testing
- fieldwork/collection using questionnaire/interview
- analysis of responses.

Erickson (1979: 210) suggested that, where a social situation is not well known, the assessor(s) should abide by the following process.

1. Identify the actors (i.e. the individuals who interact in the social system).
2. Establish the physical environment in which the actors interact.
3. Determine the motivation of individual actors.
4. Determine the cultural context (the rules governing behaviour).

Others adopt a similar approach, essentially recognizing the following three steps for which techniques will be needed (Dietz, 1987: 56–7).

1. Identification: assessor has to know the social system, understand the people and their needs, etc.
2. Analysis: assessor assigns probabilities and significance to identified impacts.
3. Evaluation: integration of Stages 1 and 2 to reach and present clear, informative findings.

Surveys may be the starting point for another technique; for instance, a telephone questionnaire survey may be used to assemble a focus group (*see* below), or can even be a tentative first exploration to assess how next to proceed. Personal interviews allow the assessor to check responses and gain additional insights, but tend to cost more than secondary data surveys or telephone surveys. Survey samples may be selected at random, by focusing on some characteristic (a stratified sample); sampling a particular age group, class or educational background; or as a cluster sample, with people selected from a particular locality.

Clearly, surveys have limitations and biases, and those using them for SIA must check what these are. For example, a telephone survey in a Brazilian city would miss a large portion of the people who are unable to afford a (relatively expensive) home telephone. Survey techniques must be selected to suit time and funding constraints in order to provide the required data as accurately as possible.

Questionnaires

These are widely used as a technique in SIA, and can rapidly provide information on individual and group opinions. A wide variety of questionnaires has been developed by sociologists, psychologists, market researchers and professionals from other disciplines. As with other techniques, they can be poorly conducted, mishandled or misinterpreted. For example, a 'random' questionnaire survey of shoppers conducted between 11am and 3pm on a weekday outside a high-quality clothing shop in an affluent city is anything but random: those questioned have already selected themselves from the ranks of the relatively affluent, probably non-working adult female population. Questionnaires must be presented with full information on the circumstances of data collection and the sample frame adopted.

Interviews furnish qualitative data, and may allow in-depth questioning and probing on specific points. Usually an interview is one-to-one and takes several minutes, so to gather a reasonable sample can take time. To ensure that each interview is reasonably comparable, the interviewer should be closely guided by a set of guidelines or a checklist (even in unstructured interviews, where there may be no pre-arranged set of actual questions, to avoid variations in time, venue, number of people present, style of questioning and so on).

Ideally an interview (and other survey forms) should be tested before being fully conducted in case modifications are needed. There is a risk that an interviewer may consciously, or unwittingly, prompt answers, and that the interviewee may give false information – care in interpretation is therefore vital. In market research it is not unusual for interviewees to be attracted to the interview by a reward of some kind. Assessors sometimes select an agreed, perhaps recognized standard mix of people, by reference to incomes, postcodes (zip codes), buying habits, etc.

Expert opinion and key informants

Survey methods may involve the collection of data from key informants, rather than struggling to obtain a representative sample of randomly selected people; this has the advantage of saving time and money, and may offer a deeper insight (Derman, 1990). The assessor(s) must select key informants who know a situation or the opinion of a group of people, e.g. experts, local newspaper staff, representatives of special interest groups, village school teachers, priests and specialist workers.

Expert opinion can quickly be gathered and may appeal to decision-makers as having 'weight'; however, experts have been known to be wrong! One tool used to 'pool' expert opinion is the Delphi technique (*see* below).

Participant observation methods

Two things can be invaluable to those contemplating development: traditional or indigenous knowledge, and the current perceptions of local people.

Anthropological studies can establish the former, and there are many methods for gathering information on the latter (for example, key informant interviews). Alternatively, an assessor, or assessors, can observe people, openly or covertly, or involve people in role-play or game-play situations (*see* the discussion of workshops later on in this chapter). At its most extreme, this type of rersearch may call for an assessor may work, or live and work, with a group for an extended period hoping to be accepted as 'one of them' – an ethnographic approach. An example of this might be a social psychologist researching employee–employer relations in a 'problem' factory; another example might be an anthropologist living with a group of indigenous people to observe their perceptions and traditional knowledge. A more mundane example of how observation may be used is the situation where, rather than constructing paths on a new housing estate, it makes sense to leave things as they are and see where people habitually walk, then lay paving along those routes. Rural development agencies commonly encourage villagers and farmers to map their activities; western industries have long used time-and-motion studies observers (nowadays, these are more likely to be called 'ergonomics experts') to assess how activities are conducted. There has been considerable growth in recent years in participatory rural appraisal (PRA), and in the related field of rapid rural appraisal (RRA). These both adopt a multidisciplinary approach and often encourage villager or farmer participation to assess current livelihood situations, and to try and predict future challenges and opportunities (for example, Barrow, 1997: 32; Chambers, 1991 and 1983).

Public meetings

The public meeting is still a widely adopted technique, but it is also one that can be steered by public relations teams to favour the developer (*see* Chapter 4).

Stakeholder analysis

Stakeholder analysis (*see* Glossary) is the identification of all stakeholders (i.e. groups affected by a development) and the assessment of all significant impacts upon them (Finsterbusch, 1995: 248).

Modelling

Given the diversity of modelling techniques and their widespread use, it is difficult to offer more than a selective and brief overview of this method. Models can be used to simplify complex situations so that they can be understood and perhaps managed, or future projections made. Models can show opportunities or help evaluate masses of complex data. They may take the form of word models, computer models or analogue models (scale reconstructions of a situation – such as a tidal erosion model or mechanical models). Models can also be used to construct various alternative scenarios by manipulating the variables involved. (It must be stressed that models are based on assumptions that are inherently uncertain, by data that may be imperfect or insufficient; they thus present abstractions of reality.)

Input–output models are widely used by project planners, economists and regional administrators, mainly for economic and employment forecasting. These methods can be used for assessment at national, state, regional and local levels. For regional impact studies, regional input–output models have been in use since the 1970s. There are various approaches, some relying on available secondary data. Though imperfect, input–output models have some advantages over methods like the export base model (or economic base model) (Leistritz and Murdock, 1981: 27–39).

SWOT analysis

This is an assessment of:
Strengths (S)
Weaknesses (W)
Opportunities (O)
Threats (T)
usually tabulated as a matrix (see Table 6.2), so that overall costs and benefits can be compared.

Trend analysis

Possibly one of the most widely used techniques, trend analysis is basically the presentation of time-series data in order to show fluctuations in the past, and perhaps allow future projections to be made. It is important that observations are not too infrequent or subtle fluctuations will be missed. The data must also be checked to ensure that it has not been statistically 'smoothed' (transformed).

Venn-type diagram

Venn diagrams are used to illustrate informants' perceptions. The diagram typically consists of symbols assigned a size to indicate their importance, shape to indicate character and distance from a centre to convey how high a regard the informant has for it. Symbols may also be varied to show change over a period of time (say surveys at five-year intervals). For example, a village may hold traditional healers in less respect than it did eight years ago and hospital care may have gained in importance; a Venn-type diagram could be used to recognize this.

Simulation techniques

For scenario simulation, the assessor seeks to establish the logical sequence of events to see how a situation is likely to evolve in the future. Social

TABLE 6.2 Example of a SWOT analysis

	S	W	O	T
alternative 1	*		*	
alternative 2		*		
alternative 3		*	*	*

simulation involves the study of social intervention under controlled ('reproducible') simulated conditions, in order to develop predictive models (Boskma, 1986; Conner, 1981). Naik (1981: 122) noted that scenario simulation could investigate the past and suggest possible future situations, and is especially able to handle uncertainty (weak data and rapid change). Modelling and role-playing can be used to predict likely future scenarios (Clapham and Pestel, 1979).

Workshops

Workshops are structured group meetings in which stakeholders share knowledge and seek a common strategy. The workshop (like a focus group) is usually guided by a chairperson or facilitator, and there may be formal outcomes. The facilitator may need to prompt participants toward consensus, and help to prioritize objectives. Workshops are a good way for a researcher to encourage informants to collaborate. They can show how the 'group mind' develops in dialogue with a development agency, other affected parties, etc. In some cases they can take a gaming form so that participants 'discover through play'. Workshops may involve a mix of stakeholders, or just a particular interest group. Role-playing is a way of getting people to step back from established perspectives and gain an insight into other people's predicaments; from this it may be possible to predict likely future scenarios.

Focus groups

Focus group interviewing is widely used in market research and has spread to non-profit and research sectors. Focus groups are a good means of collecting qualitative data. Groups foster a dialogue in which individuals participate in debate or discussion. Groups are comprised of 5–15 individuals, selected (typically by phone contact) to ensure that they are of similar social standing and have other things in common but, ideally, do not know each other. The group is managed by a skilled, largely passive moderator who feeds prepared questions for group discussion. The assessor should prepare and issue ground rules at the outset to guide discussion and reassure those involved about confidentiality, etc. Obviously, assessors should not mix people likely to come into conflict (landlords and tenants, for example). After sufficient interaction, the discussion is terminated and a careful analysis made of what has been said. The process is then continued a number of times, with different groups but similar questions. If conducted well, in an environment that does not threaten the participants, the process should allow group interaction and help show how opinions are formed (Kruger, 1994).

Focus groups are a qualitative technique, a means of interviewing several people together as a group, and thus benefiting from the way opinions develop through discussion (Finsterbusch, 1995: 245). The approach can show attitudes and experiences, but the sessions are relatively uncontrolled by the assessors (in some respects they are like college tutorial-group discussions – apparently similar groups can function moderately well, fail or 'take off' under almost identical conditions). While a cheap and speedy method, it is not suitable if the environment is emotionally charged or to be used for making future projections. There is also limited opportunity to following it up or check results. Unscrupulous politicians, and other decision-makers, may be tempted to use focus groups to avoid being held accountable; if things go wrong they can resort to the plea: 'I did what the focus group advised . . . it was what the people wanted.' A cynic might be tempted to say this is one reason why participation has become so popular in recent years.

Although used extensively in market research to reveal the reasons behind people's choices, it is less often adopted by sociologists (Morgan and Spanish, 1984). Focus groups do not give very precise or objective results (Greenbaum, 1998; Merton *et al.*, 1994; Morgan, 1993; Morgan and Kruger, 1997). Nevertheless, they are a way of gathering baseline data, and can be good for obtaining information on sensitive political, economic or moral issues (Roche, 1999: 119–23). Finsterbusch (1995) calls for SIA to make more use of focus group interviews, and notes their value in developing countries where private one-to-one interviews may give rise to fear and suspicion (a group is better able to support and 'police' its members, making a useful exchange of information more likely). Focus groups can reveal people's needs, concerns, attitudes, wants, values, etc., and have the advantage over one-to-one interviewing in that members of the group may be prompted to respond by each other as well as by the interviewer.

Aesthetic impacts

Change in visual or other aesthetic features of the environment can have a considerable social impact: on feelings of well-being (individual or community), stress-levels, property prices, creativity and so on. Landscape planners, architects, behavioural geographers, anthropologists and social psychologists have developed a range of techniques to measure and assess aesthetic qualities, and to predict impacts. Photography and digital techniques permit assessors to simulate future impacts as TV presentations, pictures, etc.

Once aesthetic impacts have been identified, it may be possible to avoid damage, camouflage or hide negative impacts or site them away from direct view. With the bulk of these techniques, the problem is to convert, often widely varying, subjective judgement of observers, to as objective a scale or system as possible.

Cognitive mapping

Respondents are asked to draw a map of an area, noting features that are important to them. This technique is widely used in PRA and RRA. Cognitive mapping is used to gather information about people's psychological outlook, it is also useful where the informants are illiterate or suspicious of outsiders. It is an approach that is helpful for gathering people's feelings on sensitive subjects (for example, studies of political, income or sexual issues).

Identifying and assessing indirect and cumulative impacts

The need to identify cumulative impacts has generated a sub-specialism within EIA and SIA: cumulative impact assessment. The techniques are still a long way from adequate. Because of the longer time-frame involved, there is some overlap with futures studies and futures forecasting, and strategic environmental assessment (*see* Chapter 4). The approach also needs to be as holistic as possible. Smit and Spaling (1995) reviewed a variety of cumulative impact assessment techniques, including geographical information systems (GIS), matrix multiplication, causal analysis and simulation modelling.

Planners and managers are increasingly faced with the need for a holistic approach to dealing with complex development issues, and the consideration of different sectors or issues from local up to national or even global level, and from project-scale up to policy level (Ravetz, 1998).

Computer-assisted SIA

There have been numerous attempts to perfect computer-aided SIA, generally using modelling approaches and systems analysis (McDonald, 1980). Expert systems have also been used to assist SIA.

Expert systems

These are computer programs that store a body of knowledge and, with it, help the user to perform tasks that would normally demand input from a human expert (Barrow, 1997: 52–3; Goldsborough and Van Koppen, 1988). Expert systems are of particular value where there is a shortage of skills: for example, in developing countries. Although used by EIA, environmental assessment, the legal profession, healthcare, risk assessment and regional planning, there has been relatively limited use by SIA (Meyer, 1992).

Logical framework analysis

This is largely a tool of project planning. Also known as the project framework approach (and commonly abbreviated to 'LogFrame' or LFA), logical framework analysis is a tool borrowed from management studies by development planners, evaluation and project appraisal practitioners more than by SIA. Initially developed by USAID between 1969 and 1970, it is a way of establishing a structure to describe a project, and is used to test the logic of a plan of action in terms of means and ends. It helps to clarify how the planned activities will achieve objectives; and also highlights the implications of carrying out a planned action – and so can be useful for SIA (Akroyd, 1999). LFA takes the form of a matrix which provides a visual summary of project design. The matrix emphasizes the results expected if the project is completed successfully. The results are presented in terms of objectively verifiable indicators. One variant of LFA adapted for participatory methods of assessment is the Zentrale Orienterte Projekt Plannung (ZOPP) (objective-oriented project planning) method, originally developed by the GTZ in 1987.

Project developers see it as an aid to logical thinking that is especially useful in the early stages to help develop management skills and establish communication between various parties. The technique can check means against ends and show how objectives will be achieved. It can also stimulate discussion of feasibility (Akroyd, 1999; Barrow, 1997: 21–2; Gosling and Edwards, 1995). Software to assist with LFA can be found on the internet at http://www.mdf.nl, and can also be accessed by e-mail at planbud@mdf.nl (June 2000).

REFERENCES

Akroyd, D. (1999) Logical framework approaches to project planning, socio-economic analysis and to monitoring and evaluation services: a smallholder rice project. *Impact Assessment Bulletin* **17(1)**, 54–66.

Albrecht, S.L. and **Thompson, J.G.** (1988) The place of attitudes and perceptions in social impact assessment. *Society and Natural Resources* **1(1)**, 69–80.

Ament, R,H. (1970) Comparison of delphi forecasting studies. *Futures* **2(1)**, 35–44.

Arksey, H. (1999) *Interviewing for Social Scientists: an introductory resource with examples*. Sage, London.

Armour, A. (1988) Methodological problems in social impact assessment. *Environmental Impact Assessment Review* **8(3)**, 249–65.

Atkinson, R. (1998) *The Life Story Interview*. Sage, London.

Barbour, R. (ed.) (1998) *Developing Focus Group Research: politics, theory and practice*. Sage, London.

Barrow, C.J. (1997) *Environmental and Social Impact Assessment: an introduction*. Arnold, London.

Baster, N. (ed.) (1972) Measuring development, special issue of *Journal of Development Studies* **8(3)**.

Bauer, R. (ed.) (1967) *Social Indicators*. MIT Press, Cambridge (MA).

Becker, H.A. (1988) Social impact assessment by scenario projections combining quantitative and qualitative analysis. *Impact Assessment Bulletin* **6(1)**, 89–102.

Becker, H.A. (1990) Social consequences of demographic change, in C.A. Hazeu and G.A.B. Finking (eds), *Emerging Issues in Demographic Research*. Elsevier, Amsterdam, 77–125.

Becker, H.A. (1997) *Social Impact Assessment: method and experience in Europe, North America and the developing world*. University College London Press, London.

Boskma, B. (1986) Social impact assessment by social simulation. *Impact Assessment Bulletin* **4(3–4)**, 135–48.

Burningham, K. (1995) Attitudes, accounts and impact assessment. *Sociological Review* **43(1)**, 100–22.

Buzzard, S. (1990) Surveys: avoiding the common problems, in K. Finsterbusch., J. Ingersol and L. Llewellyn (eds), *Methods for Social Analysis in Developing Countries*. Westview, Boulder (CO), 71–87.

Canter, L.W. (1977) Prediction and assessment of impacts on the socioeconomic environment, in L.W. Canter (ed.), *Environmental Impact Assessment*. McGraw-Hill, New York (NY), 163–72.

Carley, M.J. (1981) *Social Measurement and Social Indicators: issues of policy and theory*. George Allen and Unwin, London.

Carley, M.J. (1984) *Cumulative Socio-economic Monitoring*. Northern Economic Planning Branch, Indian and Northern Affairs Canada, Ottawa.

Carley, M. and **Wathey, A.** (1981) Explaining some key elements in SIA, in F. Tester and W. Mykes (eds), *Social Impact Assessment: theory, methods and practice*. Detselig Enterprises Ltd, Calgary (Canada), 13–22.

Chambers, R. (1983) *Rural Development: putting the last first*. Longman, Harlow.

Chambers, R. (1991) Rapid rural appraisal: rationale and repertoire. *Public Administration and Development* **1(1)**, 95–106.

Clapham, W.B. Jnr and **Pestel, R.F.** (1979) On the scenario approach to simulation modelling for complex policy assessment and design. *Policy Sciences* **11(2)**, 157–77.

Cochran, N. (1979) On the limiting properties of social indicators. *Evaluation and Program Planning* **2(1)**, 1–4.

Conner, R.F. (1981) *Methodological Advances in Evaluation Research*. Sage, Beverly Hills (CA).

Cox, G. (1995) *Techniques for Effective Social Impact Assessment: a practical guide*. NSW Office on Social Policy, Sydney.

Cracknell, B.E. (ed.) (1983) *The Evaluation of Aid Projects and Programmes*. HMSO, London.

Dale, A.P. and **Lane, M.B.** (1994) Strategic perspectives analysis: a procedure for participatory and political SIA. *Society and Natural Resources* **7(3)**, 253–67.

Derman, W. (1990) Informant interviewing in international social impact assessment, in K. Finsterbusch, J. Ingersol and L, Llewellyn (eds), *Methods for Social Analysis in Developing Countries*. Westview, Boulder (CO), 107–26.

Diener, E.S.E. (1997) Measuring quality of life: economic, social, and subjective indicators. *Social Indicators Research* **40(1–2)**, 189–216.

Dietz, T. (1987) Theory and method in social impact assessment. *Sociological Inquiry* No. 57, 54–69.

Erickson, P.A. (1979) *Environmental Impact Assessment: principles and appliances*. Academic Press, New York (NY).

Fink, A. and **Kosecoff, J.** (1998) *How to Conduct Surveys: a step-by-step guide* (2nd edn). Sage, Thousand Oaks (CA).

Finsterbusch, K. (1985) State of the art in social impact assessment. *Environment and Behavior* **17(2)**, 193–221.

Finsterbusch, K. (1995) In praise of SIA – a personal review of the field of social impact assessment: feasibility, justification, history, methods, issues. *Impact Assessment* **13(3)**, 229–52.

Finsterbusch, K. and **Wolf, C.P.** (eds) (1981) *Methodology of Social Impact Assessment* (2nd edn). Dowden, Hutchinson and Ross, Stroudsburg (PA) (1st edn 1977).

Force, J.E. and **Machlis, G.E.** (1997) The human ecosystem 2: social indicators in ecosystem management. *Society and Natural Resources* **10(4)**, 369–82.

Fox, K.A. (1974) *Social Indicators and Social Theory*. Wiley, New York.

Freeman, H.E. Rossi, P.H. and **Wright, S.R.** (1979) *Evaluating Social Projects in Developing Countries*. OECD, Paris.

Gardner, G. (1978) *Social Surveys for Social Planners*. Open University Press, Milton Keynes.

Geisler. C.G. (1993) Rethinking SIA: why ex-ante research isn't enough. *Society and Natural Resources* **6(4)**, 327–38.

Gold, R.L. (1978) Linking social with other impact assessments, in R.K. Jain and B.L. Hutchings (eds), *Environmental Impact Analysis: emerging issues in planning*. University of Illinois Press, Urbana (IL), 105–16.

Goldsborough, D.G. and **Van Koppen, C.S.A.** (1988) Expert systems in environmental protection: myths and possibilities. *Milieu* **3(5)**, 137–42.

Gosling, L. and **Edwards, M.** (1995) *Toolkits: a practical guide to assessment, monitoring, review and evaluation* (Development Manual No. 5). Save the Children Fund, London, 178–92.

Gramling, R. (1992) Employment data and social impact assessment. *Evaluation and Program Planning* **15(3)**, 219–25.

Greenbaum, T.L. (1998) *The Handbook for Focus Group Research* (2nd edn). Sage, London.

Griffiths, C.R. (1980) Assessing community cohesion impact through network analysis. *Journal of Environmental Systems* **9(2)**, 161–7.

Helmer, O. (1968) Analysis of the future: the Delphi method, in J.R. Bright (ed.), *Technological Forecasting for Industry and Government*. Prentice-Hall, Englewood Cliffs (NJ), 116–22.

Henshel, R.L. (1976) *On the Future of Social Predictions*. Bobbs-Merrill, Indianapolis (IN).

Henshel, R.L. (1982) Sociology and social forecasting. *Annual Review of Sociology* **8**, 57–79.

Hill, K.Q. and **Fowles, J.** (1975) The methodological worth of the Delphi forecasting technique. *Technological Forecasting and Social Change* **7(2)**, 179–92.

Interorganizational Committee on Guidelines and Principles (1994) *Guidelines for Social Impact Assessment*. NOAA, Washington. (Also published in *Impact Assessment* **12(2)**, 107–152 and *Impact Assessment Review* **15(1)**, 11–43.)

Johnston, D.F. (1970) Forecasting methods in the social sciences. *Technological Forecasting and Social Change* **2(1)**, 173–87.

King, B.K. (1981) *What is SAM? A Laymans Guide to Social Accounting Matrices* (World Bank Staff Working Paper No. 463). The World Bank, Washington (DC).

Kruger, R.A. (1994) *Focus Groups: a practical guide for applied research* (2nd edn). Sage, Thousand Oaks (CA).

Kvale, S. (1996) *InterViews: an introduction to qualitative research interviewing*. Sage, London.

Land, K.C. (1970) Social indicators, in B. Smith (ed.), *Social Science Methods*. Free Press, New York.

Lawrence, D. (1993) Quantitative *versus* qualitative evaluation: a false dichotomy. *Environmental Impact Assessment Review* **13(1)**, 3–11.

Leistritz, F.L. and **Murdock, S.H.** (1981) *The Socioeconomic Impact of Resource Development: Methods of Assessment*. Westview, Boulder (CO).

Linstone, H.A. (1985) The Delphi technique, in V.T. Covello, J.L. Mumpower, P.J.M. Stallen and V.R.R. Uppuluri (eds) (1985) *Environmental Impact Assessment, Technology Assessment, and Risk Analysis: contributions from the psychological and decision sciences*. Springer-Verlag, Berlin, 621–50.

Llewellyn, L.G., Wolf, C.P. and **Finsterbusch, K.** (1983) *Social Impact Assessment Methods*. Sage, Beverly Hills (CA).

McDonald, J.M. (ed.) (1980) *Computer Models and Forecasting Socio-Economic Impacts of Growth and Development*. University of Alberta, Faculty of Extension, Edmonton (Canada).

Macfarlane, M. (1999) An Evaluation of Social Impact Assessment Methodologies in the Mining Industry. PhD thesis, University of Bath, Bath (UK).

Meissen, G.J. and **Cipriani, J.A.** (1984) Community psychology and social impact assessment: an action model. *American Journal of Community Psychology* **12(3)**, 369–86.

Merton, R.K., Fiske, M. and **Kendall, P.L.** (1994) *The Focused Interview* (2nd edn). The Free Press, Glencoe (IL).

Meyer, M.A. (1992) How to apply the anthropological technique of participant observation to knowledge acquisition for expert systems. *IEEE Transactions on Systems, Man and Cybernetics* **22(3)**, 983–91.

Miller, A. and **Cuff, N.** (1986) The Delphi approach to the mediation of environmental disputes. *Environmental Management* **10(3)**, 321–30.

Morgan, D.L. (ed.) (1993) *Successful Focus Groups*. Sage, Newbury Park (CA).

Morgan, D.L. and **Kruger, R.A.** (1997) *Focus Group Kit* (six vols). Sage London.

Morgan, D.L. and **Spanish, M.T.** (1984) Focus groups: a new tool for qualitative research. *Qualitative Sociology* **7(3)**, 253–70.

Moser, C.H. and **Kalton, S.** (1979) *Survey Methods in Social Investigation*. Heinemann, London.

Muth, R.M. and **Lee, R.G.** (1986) Social impact assessment in natural resource decision making: toward a structural paradigm. *Impact Assessment Bulletin* **4(3–4)**, 168–83.

Naik, H. (1981) Evaluation of social intangibles with special reference to floodplain management, in F.J. Tester and W. Mykes (eds), *Social Impact Assessment: theory, methods and practice*. Detselig Enterprises, Calgary (Canada), 110–33.

Patton, M. (1987) *Qualitative Methods in Evaluation*. Sage, London.

Peters, H.P. (1986) Social impact analysis of four energy sources. *Impact Assessment Bulletin* **4(3–4)**, 149–67.

Pill, J. (1971) The Delphi method: substance, context, a critique and annotated bibliography. *Socioeconomic Planning Sciences* **5(1)**, 57–71.

Ravetz, J. (1998) Integrated assessment models – from global to local. *Impact Assessment and Project Appraisal* **16(2)**, 147–54.

Rickson, R.E., Hundloe, T., McDonald, G.T. and **Burdge, R.J.** (eds) (1990) Social impact of development: putting theory and methods into practice. *Environmental Impact Assessment Review* special issue **10(1–2)**.

Roche, C. (1999) *Impact Assessment for Development Agencies: learning to value change*. Oxfam (with Novib), Oxford.

Rossi, P.J. and **Freeman, E.** (1982) *Evaluation: a systematic approach* (2nd edn). Sage, Beverly Hills (CA).

Rossi, P.J. and **Gilmartin, K.J.** (1980) *The Handbook of Social Indicators: sources, characteristics, and analysis*. Garland (STPM Press), New York (NY).

Sapsford, R. (1999) *Survey Research*. Sage, London.

Schonfield, A. and **Shaw, S.** (eds) (1972) *Social Indicators and Social Policy*. Heinemann, London.

Sheldon, E.B. and **Freeman, H.E.** (1970) Note on social indicators: promises and potential. *Policy Sciences* **1(1)**, 97–111.

Shields, M.A. (1975) Social impact assessment: an expository analysis. *Environment and Behavior* **7(3)**, 265–84.

Smit, B. and **Spaling, H.** (1995) Methods for cumulative effects assessment. *Environmental Impact Assessment Review* **15(1)**, 81–106.

Soderstrom, E.J. (1981) *Social Impact Assessment: experimental methods and applications*. Praeger, New York (NY).

Vlachos, E. (1981) Figure 1, in K. Finsterbusch and C.P. Wolf (eds), *Methodology of Social Impact Assessment* (2nd edn). Hutchinson Ross Publishing, Stroudsburg (PA), 168 (Figure 1).

Vogel, J. (1997) The future of social indicator research. *Social Indicators Research* **42(2)**, 103–16.

Wildavsky, A. (1996) *Speaking truth to Power: the art and craft of policy analysis* (2nd edn). Transaction Publishers, New Brunswick (1st edn 1979 – Little, Brown & Co., Boston, MA).

Wildman, P. (1990) Methodological and social policy issues in social impact assessment. *Environmental Impact Assessment Review* **10(1–2)**, 69–79.

Wolf, C.P. (1983) Social impact assessment: a methodological overview, in K. Finsterbusch, L.G. Llewellyn and C.P. Wolf (eds), *Social Impact Assessment Methods*. Sage, Beverly Hills (CA), 25–33.

Yong, Y.W., Keng, K.A. and **Leng, T.L.** (1989) A Delphi forecast for the Singapore tourism industry: future scenario and marketing implications. *International Marketing Review* **6(3)**, 35–46.

7

SIA IN PRACTICE: DEVELOPING COUNTRIES

'SIA is a product of Western culture, steeped in the positivist tradition, often overstating its scientific strength and efficacy' (Derman and Whiteford, 1985: 15)

THE SPREAD OF SIA IN DEVELOPING COUNTRIES

Since the 1950s it has become all too apparent that efforts to assist developing countries have frequently failed to yield optimum results and, in some cases, 'unexpected' social impacts have significantly or totally overshadowed any benefits, and have perhaps even made conditions worse than they were prior to intervention. There are many cases of this: for example, numerous large dam projects; Amazonian road developments; the effects of structural adjustment policies worldwide; and transmigration in Indonesia (Adams and Solomon, 1985; Hayter, 1971; Hayter and Warren, 1985). Some of the issues covered in Chapter 8 are often encountered in developing countries – notably SIA and indigenous peoples, SIA and marginalized people, SIA and relocatees, SIA and vulnerable communities.

Many of those active in aid agencies, funding bodies, development studies, development planning and policy-making have realized the importance of SIA as a way of reducing development failures and of improving the benefits and sustainability of successes (*Environmental Impact Assessment Review* **10(1–2)**, special issue 'Social impacts of development: putting theory into practice'; Freeman and Frey, 1990; Vanclay and Bronstein, 1995: 35). Given the magnitude of the problem, it is surprising how little SIA has been applied to poverty. Poverty has huge impacts: on health, life expectancy, educational achievement, human rights, political stability and many aspects of life. The rich have been slow to realize, or admit, that poverty can affect their health, wealth and security; this message was clearly stated by the Brandt Report

(Independent Commission on International Development Issues, 1980). World peace, sustainable development and healthy international trade are threatened by poverty; SIA, however, could help to unravel the causes and likely effects of poverty.

The spread of SIA to developing countries has largely been through its being required by aid and funding agencies, and more recently by some large companies and NGOs. Not all countries have welcomed it: some administrations have failed to perceive the need and more than a few are hostile. NEPA (1970), plus the New Direction Legislation for Development Assistance (1973), effectively forced all US donor agencies as well as federal bodies to conduct SIA. In 1975 the main US foreign aid body, the US Agency for International Development (USAID), introduced the requirement that a social soundness analysis (a proactive process similar to SIA) be undertaken as part of project preparation and approval (Asian Development Bank, 1992; Hansen, 1985; Ingersoll *et al.*, 1981). This was to consider socio-cultural feasibility, potential spread effects and social impacts, and would consider which groups benefited and which suffered. There is a well-developed literature and thriving consultancy activity focused on project evaluation, analysis or assessment; however, much of this is retrospective or reviews the current situation (Cracknell, 1983; Freeman *et al.*, 1980; Peil, 1982). There has also been more of an emphasis on economic issues (often using cost–benefit analysis), rather than social impacts (Abelson, 1996; Bulmer and Warwick, 1983; Curry and Weiss, 1993).

During 1974 the World Bank appointed a full-time sociologist and began to build a team for social impact assessments. In 1985 it issued guidelines for social aspects of project appraisal, and soon the Bank and other agencies required social analysis, social soundness analysis and SIA, and had established procedures for implementing them (Asian Development Bank, 1992; ODA, 1995; USAID, 1994). Since the mid-1980s NGOs in developed and developing countries have pressured bodies like the World Bank to improve EIA and SIA.

There has been considerable development of social assessment, social research, and social analysis techniques for foreign aid and rural development (Becker, 1997; Cernea, 1985; Dawson, 1998; Finsterbusch and VanWicklin, 1989; Finsterbusch *et al.*, 1990; Francis and Jacobs, 1999; Green, 1986; Leistritz and Murdock, 1981; Llewellyn *et al.*, 1990). One aspect has been the trend in recent years for a shift from post-ante to ex-ante SIA (i.e. from evaluation after development has been started to proactive assessment), and growing interest in integrated approaches to impact assessment (Sholten and Post, 1999).

SIA appeals to development agencies and NGOs because it has the potential to give a better rate of development success, and it offers a way of helping to ensure that benefits are shared equitably. SIA can be used, for example, to check how a development might improve or worsen the welfare of women or a minority group. SIA, or EIA modified to address social issues, can be useful to support both community development and sustainable development (Roche, 1999). The latter has increasingly attracted attention, while the former has generated less interest, although it has been tried in the Caribbean (Brown and Jacobs, 1996). There has been resistance to SIA from some administrators and companies involved in development, who argue that it is an expensive luxury that can delay development.

Increasingly, the world's planners accept that SIA saves money in the long run and that the costs of failure to conduct assessments in developing countries are possibly higher than in developed countries because they are felt by the public rather than the private sector, and because people are more vulnerable, having less savings or flexibility of employment to enable them to avoid impacts (Burdge, 1990 and 1994; Henry, 1990). Negative and positive social impacts tend to affect weak social groups the most; the very poor include the unemployed and under-employed, the sick, injured and elderly, and other 'underclasses'. In developing countries, improvements to healthcare mean that more people are now surviving to old age in societies where the traditional arrangements for care are breaking down, and where there is little or no provision for pensions (*see* Chapter 10's coverage of ageing populations).

ADAPTING SIA TO THE NEEDS OF DEVELOPING COUNTRIES

SIA appeared in North America, much influenced by NEPA, and has largely evolved there and in other developed countries; to work effectively in developing countries, it must be adapted to their social, environmental and cultural conditions, regulatory procedures, education level of the population and so on (Ingersoll, 1990; Khan, 1990). Even within North America there are considerable differences between cultures, and powerful special interest groups, underclasses and indigenous peoples. Both EIA and SIA have been developing methods to deal with these challenges (Lemons and Porter, 1994). Those conducting SIAs must try to remain objective (neutral), alert and diligent, and should avoid making the assumption that 'the developer knows best', that proposed changes are the only options or are inevitable (Derman and Whiteford, 1985: 5). It is also vital that SIA assessors are properly trained, have relevant experience and are capable, and it is desirable that they are nationals of the country in which they are working, to help avoid dependency and to ensure that prompt follow-up studies are possible.

Improving the adoption of SIA and ensuring that it is properly adapted may not be easy; Henry (1990: 92) noted that the forces that propel development in developing countries are often institutionalized, and so will be difficult to change. The decision-makers in developing countries are faced with growing national debts and terms of office that discourage them from planning more than a few years ahead; hence, they may have little incentive to adopt measures like SIA. With planning and decision-making in developing countries often compartmentalized by discipline or sector, the multidisciplinary co-ordination and integration required for effective SIA can be difficult to achieve. In the meantime its effective function is hindered. In addition, there are fewer, or indeed none, of the legal and administrative frameworks that support the SIA process in richer nations; this makes effective assessment difficult and gives little support to encourage the use of its findings. Often the process is at least partly 'tokenism', and if an SIA predicts negative impacts it may simply be shelved and ignored.

In developing countries, SIA has, in the main, been project-focused, sometimes undertaken as part of pre-development planning, but too often only after the choice of development option has been made or as part of project analysis/appraisal (*see* Chapter 6) (Burdge, 1990; Curry and Weiss, 1993; Little and Mirlees, 1974; *see also* special issue on 'Project appraisal in developing countries', *Journal of International Development* **6(1)**, 1994). Project analysis and appraisal often has a dominant economic focus.

When SIA is supported in a developing country there are seldom follow-up studies, and the accuracy of predictions has rarely been evaluated by ex-post SIA audit. Assessments focus on impacts taking place during development implementation and much less attention is given to what happens after that phase. Overall, according to Rickson *et al.* (1990) the application of SIA in developing countries has been more passive than in developed countries. There is also a need for better communications between assessor(s) and the assessed. Partly as a result of these problems, and because discussion about how to improve impact assessment tends to emphasize methodological issues rather than structural or political issues or the nature of the relationship between SIA and development planning, developing country applications have been slow to improve (Rakowski, 1995: 526).

Anthropological and sociological studies have helped highlight the risks of professionals and expatriates misreading the abilities, condition and views of local people (culturally embedded interpretation and bias). Henry (1990) stressed the need for developing-country SIA to use local knowledge and expertise, to ensure it was adapted to needs and to reduce dependency. Like EIA, it should also be flexible and adaptable to cope with inadequate availability of data and uncertainty (Holling, 1978: 17; Walters, 1986). People's attitudes to a development may well alter over time: something welcomed before construction may be hated by locals a few years later. The spread of new technology has had, is having and will have a huge social impact on developing countries; this is particularly true of agricultural innovations (the 'green revolution' has affected millions since the 1930s), modern healthcare, improved communications and biotechnology, and is likely to be felt increasingly in coming decades (*see also* the discussion of this in Chapters 9, 10 and 12).

SIA can draw on considerable experience of relocation and resettlement, much of it generated by large dam projects (Barrow, 1981). Some in Africa were already under way by the early 1970s (Chambers, 1970; Colson, 1971) (*see* Chapter 8). Other fields in which SIA has acquired fairly good hindsight include: highway construction (*see* Chapter 9); natural resource developments that impinge on indigenous peoples (*see* Chapter 8); tourism (*see* Chapter 11); boomtowns (*see* Chapter 8); structural adjustment programmes (*see*

Chapter 11); agricultural modernization (*see* Chapter 12); and healthcare changes (*see* Chapter 10). Reviewing the value of SIA for reducing the social impacts of biotechnology innovations and for improving the chances of achieving sustainable development, Hindmarsh (1990) noted its potential but came to pessimistic conclusions. Biotechnology is still largely at a stage where evaluation and controlled proactive management is theoretically possible; whether SIA can work in the political economic conditions of developing countries to ensure that this happens is doubtful according to Hindmarsh (1990). For SIA to be effective in controlling biotechnology in developing countries, he argued, it would have to be 'vastly more sophisticated', proactive in operation and focused on Third-World priorities. Given the size of the biotechnological revolution – at the time of writing (spring 2000) it was likely to be worth between US$50 to US$100 billion a year by 2000 – and the fact that multinational corporations (MNCs) and transnational corporations (TNCs) control most of it, SIA faces powerful forces.

There is a risk that the application of SIA in developing countries will be similar to the experience with EIA: it will be used as a 'tool' by planners and administrators who will fail to engender adequate public participation, or to ensure that recommendations are acted upon. In developed countries, public participation presents fewer problems because there is considerable freedom of access to information and democratic decision-making is established; in addition, there are relatively unrestrained media and NGOs, and some degree of political accountability through the election process. In stark contrast, many developing countries have evolved planning and decision-making systems that are paternalistic, authoritarian and subject to little political accountability; SIA does not easily transfer to such situations (Fu-Keung Ip, 1990; Ingersoll, 1990; Jiggens, 1995; Suprapto, 1990; Wisner, 1985).

There has been a tendency to emphasize the negative aspects of SIA and to miss the positive; there may also be other subtle benefits from SIA in developing countries, in addition to those usually expected: it can identify research priorities, uncover useful indigenous knowledge, help educate administrators to the problems and needs of those impacted (even if nothing immediate is done to aid them), generate discussion and debate, and so raise peoples' consciousness and awareness of social issues, make explicit who benefits and who loses as a result of a development or policy, and it can stimulate third-party involvement. In the words of Rakowski (1995: 538), 'The SIA experience and resulting report may generate long-term outcomes not readily identifiable in the short run ... there may be indirect positive impacts. ... These outcomes may be as important as those recommended.'

Issues like tourism, free trade, structural adjustment, heath changes, global environmental change, urbanization and technology innovation are felt acutely in developing countries. SIA has been applied to these sectors (which are dealt with in other chapters rather than in the present context of developing countries).

Roche (1999) examined the NGOs experience with impact assessment (including SIA), focusing on the needs of practitioners and evaluation specialists. On the whole, Roche found that the approach adopted was participatory. He also examined a number of case studies to establish how well various approaches and methods of impact assessment worked.

People may react very differently to challenges and opportunities; even the same group of people, facing a repeated challenge, could follow a very different path. Add to this unpredictability the growing likelihood that various 'development pressures' have altered or destroyed the coping strategies that may have evolved, plus the possibility of global environmental change, and the likelihood of social and economic change, and the planners and managers of developing countries face great uncertainty. SIA may help to reduce this.

REFERENCES

Abelson, P. (1996) *Project Appraisal and Valuation of the Environment*. Macmillan, London.

Adams, P. and **Solomon, L.** (1985) *In the Name of Progress: the underside of foreign aid*. Earthscan, London.

Asian Development Bank (1992) *Guidelines for Social Analysis of Development Projects* (Operational Summary, June 1991). Asian Development Bank, Manilla.

Barrow, C.J. (1981) Health and resettlement consequences and opportunities created as a result of river impoundment in developing countries. *Water Supply & Management* **5(1)**, 135–49.

Becker, H.A. (1997) *Social Impact Assessment: method and experience in Europe, North America and the developing world*. University College London Press, London.

Brown, D. and **Jacobs, P.** (1996) Adapting environmental impact assessment to sustain the community development process. *Habitat International* **20(3)**, 493–507.

Bulmer, M. and **Warwick, D.P.** (eds) (1983) *Social Research Methods in Developing Countries*. Wiley, New York (NY).

Burdge, R.J. (1990) The benefits of social impact assessment in Third World development. *Environmental Impact Assessment Review* **10(1–2)**, 123–34.

Burdge, R.J. (1994) The benefits of social impact assessment in Third World development, in R.J. Burdge (ed.), *A Conceptual Approach to Social Impact Assessment: collection of readings*. Social Ecology Press, Middleton (WI), 239–56.

Cernea, M.M. (ed.) (1985) *Putting People First: sociological variables in rural development*. Oxford University Press, New York (NY).

Chambers, R. (1970) *Volta Resettlement Experience*. Pall Mall Press, London.

Colson, E. (1971) *The Social Consequences of Resettlement: Kariba studies IV, the impact of Kariba resettlement upon the Gwembe Tonga*. Manchester University Press, Manchester.

Cracknell, B.E. (ed.) (1983) *The Evaluation of Aid Projects and Programmes*. HMSO, London.

Curry, S. and **Weiss, J.** (1993) *Project Analysis in Developing Countries*. Macmillan, London.

Dawson, E. (1998) *Assessing the Impact of Emergency Aid: a discussion paper*. Oxfam, Oxford.

Derman, W. and **Whiteford, S.** (eds) (1985) *Social Impact Analysis and Development Planning in the Third World*. Westview, Boulder (CO).

Finsterbusch, K. and **VanWicklin, W.A.** (1989) Project problems and shortfalls: the need for social impact assessment in AID projects, in S.S. Nagel and R.V. Bartlett (eds), *Policy Through Impact Assessment: institutionalized analysis as a policy strategy*. Greenwood Press, New York (NY), 73–84.

Finsterbusch, K., Ingersol, J. and **Llewellyn, L.G.** (eds) (1990) *Methods for Social Analysis in Developing Countries*. Westview, Boulder (CO).

Francis, P. and **Jacobs, S.** (1999) Institutionalizing social analysis at The World Bank. *Environmental Impact Assessment Review* **19(3)**, 341–57.

Freeman, D. and **Frey, R.S.** (1990) A modest proposal for assessing social impacts of natural resource policies. *Journal of Environmental Systems* **20(4)**, 375–404.

Freeman, H.E., Rossi, P.H. and **Wright, S.R.** (1980) *Evaluating Social Projects in Developing Countries*. OECD, Paris.

Fu-Keung Ip, D. (1990) Difficulties in implementing social impact assessment in China: methodological considerations. *Environmental Impact Assessment Review* **10(1–2)**, 113–22.

Green, E.C. (1986) *Practising Development Anthropology*. Westview, Boulder.

Hansen, D.O. (1985) Social soundness analysis: an institutional role for social scientists in AID's assistance program. *The Rural Sociologist* **5(1)**, 37–42.

Hayter, T (1971) *Aid as Imperialism*. Penguin, Harmondsworth.

Hayter, T. and **Warren, C.** (1985) *Aid Rhetoric and Reality*. Pluto Press, London.

Henry, R.J. (1990) Implementing social impact assessment in developing countries: a comparative approach to structural problems. *Environmental Impact Assessment Review* **10(1–2)**, 91–101.

Hindmarsh, R. (1990) The need for effective assessment: sustainable development and the social impacts of biotechnology in the Third World. *Environmental Impact Assessment Review* **10(1–2)**, 195–208.

Holling, C.S. (ed.) (1978) *Adaptive Environmental Assessment and Management*. Wiley, Chichester.

Independent Commission on International Development Issues, The (1980) *North–South: a programme for survival* (the Brandt Report). Pan Books, London.

Ingersoll, J. (1990) Introduction: social impact assessment – for richer and for poorer, in K. Finsterbusch, J. Ingersoll and L.G Llewellyn (eds), *Methods for Social Analysis in Developing Countries*. Westview, Boulder (CO), 1–35.

Ingersoll, J., Sullivan, M. and **Lenkerd, B.** (1981) *Social Analysis of AID Projects: a review of the experience*. Agency for International Development, Report of the Bureau for Science and Technology, Washington (DC).

Jiggens, J. (1995) Development impact assessment: impact assessment of aid projects in nonwestern countries, in F. Vanclay and D.A. Bronstein (eds) (1995) *Environmental and Social Impact Assessment*. Wiley, Chichester, 265–81.

Khan, J. (1990) Social impact assessment: a critique from the perspective of the third world countries with special reference to the construction of Chashma Right Bank Canal in the Dera Ismail Khan District of Pakistan. *Journal of Development Studies (IDS, NWFP Agricultural University, Peshwar)* **10(1)**, 71–89.

Leistritz, F.L. and **Murdock, S.H.** (1981) *The Socioeconomic Impact of Resource Development: methods of assessment*. Westview, Boulder (CO).

Lemons, K. and **Porter, A.** (1994) A comparative study of impact assessment methods in developed and developing countries. *Impact Assessment Bulletin* **10(1)**, 57–65.

Little, I.M.D. and **Mirlees, J.** (1974) *Project Appraisal and Planning for Developing Countries*. Heinemann, London.

Llewellyn, L.G., Ingersol, J. and **Finsterbusch, K.** (1990) *Methods for Social Analysis in Developing Countries*. Westview, Boulder (CO).

ODA (1995) *A Guide to Social Analysis for Developing Countries* (Overseas Development Administration). HMSO, London.

Peil, M. (1982) *Social Research Methods: an African handbook*. Hodder and Stoughton, London.

Rakowski, C.A. (1995) Evaluating a social impact assessment: short-term and long-term outcomes in a developing country. *Society and Natural Resources* **8(6)**, 525–40.

Rickson, R., Burdge, R.J., Hundloe, T. and **McDonald, G.T.** (1990) Institutional constraints to adoption of social impact assessment as a decision-making and planning tool. *Environmental Impact Assessment Review* **10(1–2)**, 233–43.

Roche, C. (1999) *Impact Assessment for Development Agencies: learning to value change*. Oxfam (with Novib), Oxford.

Sholten, J.J. and **Post, R.A.M.** (1999) Strengthening the integrated approach to impact assessments in development cooperation. *Environmental Impact Assessment Review* **19(3)**, 233–43.

Suprapto, R.A. (1990) Social impact assessment and planning: the Indonesian experience. *Impact Assessment Bulletin* **8(1–2)**, 25–30.

USAID (1994) *Social Soundness Analysis*. US Agency for International Development, Washington (DC).

Vanclay, F. and **Bronstein, D.A.** (eds) (1995) *Environmental and Social Impact Assessment*. Wiley, Chichester.

Walters, C. (1986) *Adaptive Management of Renewable Resources*. Macmillan, New York (NY).

Wisner, B. (1985) Social impact, socialism, and the case of Mozambique, in W. Derman and S. Whiteford (eds), *Social Impact Analysis and Planning in the Third World*. Westview, Boulder (CO), 262–83.

8

SIA IN PRACTICE: WEAK AND VULNERABLE GROUPS, CRIME AND JUSTICE, GENDER, FAMILY STRIFE AND CIVIL UNREST

There are so many weak and vulnerable groups that it is difficult to cover even a representative section. This chapter focuses on displaced people, indigenous peoples, small communities, small islands, boomtowns, those affected by family strife and civil unrest, those affected by social and religious movements, those vulnerable because of their gender, and those affected by crime and measures designed to counter crime. To some extent this selection has been determined by the areas to which SIA has been applied. While those affected by poverty are numerous and include the most vulnerable, SIA has been little applied to them. (The elderly are considered in Chapter 10.)

Displaced people have been the subject of quite a few SIAs. People forced or encouraged to move from areas where they have established livelihoods and 'roots' (relocatees) may be divided into the following categories.

- Permanent or semi-permanent socio-economic migrants: those who choose to move, and those forced to move by circumstances, rather than compelled by authority, in order to try to earn enough to live as they would like. They may return home from time to time or send cash back to relatives. Some countries, like the Gulf States, are heavily dependent on such relocatees as cheap labour. Socio-economic migrants may congregate in shanty towns on the fringes of cities, and have considerable socio-economic impact on urban conditions and national economies (Vargas *et al.*, 1995), or they may seek to move overseas. Migrants may form largely single-sex communities with a quite narrow age range (for example, young men who move to work in mines, or women in domestic service). The area migrants have left may suffer a shortage of able-bodied labour, leading to the breakdown of traditional livelihoods, difficulties for some in finding marriage partners, and sometimes land degradation through labour shortages. Another type of migrant are the permanent elderly relocatees, who choose to retire to warmer, more secure and possibly cheaper locations (for example, Florida in the USA or the south-west of the UK. In some places such migrants outnumber the host population and considerably distort retail service provision as well as healthcare and housing provision.

- Short-term and seasonal migrants: these people choose, or are forced, to move for part of the year on a regular basis or for a short time as a temporary measure. They can be relatively affluent, even better off than the host population. In the UK and other countries, 'commuters' live more or less permanently in a locality, but journey daily or on a weekly basis to work in cities; and city people may purchase second homes in the country that they occupy at weekends and during vacations. These migrants may come into conflict with local people if they swamp the host population culture or drive up housing prices beyond the reach of locals. In Wales, Welsh-speaking rural areas have expressed concern at the excessive numbers of English-speaking second-home buyers, and there are similar problems in parts of the Alps, the eastern USA, the Balearics, coastal Spain and elsewhere. Commuter settlement patterns can change swiftly with fashion and communication developments, and as technology makes home-based work easier.

  Where environments are harsh for part of the year, or offer seasonal opportunities, people may practice transmigration. This is a regularized pattern of movement; farmers, for example, move upslope with their livestock in spring in upland areas, or in more level regions move to better-watered areas during dry periods. In British Colonial India, Ceylon and Malaya, seasonal migration to cool upland 'hill stations' became fashionable and led to considerable communications and town development. In some developed countries, there are groups of 'younger' retired people who buy mobile homes and move between resorts (notably in Australia and parts of the USA).
- Relocatees: these can be people who involuntarily leave their homes as a result of social unrest (such as war, civil war or discrimination) (Asthana, 1996). The move often takes place with little warning, in which case the relocatees are usually termed 'refugees'. This term is somewhat contentious, but generally suggests a move across a national border to a place of safety. This may involve a risk in exiting a country and travelling to another, as faced by the Vietnamese 'Boat People' and Cuban refugees. Relocatees can also be people forced into involuntary relocation by developments such as large dams, nuclear contamination, irrigation projects and so on. Some of these developments may also attract voluntary

relocatees seeking opportunities, who may compete with, or come into conflict with, involuntary relocatees and possibly the host population too. Where relocation has been caused by a 'natural' event such as flooding, drought, soil degradation or quasi-natural changes like global warming or sea-level rise, the trend has been to describe the resulting relocatees as 'eco-refugees' (*see also* Chapter 13). Refugees dislocated by political or social unrest are more likely to get a chance to return to their old homes than eco-refugees or those forced to move by serious pollution. The final group that comes under this title is that of economic relocatees, or migrants, who have moved in order to seek better livelihood opportunities.

DISPLACED PEOPLE: RELOCATION AND RESETTLEMENT

There is much overlap between the groups listed above; many share the trauma of leaving what is familiar – family land and homes, shrines and ancestors' graves, and secure livelihoods – as well as being forced to settle in what are, at least initially, unfamiliar and possibly harsh surroundings, often among indifferent or hostile host populations (Unruh, 1993). The numbers involved may be considerable: resettlement camps or squatter settlements may house tens of thousands of relocatees who sometimes outnumber the host population. For example, Belize (a small nation) received over 30,000 refugees from elsewhere in Central America and had to be give UN aid to assist with resettlement (Collins, 1995). In the case of modern Israel, a nation has been established by those forced or encouraged to resettle; the country is still attracting relocatees, and most would accept that the host population (the Palestinians) have been seriously impacted.

SIA can advise social workers on how best to help the relocated and how to ensure that resettlement agencies do not overlook or under-rate cultural and social features like religious sites when planning relocation (Napier, 1981; VandenBerg, 1999). Caution is required; there is some evidence from Brazilian reservoir-related resettlement, that linear, reductionist models of social change, which argue that outcomes can be predetermined by assessors, may not always work because relocation and resettlement can be highly variable and situation-specific, subject to external intervention and the evolution of new social movements. SIA must therefore be responsive to local circumstances and an ongoing process (Hall, 1994).

One of the main groups of largely voluntary relocatees is that of rural–urban migrants. Members of this group are attracted, or driven, to cities for many reasons: landlessness; deterioration of farm livelihood; lack of rural employment; drought and other natural disasters; civil unrest; or simply the 'lure' of the city. In some countries they have become a serious problem, concentrating in unhealthy, crime-ridden squatter settlements. Arrival in a city is no guarantee of adequate employment. These migrants frequently become even poorer than they had been before moving and are, in effect, trapped – unable to afford to return to the countryside where they have probably lost any land that they had. The drain of people to the city can also deprive country areas of manpower, leading to the breakdown of farming, environmental degradation and an often worsening decline of rural livelihoods. The urban migrants may place a huge strain on public services, and may hinder economic development. Squatter settlements are often populated by relatively young people and high birth rates are common.

Unlike refugees of war, persecution or sudden disasters, development-related relocatees have usually had some warning, and sometimes considerable assistance and guidance, and are able to take possessions and consider the move. However, both refugees and relocatees are likely to face unexpected challenges, they will need to adapt, and will probably suffer physical and psychological trauma ('multidimensional stress' or post-traumatic stress disorder) as well as a sense of loss. These problems may continue for a considerable period of time, often 10 years or more. Migrants and relocatees frequently have difficulty re-establishing satisfactory livelihoods and being able to settle. They may suffer health problems, especially if relatively isolated groups are concentrated and brought into contact with other people who have different endemic diseases. Relocatees are also likely to have to live in unsatisfactory conditions with poor diets, and encounter new disease vectors – factors that should be predictable if SIA is used (Prothero, 1994).

Clearly, certain social groups are less likely to relocate without distress, especially the elderly. There is a lot to be learnt from retrospective study of the ways in which people adjust to dislocation, resettlement or repatriation, how they may react to other relocatee groups and host populations, what the long-term adaptations are, and how moves can best be managed. In some cases of forced relocation, the adults may adapt poorly, but their offspring embrace the new culture, leading to inter-generational friction and cultural erosion.

It is not uncommon for relocatees to settle or be relocated on marginal land (Hirsch, 1989), often because better land has been settled. For example, when reservoir flooding drives people from the best land in the valley bottoms, what is left is likely to be vacant because it has poor soil, the risk of disease, or some other hazard. Sometimes, a few years after relocation, neglect in providing some service necessary for health or livelihood results in the appearance of marginality; this may be something like a failure to ensure that there is adequate affordable public transport. Because many relocation efforts are rapid, and then interest shifts somewhere else, mistakes are common. In practice, SIA needs to be quick and adaptive.

Resettling relocatees, such as farmers moving to a land development scheme, may seem relatively straightforward, but the real challenge may appear 20 years later when their children refuse to stay in the community. There are examples where relocation authorities have tried to pursue ambitious and often well-meaning improvements as part of resettlement, with unwanted results – they have effectively 'overstretched' the relocatees' resilience. Bringing together people from scattered settlements in new villages may make it possible to provide better infrastructure, schools, healthcare and so on, but the people may not mix well, there may be strong and incompatible cultural differences, and even deep-seated feuds between villages. SIA should be used to check for such risks, and monitoring should continue long after relocation (for at least 10 years) because many impacts are delayed.

Large dams and resettlement

Over the last 40 years or so there has been much study of the relocation and resettlement impacts associated with large dam projects (Atkinson, 1992; Colson, 1971; Gutman, 1994; Rosenberg *et al.*, 1995; Wilkes and Hildyard, 1994). The information obtained has been valuable in aiding the preparation of checklists and guidelines for future assessments (*see* Box 8.1). Some impoundment schemes, like the Volta Project, have been subject to detailed socio-economic studies, although most of this is not SIA proper (Chambers, 1970; Hart, 1980; HMSO, 1956a and 1956b; Huszar, 1956; Scudder, 1993). Other large dam projects undertaken in Africa, Asia and Latin America between the 1960s and 1990s have also provided hindsight knowledge for those undertaking SIA in the future. Particularly worthy of note are the many studies by Theyer Scudder, mainly focused on the impacts of African dam projects (e.g. Scudder, 1975). Insight into how indigenous peoples are affected by large dams has also been provided by projects in the north of Canada and Alaska (*see* the section on indigenous peoples, below), and in Amazonia (Aspelin and Coelho dos Santos, 1981).

Large dams have often encountered relocation and resettlement costs of more than one-third of total project expense. Some projects have dislocated hundreds of thousands, or even millions of people (China's Three Gorges Project will displace more than 1.25 million people, and possibly as many as 3 million) (Fearnside, 1993; Jing, 1997). In India the Narmada Valley dams (the Sardar-Sarovar Project) have caused serious controversy and unrest over relocation (Dreze *et al.*, 1999; Roy, 1999: 6–114). So, the costs of SIA can be justified.

Three problems face those conducting SIA for reservoir-related relocation.

1. There is a need for caution to ensure that local people or those from outside the area to be flooded do not panic or try to speculate. There have been cases where SIA studies have triggered in-migration of squatters seeking to profit from any relocation compensation.
2. The planners may fear that SIA will prompt more, and perhaps better-informed, protest from locals and NGOs than might otherwise have been the case.
3. Relocation and resettlement is often more hurried than expected. This may be because construction companies are often offered an early completion bonus, and SIA may be started late. Some of these lessons are relevant to other large-scale development projects.

Box 8.1 Issues disclosed by past studies of relocation and resettlement that can help in drawing up checklists and guidelines for future SIA

- Count how many people will need to be relocated: in a number of cases authorities have neglected to assist relocation because 'population in the area to be affected was light'; what is forgotten is that even one family per km^2 is significant when several thousand km^2 are flooded, polluted or otherwise affected.
- Check if there are indigenous peoples and whether these are adequately represented.
- Establish who is entitled to relocation aid or compensation.
- Establish what has been, or will be, lost.
- Explore what can be offered as compensation (new landholdings, housing, cash and so on), and whether it is adequate and will remain in the possession of those relocated.
- If cash compensation is to be offered, try to establish what the relocatees will do with it and, if necessary, advise, assist and protect.
- Check how the 'host' population might react to the relocatees or how aid measures may affect their reception.
- Check whether there is any risk that opportunistic migrants will move in and compete with relocatees.
- Explore whether there are differences between the old and new environments that may cause problems (soil, water supply, disease risks, access to common resources such as fuel/wood and so on).
- Assess whether relocatees or their children will fail to settle and will move on. According to Taylor (1973), of the 67,000–68,000 caused to relocate by the Volta Scheme, only 25,000–26,000 were still settled six years later, and about 18,000 outsiders had moved into the relocation area.
- Check whether there are likely to be cultural losses (access to shrines, family graves, etc.).
- Check whether there are especially vulnerable groups among those likely to relocate (elderly, landless, the poor, etc.).
- If providing compensation in the form of housing, land and/or employment, check that it is adequate and appropriate.
- Check whether development may generate beneficial impacts of which relocatees could take advantage (e.g. reservoir fishing, drawdown-area agriculture, tourism).
- Often, landowners or property owners are compensated, but those people (often far more numerous) without legal tenure or written contracts (which includes farm labourers, users of common land and traditional farmers without documentation) get nothing. SIA might be used to identify such cases and to try to make suitable compensatory arrangements.

Source: adapted from the UN Resolution by the UN Commission on Human Rights, on Forced Evictions (adopted 4 March 1993, Geneva)

For published resettlement guidelines, reviews and checklists, *see* the following authors in the References for this chapter: Butcher (1971); Cernea (1988); Cernea and Guggenheim (1993); Chambers (1969); Hall (1994); Hansen and Oliver-Smith (1982); Lightfoot (1979); Palmer (1974); Panos (1992); World Bank (1980 and 1994).

Land settlement schemes

People may be resettled if population growth or migration results in too little land to yield a reasonable livelihood, or if civil unrest, natural disaster or pollution necessitates their being moved. Around the world, resettlement projects have led to socio-economic impacts, yet generally little has been done to apply SIA (Dearth, 1982). Since the late 1950s Malaysia has relocated large numbers of poor farmers to land cleared from forest through Federal Land Development Authority (FELDA) schemes. FELDA has gathered information on social, economic and health impacts, including the longer-term effects (i.e. over decades), and in particular the problems of retaining second- or third-generation settlers at relocation sites.

Since the 1970s Indonesia's Transmigration Programme has been the subject of numerous evaluative studies (Hardjono, 1988) (transmigration is also discussed in Chapter 12). Recent reports suggest that it has had serious impacts on the culture and welfare of indigenous peoples like the Dayaks of Kalimantan and the Kubu of southern Sumatra, in addition to the serious socio-economic and environmental problems faced by those who have been relocated (Scholtz, 1992). Impacts on indigenous peoples are also reported by the World Rainforest Movement (1999; *see* http://jsa-44.hum.uts.edu.au/signposts/articles/Indonesia/Population/383.html).

People relocated for economic or political reasons

These are people who – while they are not forced out of a country or region (like refugees) and often get treated with some degree of sympathy – are nevertheless required to move under duress. During the Second World War Japanese-Americans were relocated to internment camps or settlements where they could be monitored and protected from public victimization. In the UK many people of German or eastern European stock were arrested between 1939 and 1945 for similar reasons. The impacts upon the Japanese-Americans have been well studied and provide some insights likely to be of use in SIAs of similar dislocated groups in the future.

A number of countries have required people to relocate to enable better provision of services or to improve agricultural productivity (often combined with a more political agenda: 'collectivization'). One of the first was the Soviet Union during the 1920s and 1930s, and more recently Kenya, Mozambique and other countries have implemented such policies. Often this involves 'villagization': the concentration of scattered small rural communities into model villages. In Malaya in the 1950s and 1960s, and in Vietnam during the Vietnam War, villagization was primarily designed to isolate rural people in order to 'protect' them and to ensure that they did not shelter or feed guerrilla troops. Villagization generally reflects central government policies; where the state favours co-operatives or collective farms, villagization will be along similar lines. Unfortunately, government policies do not always lead to socio-economic success and sustainable development

(AkwabiAmeyaw, 1997). SIA is needed before relocation to check what relocatees should be capable of, and what they need to help them achieve it.

There has been closure of long-stay hospitals, retirement homes and mental institutions in some countries, requiring inmates to relocate. Such relocatees may suffer severe trauma and may find it difficult to re-adapt; the weak and elderly tend to suffer increased rates of illness and death, and some psychiatric patients may prove a hazard to themselves and wider society if non-institutional provision is inadequate. There may also be increased pressure on existing schools and health centres as a consequence of institutional care changes. A further difficulty, which has sometimes been overlooked, is that specialist facilities may be less easy to provide once large centralized institutions are closed, and the now-scattered users have to travel a long distance to get access. In the UK, and other countries, where care in the community has replaced residential care since the mid-1980s there has been considerable publicity about the negative social impacts (and little about the positive side). Without careful social impact assessment, misassessment of the degree of success is a risk, compromises are likely to be made, and both the relocated and host communities can suffer. In addition, the families of those affected and the community may change their attitudes after de-institutionalization (to more or less opposition); SIA can help predict and manage such shifts.

Refugees

These relocatees differ from the other groups discussed above. While all relocatees suffer trauma, refugees and eco-refugees are likely to be more drastically affected because they are usually forced away from their normal home territory suddenly, by warfare, natural disasters, ethnic cleansing and other persecution; they are often unprepared for this upheaval and can suffer fear and material loss. The social impacts of war alone may be serious enough, without enforced relocation (Modell and Haggerty, 1991). Refugees may be concentrated, or may congregate, in camps or settlements which may lead to severe social and mental upset, economic hardship and physical health impacts. There has been considerable study of refugee resettlement by health researchers, anthropologists and other social scientists (Dewet, 1991). Also, there have been studies of the mental health impacts of relocation on various refugee groups, and EIA of refugee camps (Biswas and Quiroz, 1996). Such research can be drawn on by SIA.

Because refugees are often generated by sudden, or hidden, events there is seldom likely to be sufficient warning for SIA to be undertaken in advance – mostly it seeks to clarify a developing situation, or to improve resettlement or other coping responses, and gather information to help in future assessments or contingency preparations (Shami, 1993). Specialist academic journals deal with the field (for example, the *Journal of Refugee Studies'*, *International Migration*, *International Migration Review* and *Disasters*), and refugee affairs are the concern of the UN High Commission on Refugees and numerous NGOs.

Indigenous peoples

Indigenous peoples are often caught up in resource development, but in the past have often been excluded from adequate input into SIAs (Howitt, 1998). This has been recognized, but there is still the problem of 'how' to involve indigenous peoples satisfactorily in SIA. In the past there have been communication problems and, today, many assessors still do not have adequate insight into their attitudes and needs, culture, religion and society to ensure effective participation. Simple interviews are unlikely to be satisfactory; there should be negotiation and a two-way learning process to ensure that indigenous peoples' perceptions are accepted as legitimate not dismissed or devalued (Little and Krannich, 1988; O'Faircheallaigh, 1999; Ross, 1989, 1990a and 1990b). Europeans have often failed even to recognize spiritual issues and sacred sites, let alone treat them as key issues in decision-making; yet for many indigenous peoples these play a crucial role in their lives and well-being. Resource development opportunities may not be exploited without causing serious offence, unhappiness and harm to indigenous peoples. SIA must also look out for the risk that traditional leaders may lose face with their people during contact with developers. Once this happens there may be damage to social stability. There is also a risk that a few people will profit, while others get little or nothing; SIA may be able to improve equity.

Indigenous peoples are often vulnerable to introduced diseases, they may suffer discrimination, loss of self-respect and cultural identity, and have their access to natural resources hijacked by the state, large companies or settlers. Where nomadic people have encountered border restrictions, or the spread of sedentary farming and livestock rearing, or deforestation and other forms of land degradation, there are likely to be problems simply settling and earning a living in one location. Indigenous peoples may not have the same concepts of land rights or ownership as Europeans, although they may have a tradition of rights to hunt, fish or gather.

Native peoples are often vulnerable to pollution. For example: in Amazonia some rivers are badly polluted with mercury from gold extraction; in Canada rivers have also been contaminated with mercury (not through gold mining); in Australia, Mongolia (Lop Nur), test sites in the former USSR, the USA and the Pacific Islands, peoples have suffered as a consequence of atomic testing; and in a growing number of developing countries acid deposition (acid rain) is starting to affect even remote areas. The social and economic impacts are considerable: where people know there is contamination they may be forced to abandon traditional food sources and suffer poorer diets; there can be physical health impacts of pollution; and – what tends to be overlooked – some pollutants, especially mercury, have a subtle and powerful influence on mental health and on children's developmental potential. There have been assessments of environmental and health impacts, but Wheatley (1996) is one of the few to explore the social impacts.

Australia

Until recently Australian Law regarded the land as *terra nullius*: officially empty at the point of European arrival – effectively depriving native peoples (who had been present) of any rights over natural resources. Aborigines have been excluded from traditional lands by enclosure, persecution, contamination by atomic weapons testing, and have been affected throughout Australia by major mining projects and by settlement growth (Australian Institute of Aboriginal Studies, 1984; Cousins and Nieuwenhuysen, 1984; Dixon and Dillan, 1990; Government of Australia, 1984). A threat is currently facing the Mirrar Aboriginal people in the form of proposals for a large uranium mine at Jabiluka (near Kakadu National Park, Northern Territory) which could disrupt sacred sites and ecology.

There has been growing support for the view that, in order to satisfy basic social justice, it is important to inform local people and, ideally, to involve them in development (Lane and Rickson, 1997). In recent years there have been increasing efforts to empower native peoples, integrate local needs with the wider national context, and to ensure that SIA has a realistic grasp of their perspective (Gondolf and Wells, 1986; Howitt, 1989 and 1993).

It had become clear by the mid-1970s that European Australians have only a weak grasp of Aboriginal peoples' values, especially the cultural significance they place upon the landscape (Chase, 1990), a point Bruce Chatwin illustrated in his book *The Songlines* (1988). Braaf (1999) argued that indigenous peoples' viewpoints and needs were still being overlooked when global climate change impacts were being assessed. Nevertheless, by the 1980s there were cases in Australia where SIA did reflect the feelings of Aboriginal peoples, and proposed developments were halted; for example, the planned uranium and gold mines at Coronation Hill, near Corowa in the Northern Territory).

As in North America, SIA has increasingly focused on developing a community response approach to exploring how native people themselves perceive events and their impacts, using participatory techniques to do so. This could be summed up as considering impacts 'from the perspective of the whole range of groups with an interest in land use outcomes' (Lane *et al.*, 1997: 304). There has been SIA of tourism development impacts on indigenous and local peoples (*see* Chapter 12).

New Zealand

The Treaty of Waitangi in 1840 guaranteed the Maoris rights over everything they valued. However, it wasn't until the 1970s that the authorities really began to recognize that the population was not homogeneous, and started to consider Maori attitudes adequately (Nottingham, 1990). SIA has played a key role in assisting these changes, helping to ensure that developers are aware of Maori views, the impacts upon them, and what they have to offer.

The Caribbean

Cowell (1987) explored the social and economic impacts of bauxite mining on Jamaica. Most other SIAs in this region have focused on the socio-economic impacts of tourism development.

South America

Development projects that encroached on Amerindian lands (such as the ongoing Carajas Programme in Brazilian Amazonia) have had an enormous social, economic and health impact on native peoples (Treece, 1987). Protection of Amerindian peoples in Brazilian Amazonia, Columbia, Venezuela and other Latin American countries, threatened by immigrants, road, hydro-electricity or natural resource development projects, has progressed beyond the past reliance on, and to some extent control by, agencies like the National Foundation for Amazonian Indians (FUNAI) in Brazil. Nowadays, in Brazil at least, Amerindian peoples are taking their own initiatives to safeguard their traditional rights. They hire lawyers and specialist experts, elect representatives to attend Senate, send students to be educated in universities, and demand adequate SIA. However, untold damage has already been done and continues to be caused, by governments and those beyond the law, such as the itinerant gold miners (*garimpeiros*) of western Amazonia.

North America

Throughout the USA and Canada there have been SIAs involving, or actually initiated by, Native (Indian) peoples. Most have been in response to proposals to exploit mineral resources or to generate hydroelectricity. The USA and Canada have gained considerable experience in relating SIA to Native peoples' needs (Charest, 1995; Dufour, 1996; Greider, 1993; Marshall and Scott, 1983; Nordstrom *et al.*, 1977). Some of this has been retrospective, but predictive usage has also been developing, much of it relating to rapid large-scale natural resource development (Geisler *et al.*, 1982). For example, the Federation of Saskatchewan Indians commissioned its own SIA (which included hired anthropologists on the team) in response to proposals for the Wintego Dam, in order to counterbalance an assessment prepared by the Canadian Government, which they feared was biased (FSI, 1976). Waldram (1984) stressed the need for Native people to have control over the design and practice of SIA and to be involved as researchers, yet there was the problem that few may have the appropriate 'training'. To facilitate Native peoples' involvement, it may be necessary to budget for extra time in development planning (*see also* the discussion of the Berger Inquiry in Chapter 1). American Indian rights have been better recognized by the SIA process since the American Indian Religious Freedom Act (1995) and the Native American Graves Protection and Repatriation Act (1990). These have resulted in special sections in US assessments involving traditional Native American lands, relics and human remains.

Being aware of impacts on indigenous people is not enough – there must be adequate enforcement of SIA recommendations. Almost two decades ago, Jobes (1986) noted the failure of SIA to reduce impacts on reservations in North America; and there is still much progress to be made today.

Increasing reliance on snow-mobiles, modern clothing and construction materials, means that the younger generation of Native peoples in North America have, in many cases, lost their skills with dog-sleds and traditional materials for building, hunting and clothing, and would find it difficult to recover these if the need arose (a similar situation has developed in Scandinavia, Siberia and with many native peoples elsewhere). This represents the loss of a rich indigenous technology developed over tens of thousands of years (Gramling and Freudenburg, 1992: 228).

Small communities and small islands

SIA is often applied to small communities (Bowles, 1983a). Small communities may take the form of single villages or townships, or they may be groups (perhaps sharing a culture), or a small island. Small communities are often of interest to SIA because their social dynamics make them vulnerable to impacts, and also because some are isolated and may depend on one or a few natural resources for their livelihood. Hydroelectricity development, and mining and petroleum exploitation impacts on communities in the far north of the USA and Canada have generated a number of SIA studies, most of them retrospective (Bowles, 1983b; Dixon, 1980; MacDonald and MacDonald, 1979). In the UK the impact of North Sea oil exploitation stimulated some of the country's first SIA studies in the 1970s, many focusing on small mainland or island Scottish communities, such as Shetland and the Orkneys (Francis and Swan, 1973; Hill *et al.*, 1997).

Small community-focused SIA has mainly explored specific social impacts, community social viability and the state of the local economy. Because community values change, SIA needs to be dynamic and responsive (Canon and Heinessy, 1984). Palinkas *et al.* (1985) employed a systems analysis approach to SIA (*see* Chapter 6) in order to explore the potential effects of offshore oil exploitation on two rural Alaskan settlements, Unalaska and Cold Bay, and to compare it with other possible future scenarios.

Biogeographers and ecologists have learnt much from small islands, where relatively simple, isolated and well-defined conditions make research easier. The same is to some extent true for SIA. Small islands are vulnerable to the physical, social and economic impacts of development. Some are isolated, many have precarious and poorly diversified economies, often they are vulnerable to storms or other natural disasters, some host numbers of tourists or the personnel of military stations which match or outnumber the native population. There is now a good deal of experience with island development-related EIA (*see* the UNEP island environmental management website at http://www.unep.ch/islands/siem2.htm; *see also* special issue of *Geographische Zeitscrift* **84(2)**, 1996; Lockhart *et al.*, 1994). Development planning for small islands must pay attention to the need for sustainable development, given the limited space, restricted range of development alternatives, and the cost of having to bring in any commodity or service that is unsustained (McElroy *et al.*, 1987; Tisdell, 1993). SIA can play an important part in improving chances of attaining sustainable development (*see* Box 8.2).

Boomtowns and company towns

Boomtowns form for a number of reasons: they may be settlements servicing mining or some other type of resource development; they may lie at important crossroads, or staging points, on a busy communications route (like Skagway during the Klondike Gold Rush); they may suddenly become popular for a particular purpose (like some US retirement areas or ski resorts, or sites of religious or cultural significance); or they may be associated with a strategic activity (e.g. Los Alamos, USA, or Pearl Harbor, Hawaii). Boomtown and company town problems vary through time:

- at first there is rapid growth which overwhelms planning and services
- then there may be a sudden reduction or loss of the factor(s) that sustained the boom
- finally, there may be a more or less prolonged struggle to adapt and develop alternative livelihoods for as many people as can be supported.

So, development changes its character and the areas affected alter as time progresses. SIA focused on one phase will provide only a partial snapshot of the situation (Gramling and Freudenburg, 1992).

Boomtowns have generated a great many SIA studies, the literature focusing especially on steel towns and mining communities (Detomasi and Gartrell, 1984; England and Albrecht, 1984; Freudenburg, 1984a; Gold, 1978; Gulliford, 1989), offshore oil, and also on retirement and tourism boom areas, such as the US 'sun belt' (Gramling and Brabant, 1986). In the UK, concern about the socio-economic impacts of North Sea oil exploitation helped prompt UK interest in EIA. Boomtown SIA must often predict employment changes (as discussed in Chapter 10), emphasize conditions that affect health and community cohesion (as boomtowns bust, there are often elevated rates of crime and clinical depression (Bacigalupi and Freudenburg, 1983), stress-related diseases and suicides). Studies of boomtown impacts have been undertaken by sociologists (Cortese and Jones, 1977), historians, regional planners, criminologists, geographers and anthropologists (the impact of oil and other natural resource extraction booms is considered in Chapter 11).

Box 8.2 Examples of vulnerable small islands communities

Nauru Island (Pacific)

Mined for phosphates for over 90 years during Colonial times. As a consequence, the island suffered extensive loss of topsoil and reef damage, as well as the removal of mineral resources. Some years after independence (in 1967) Nauru made a claim for damages through the International Court of Justice (Anderson, 1992). This case has helped to establish the rights of other small communities, former colonies or protectorates (and is relevant today with respect to exploitation by commercial bodies) to compensation for past resource extraction which has failed to provide an alternative livelihood. The case has also been a test of the 'polluter pays' principle, and the ability of a relatively weak group to pursue their grievances retrospectively to compensate for impacts suffered in the past.

Tristan da Cunha (South Atlantic)

One of the world's most isolated communities. The rugged topography has prevented the construction of an airstrip, so the islanders depend on passing sea transport. The opening of the Panama Canal and subsequent changes in shipping practices have reduced the island's opportunities for trade and contact. With a small population and a precarious economy, there have been several points when tragedy has made survival difficult. In 1885, 15 of the island's 18 able-bodied males were drowned; even this relatively small number of deaths caused severe hardship for the small community. In the 1960s a volcanic eruption forced temporary evacuation (mainly to the UK). This proved so unpopular that, once the risk of eruption diminished, most relocatees made the choice to return, to the surprise of many observers (Blair, 1964).

Bikini Atoll (Republic of the Marshall Islands, Central Pacific)

Bikini Atoll was the site of a series of nuclear tests conducted by the USA in the 1940s and 1950s (islands like those of the Mururoa Atoll and Christmas Island have much in common with Bikini). The people were evacuated to other atolls in the Marshall Islands archipelago or moved further afield. There have been relatively thorough studies of most aspects of the resulting resettlement trauma, which continues nearly half a century later (Niedenthal, 1997). A clean-up of radioactive and other test debris was started in 1991 and some areas are considered relatively safe for habitation, although not food production. As in many cases where small communities have been disrupted, outsiders have grasped opportunities while native Bikinians have yet to resettle. The atoll is now host to expatriate sport diving and game fishing companies, foreign construction workers live there, and there are growing numbers of tourist visitors. Those resettled have had to live under quite crowded conditions since their evacuation (*see* http://www.bikiniatoll.com/home.html for more information).

Lessons learnt with cases like Bikini will be useful for SIA of other nuclear accident or weapons use contaminated areas and for the advance assessment of possible socio-economic impacts of global change-related sea-level rise on Pacific and other small islands.

St Kilda (Atlantic island to the west of Scotland, UK)

For a variety of reasons, but in the main the impact of twentieth-century ways, the tiny community on St Kilda was finally evacuated in 1930 to be resettled in Scotland. Everyone, young and old, suffered trauma (Steel, 1975). In the decades that have since passed, studies of how the once-isolated relocatees have adapted to the disease threats of the mainland have proved valuable for epidemiologists and health impact studies (Holohan, 1986).

Burdge *et al.* (1989) studied social history to explore the impacts on an isolated Alaskan town that boomed during the 1897–8 Klondike Gold Rush, and that was subsequently revived as a consequence of the construction of the Alaska Highway in the 1940s, and more recently (post-1970) as a consequence of tourist development. (Wien (1996) has reviewed the impacts on a west-Siberian former oil boom region.)

One of the main social impacts of boom-and-bust community development is drastic change of local employment opportunities (Grady *et al.*, 1987; Nance *et al.*, 1994). There are numerous examples of former mining communities where the abandonment of mines has led to serious socio-economic impacts (Putt and Buchan, 1987). In Louisiana, USA, towns like Morgan City had long practised shrimp fishing; in the late 1950s, however, they shifted to servicing offshore oil and lost their shrimping skills; when the oil industry began to decline in the 1980s people found it difficult to return to their old livelihoods because the processing plants had closed and skills had been lost (Gramling and Freudenburg, 1992).

Seyfrit and Sadlerhammer (1988) found that many variables affect how individuals and communities react to boom conditions; this means that results vary from place to place, making reliable generalization difficult. Boomtowns present problems as a consequence of rapid community growth, often in isolated areas with a poor infrastructure; there are also difficulties generated by novel social and economic opportunities, and often pollution and lawlessness. Some established settlements may shift to rapid growth and change without actually becoming boomtowns; in many developing countries towns and cities have grown so fast that services and infrastructure are strained (Freudenburg, 1984b; Weber and Howell, 1982).

There are many examples of a single private company or state body providing most of an areas' employment, controlling jobs, transport, welfare facilities, retail outlets and so on; this is known as a 'company town' situation (and is also the case with some boomtowns). At worst, wages may be controlled and necessary commodities priced to ensure that the population is dependent and docile, or even in debt to the company. Nowadays, though, the company is more likely to be subsidizing services and retailing, although this may still result in a form of dependence.

CRIME AND JUSTICE

Criminal behaviour has often been associated with rapid community change, alteration of attitudes, settlement growth and the movement of people (Freudenburg and Gramling, 1992; Freudenburg and Jones, 1992). SIA can be used to explore the effects of such changes, and also the likely crime impacts, resulting from changes in the justice system, policing and security measures (Heilbrun and Heilbrun, 1986; Morash, 1983). Criminals often adopt predictable patterns of behaviour; indeed, an animal behaviourist recently commented on similarities in the behaviour of predators in the Serengeti and human perpetrators of violence. Insurance companies and police forces have examined the effects of alterations in street lighting, the introduction of neighbourhood watch groups, and the installation of closed-circuit TV (CCTV) security and surveillance cameras. The latter are providing valuable information which should help with the future forecasting of crime as well as helping with its deterrence. Rapid community growth has also been seen to result in altered crime rates and patterns.

New communication links may affect crime by aiding the movements of criminals; forewarned of the effect of improved road or other links, the police may install security measures, like cameras, at strategic points. New telecommunications technology, notably mobile telephones, and the spread of computers and programming skills are leading to new types of crime: from internet fraud to industrial espionage, and even full-scale global terrorism or cyber-warfare (for instance, a government, NGO or terrorist can disrupt crucial communications and data control systems in a target country or organization without minimal risk and little effort). Mobile phones may facilitate drug-dealing, allow a burglar to assess whether a building is unoccupied from just outside and, unless already under suspicion, with relatively little risk of the authorities intercepting the calls. If improved encryption is not adopted, computer fraud is likely to increase. There are already criminals who can target victims worldwide, at little cost or risk of detection, via the internet.

Policy-makers are beginning to use SIA to explore the likely effects of altering criminal justice measures before enacting costly new legislation. For example, studies in Europe on the likely impacts of legalizing cannabis or hard drugs and, in the USA, the ongoing debates and assessments of the effects of enacting, or failing to enact, gun control laws.

In many parts of the world, crime issues play a significant part in determining people's sense of well-being and may significantly affect the economy in a positive or negative way. There are cities and countries where crime is a major source of regional or national income, and a significant generator of employment and overseas earnings, notably through the narcotics trade. But, for many people, urban crime or rural banditry makes life a misery, and damages real estate prices and commerce. For example, once crime is established, insurance premiums may be several times those of less lawless neighbourhoods, or insurance may even be virtually unobtainable.

Developments can be rapid, and the spread of new weapons, the establishment of drug-trafficking and the rapid growth of a culture of violence may catch authorities poorly prepared, and quickly deter tourism and business investment. Altered communications and the provision of services like those mentioned above (street lighting and CCTV for security monitoring) have a marked impact on crime rates and character, and on the stress and risks suffered by the public. In the UK, increased use of CCTV in towns seems to be driving criminals to prey more on those in rural areas where there is much less surveillance. The way criminals are dealt with also has a marked social impact: proposals for tagging and release, and the siting of detention centres, bail hostels or prisons can generate intense protest from local people worried for their safety or property values (Morash, 1983). Certain groups in a community may especially fear crime; for example, the elderly, women and students, who make significant changes to their lifestyle as a consequence. Where people distrust crime control they often resort to high-security housing estates, and areas may be abandoned entirely by those able to afford to move out, leading to the creation of deprived areas and even no-go areas for the police.

The risk of crime can be assessed in advance, within certain limits. In many countries, insurance companies have long had 'maps of risk' that they use to determine their customers' premium payments. Trends can be seen from published crime statistics: rising drug use, for example, is likely to mean more burglary and perhaps street violence; rapid urban growth is often equated with increasing crime rates. SIA could be applied to predicting future crime scenarios so that the authorities could be better prepared.

GENDER ISSUES

A number of assessments have sought to ascertain how various developments affect women; most of these studies have been retrospective (Bamberger, 1997; Dawson, 1995; ICPE, 1993; Jacobs, 1991; Moen, 1981; Rao *et al.*, 1996; Scholten and Post, 1999: 237). These studies should help improve the ability of SIA to explore how women will be affected by future developments; for example, the introduction of new technology (Anon., 1993).

Studies have explored why men in some countries are less likely than women to seek preventative healthcare (and vice versa in others). It is vital to have some understanding of gender differences in order to predict responses to new health treatments or services (gender impact assessment is discussed in Chapter 4).

FAMILY STRIFE AND CIVIL UNREST

In many western countries families have become increasingly isolated, lacking the diversity of linkages common in the past. Within these 'isolated' nuclear families, there are increasingly fewer siblings, parents are more likely to work longer hours than in the past and, with real and perceived dangers outside the home, children are more likely to be confined to the house outside school hours. Added to these problems there has been a marked rise in divorce rates, which adds to the stress suffered by children and parents (Henning *et al.*, 1996). In developing countries, changes such as structural adjustment programmes have also prompted adults to work longer hours and mean that there is less money for family commitments to education, care of the elderly and children (for a further discussion of this, *see* Chapter 11).

In some western countries there has been a rise in the number of lone-parent families, the parents involved being predominantly younger females who have borne children outside marriage. Some would argue that this would have as many positive as negative impacts; however, in practice these families are often vulnerable and deprived, and are usually perceived to be a burden on public funding and likely to produce problem adolescents. In parts of the USA the increase in lone-parent families is seen as a sufficient problem to warrant legislative measures to discourage illegitimacy and to prompt mothers to offer up children for adoption. Measures like the reduction or withdrawal of child support funds for the second or third offspring of single mothers has roused controversy. There has also been a move in western countries to accept non-traditional groupings as families (two partners of the same sex, for example). What is needed is objective SIA to assess the real impacts of such developments.

In the UK, the response to a trend of increased marital breakdown has been the establishment of the Child Support Agency (CSA), which is charged with finding fathers and ensuring that they pay adequate maintenance for their offspring. Clearly there are marked social changes taking place in the West, and it would make sense to conduct more thorough SIA to establish the impacts of these, and what they are likely to be in future, rather than taking measures prompted by ill-informed political dogma, knee-jerk reactions, or political correctness.

Troubles in Belfast, Beirut, El Salvador, Honduras, Rwanda, East Timor and the Balkans, and many other places of conflict, have had huge impacts on citizens, especially children (Walton *et al.*, 1997). Retrospective studies by psychologists, medics, educationalists, aid and care workers provide SIA with some idea of the impacts likely to arise as a consequence of future civil unrest and warfare (McCarney, 1996) (refugees are discussed earlier in this chapter).

Social and religious movements

Defining exactly what constitutes a social movement presents a challenge; broadly it is a trend in the way society behaves and in people's outlooks. Social movements can have the potential to change society or may be the sign of a change in society itself. A social movement is likely to be well under way before it attracts the attention of impact assessors. Social movements which have generated, or which are generating, impacts include: post-modernism, civil rights, political correctness, secularization, democratization and environmentalism (although some may dispute whether these are all 'social movements' or merely components thereof). Social movements can alter, or are indicative of change in, the political process (Andrews, 1997), attitudes, morals and ethics, fashions and beliefs.

Religious movements can have a marked socio-economic impact. The world's cultures are largely shaped by established beliefs, in spite of shifts towards secularism in the West and the Communist Bloc since the French Revolution (around 1798). There have been retrospective studies of the impact of evangelical or missionary activity in various parts of the world (e.g. Oshin, 1994; Smith, 1998), but less seeking to predict such activity's future impacts.

New religious groups may seek to convert followers or express their viewpoint forcibly, even when small in numbers, and some may rapidly gain support and power (Payulpitack, 1992). European colonial expansion was aided by the work of missionaries. Today, in some countries, a strong expansion of religion is affecting culture, education, judicial systems, economic policy and much more. While, unfortunately, social and religious change may result in civil unrest and persecution of other groups, many of the world's humanitarian and aid agencies are linked, at least in the popular mind, to religions – for example, the Red Crescent, Christian Aid and so on.

Recently, a number of religious groups or small sects have attracted media attention following mass suicides, kidnappings, brainwashing, murders and the attempted assassination of important people. One of the more significant developments is the potential for such groups to acquire and use weapons of mass destruction, as was demonstrated, fortunately with limited casualties, in Tokyo a few years ago when nerve gas was released in city's the metro system. So, even small and obscure groups may have serious impacts on family welfare and on public security; more established religions may quickly have considerable social and cultural impact. SIA could be used to forecast the impact of new beliefs (the need to cover spirituality and sacred sites in SIA has already been discussed, above).

REFERENCES

AkwabiAmeyaw, K. (1997) Producer cooperative resettlement projects in Zimbabwe: lessons from a failed agricultural development strategy. *World Development* **25(3)**, 437–56.

Anderson, I. (1992) Can Nauru clean up after the colonialists? *New Scientist* **135(1830)**, 12–13.

Andrews, K.T. (1997) The impacts of social movement on the political process: the Civil Rights Movement and Black electoral politics in Mississippi. *American Sociological Review* **62(5)**, 800–19.

Anon. (1993) Social impact assessment of investment/acquisition of technology projects in developing countries, with particular reference to the position of women. *Public Enterprise* **13(3–4)**, 239–56.

Aspelin, P.L. and **Coelho dos Santos, S.** (1981) *Indian Areas Threatened by Hydro-electric Projects in Brazil* (IWGIA Document No. 44). International Work Group for Indigenous Affairs, Copenhagen.

Asthana, R. (1996) Involuntary resettlement: survey of international experience. *Economic and Political Weekly* **31(24)**, 1468–75.

Atkinson, J. (1992) *Narmada Dam: environmental and social impact of a World Bank Project*. Community Action Abroad, Fitzroy (Victoria).

Australian Institute of Aboriginal Studies (1984) *Social Impact of Uranium Mining on the Aborigines of the Northern Territory* (Australian Institute of Aboriginal Studies, Canberra). Australian Government Printing Service, Canberra.

Bacigalupi, L.M. and **Freudenburg, W.R.** (1983) Increased mental health caseloads in an energy boomtown. *Administration in Mental Health* **10(4)**, 306–22.

Bamberger, M. (1997) Understanding the impact of development projects on women: the Tunisia Institutional Development Fund Project, in E. Chelimsky and W.R. Shadish (eds), *Evaluation for the 21st Century: a handbook*. Sage, Thousand Oaks (CA), 260–71.

Biswas, A.K. and **Quiroz, C.T.** (1996) Environmental impacts of refugees. *Impact Assessment* **14(1)**, 21–39.

Blair, J. (1964) Home to Tristan da Cunha. *The National Geographical Magazine* **125(1)**, 60–81.

Bowles, R.T. (1983a) *Social Impact Assessment in Small Communities: an integrative review of selected literature*. Butterworth & Co., Toronto (1st edn 1981).

Bowles, R.T. (ed.) (1983b) *Little Communities and Big Industries*. Westview, Boulder (CO).

Braaf, R.R. (1999) Improving impact assessment methods: climate change and the health of indigenous Australians. *Global Environmental Change: Human Policy Dimensions* **9(2)**, 95–104.

Burdge, R.J., Field, D. and **Wells, S.R.** (1989) Utilizing social history to identify impacts of resource development on isolated communities: the case of Skagway (AL). *Impact Assessment Review* **6(2)**, 37–54.

Butcher, D.P. (1971) *An Operational Manual for Resettlement: a systematic approach to the resettlement problem created by man-made lakes, with special reference for West Africa*. FAO, Rome.

Canon, P. and **Heinessy, M.** (1984) Teaching community-based social impact assessment in a practicum setting. *Impact Assessment Bulletin* **3(2)**, 68–75.

Cernea, M.M. (1988) *Involuntary Resettlement in Development Projects: policy guidelines in World Bank-financed projects* (World Bank Technical Paper No. 180). The World Bank, Washington (DC).

Cernea, M.M. and **Guggenheim, S.E.** (1993) *Anthropological Approaches to Resettlement: policy, practice and theory*. Westview, Boulder (CO).

Chambers, R. (1969) *Settlement Schemes in Tropical Africa*. Routledge and Kegan Paul, London.

Chambers, R. (1970) *Volta Resettlement Experience*. Pall Mall Press, London.

Charest, P. (1995) Aboriginal attitudes to mega projects and their environmental and social impacts. *Impact Assessment* **13(4)**, 371–86.

Chase, A. (1990) Anthropology and impact assessment: development pressures and indigenous interests in Australia. *Environmental Impact Assessment Review* **10(1–2)**, 11–23.

Chatwin, B. (1988) *The Songlines*. Picador (Pan Books), London.

Collins, C.O. (1995) Refugee resettlement in Belize. *Geographical Review* **85(1)**, 20–30.

Colson, E. (1971) *The Social Consequences of Resettlement: Kariba Studies IV, the impact of the Kariba resettlement upon the Gwembe Tonga*. Manchester University Press, Manchester.

Cortese, C.F. and **Jones, B.** (1977) The sociology of boomtowns. *Western Sociological Review* **8(1)**, 76–90.

Cousins, D. and **Nieuwenhuysen, J.** (1984) *Aboriginals and the Mining Industry: case studies of the Australian experience*. Allen and Unwin, Sydney.

Cowell, N.M. (1987) The impact of bauxite mining on peasant and community relations in Jamaica. *Social and Economic Studies* **36(1)**, 171–216.

Dawson, E. (1995) *Women, Gender and Impact Assessment: a discussion*. Oxfam, Oxford.

Dearth, C. (1982) Social impact assessment: a critical tool in land development planning. *International Social Science Journal* **34(3)**, 441–50.

Detomasi, D.D. and **Gartrell, J.W.** (eds) (1984) *Resource Communities: a decade of destruction*. Westview, Boulder (CO).

Dewet, C. (1991) Recent deliberations on the state and future of resettlement anthropology. *Human Organization* **50(1)**, 104–9.

Dixon, M. (1980) *What Happened to Fairbanks? The effects of the trans-Alaska oil pipeline on the community of Fairbanks, Alaska*. Westview, Boulder (CO).

Dixon, R. and **Dillan, M.** (1990) *Aborigines and Mining*. University of Western Australia Perth, Perth.

Dreze, J., Samson, M. and **Singh, S.** (1999) The dam and the nation: displacement and resettlement in the Narmada Valley. *Journal of Asian Studies* **58(1)**, 229–30.

Dufour, J. (1996) The Grande Baleine Project and the future of aboriginal communities in Quebec. *Cahiers de Geographie du Quebec* **40(110)**, 233–52.

England, J.L. and **Albrecht, S.L.** (1984) Boomtowns and social disruption. *Rural Sociology* **49(3)**, 230–46.

Fearnside, P. (1993) Resettlement plans for China's Three Gorges Dam, in M. Barber and G. Ryder (eds), *Discovering the Three Gorges: what dam builders don't want you to know (a critique of the Three Gorges Water Control Project Feasibility Study)* (2nd edn). Earthscan, London, 34–58.

Francis, J. and **Swan, N.** (1973) *Scotland in Turmoil: a social and environmental assessment of the impact of North Sea oil and gas on communities in the north of Scotland.* St Andrew Press (for the Church of Scotland Home Board), Edinburgh.

Freudenburg, W.R. (1984a) Boomtown's youth: the differential impacts of rapid community growth on adolescents and adults. *American Sociological Review* **49(5)**, 697–705.

Freudenburg, W.R. (1984b) Differential impacts of rapid community growth. *American Sociological Review* **49(5)**, 697–705.

Freudenburg, W.R. and **Gamling, R.** (1992) Criminal behavior and rapid community change: toward a longitudinal perspective. *Social Forces* **70(4)**, 619–45.

Freudenburg, W.R. and **Jones, R.E.** (1992) Criminal behavior and rapid community growth. *Rural Sociology* **56(4)**, 619–45.

FSI (1976) *Aski-Puko: the land alone* (Report on the expected effects of the proposed hydro electric installation of Wintego Rapids upon the Cree of the Peter Ballantyne and Lac LaRonge Bands). Federation of Saskatchewan Indians, Saskatoon.

Geisler, C.C., Green, R., Usner, D. and **West, P.C.** (eds) (1982) *Indian SIA: social* *impact assessment of rapid resource development on native peoples*. University of Michigan, Natural Resources Sociology Research Laboratory Monograph No. 43, Ann Arbor (MI).

Gold, R.L. (1978) Social science literature on the energy boomtown. *Social Science Energy Review* **1(1)**, 8–30.

Gondolf, E.W. and **Wells, S.R.** (1986) Empowered native community, modified SIA: the case of Hydaburg, Alaska. *Environmental Impact Assessment Review* **6(3)**, 373–83.

Government of Australia (1984) *Aborigines and Uranium: consolidated report on the social impact of uranium mining on the Aborigines of the Northern Territory*. Australian Government Printer, Canberra.

Grady, S.R., Braid, R., Bradbury, J. and **Kerley, C.** (1987) Socio-economic assessment of plant closure: three case-studies of large manufacturing facilities. *Environmental Impact Assessment Review* **26(2)**, 151–165.

Gramling, R. (1992) Employment data and social impact assessment. *Evaluation and Program Planning* **15(3)**, 219–25.

Gramling, R. and **Brabant, S.** (1986) Boom towns and offshore energy impact assessment: the development of a comprehensive model. *Sociological Perspectives* **29(2)**, 177–201.

Gramling, R. and **Freudenburg, W.R.** (1992) Opportunity–threat, development, and adaption: toward a comprehensive framework for social impact assessment. *Rural Sociology* **57(2)**, 216–34.

Greider, T. (1993) Aircraft noise and the practice of Indian medicine: the symbolic transformation of the environment. *Human Organization* **52(1)**, 76–82.

Gulliford, A. (1989) *Boomtown Blues: Colorado oil shale 1985–1985*. University of Colorado Press, Niwot (CO).

Gutman, P.S. (1994) Involuntary resettlement in hydropower projects. *Annual Review of Energy and the Environment* **19**, 189–210.

Hall, A. (1994) Grass-roots action for resettlement planning: Brazil and beyond. *World Development* **22(12)**, 1793–810.

Hansen, A. and **Oliver-Smith, A.** (eds) (1982) *Involuntary Migration and Resettlement: the problems and responses of dislocated people*. Westview, Boulder (CO).

Hardjono, J. (1988) The Indonesian Transmigration Program in Historical Perspective. *International Migration* **26(4)**, 427–39.

Hart, D. (1980) *The Volta River Project. A Case Study in Politics and Technology*. Edinburgh University Press, Edinburgh.

Heilbrun, A.B. and **Heilbrun, M.R.** (1986) The treatment of women within the criminal justice system: an inquiry into the social impact of the womens rights movement. *Psychology of Women Quarterly* **10(3)**, 240–50.

Henning, K., Leitenberg, H., Coffey, P., Turner, T. and **Bennett, R.T.** (1996) Long-term psychological and social impact of witnessing physical conflict between parents. *Journal of Interpersonal Violence* **11(1)**, 35–51.

Hill, A.T., Seyfrit, C.L. and **Danner, M.J.E.** (1997) Oil development and social change in the Shetland Islands 1971–1991. *Impact Assessment and Project Appraisal* **16(1)**, 15–25.

Hirsch, P. (1989) Settlement and resettlement on marginal land: a case study from Thailand. *Australian Geographer* **20(1)**, 80–9.

HMSO (1956a) *Volta River Project I: report of the Preparatory Commission*. Government of the UK and Gold Coast, London and Accra.

HMSO (1956b) *Volta River Project II: appendices to the report of the Preparatory Commission*. Government of the UK and Gold Coast, London and Accra.

Holohan, A.M. (1986) St Kilda emigrants and disease. *Scottish Medical Journal* **31(1)**, 46–9.

Howitt, R. (1989) Social impact assessment and resource development: issues from the Australian experience. *Australian Geographer* **20(2)**, 153–66.

Howitt, R. (1993) Social impact assessment as 'applied peoples' geography'. *Australian Geographical Studies* **31(2)**, 127–40.

Howitt, R. (1998) *Rethinking Resource Management: justice, sustainability and indigenous peoples*. Routledge, London.

Huszar, L. (1956) The Volta Resettlement Scheme. *Town Planning Institute Journal* **51(3)**, 279–82.

ICPE (1993) Social impact assessment of investment/acquisition of technology projects in developing countries, with particular reference to the position of women. *Public Enterprise* **13(3–4)**, 167–74.

Jacobs, S. (1991) Land resettlement and gender in Zimbabwe: some findings. *Journal of Modern African Studies* **29(3)**, 521–8.

Jing, J. (1997) Rural resettlement: past lessons for the Three Gorges Project. *China Journal* **38(1)**, 65–92.

Jobes, P.C. (1986) Assessing impacts on reservations: a failure of social impact assessment. Environmental Impact Assessment Review **6(3)**, 385–94.

Lane, M.B. and **Rickson, R.E.** (1997) Resource development and resource dependency of indigenous communities: Australia's Jawoyn Aborigines and mining at Coronation Hill. *Society and Natural Resources* **10(2)**, 121–42.

Lane, M.B., Ross, H. and **Dale, A.P.** (1997) Social impact research: integrating the technical, political, and planning paradigm. *Human Organization* **56(3)**, 302–10.

Lightfoot, R.P. (1979) Planning reservoir-related resettlement programmes in Northeast Thailand. *Journal of Tropical Geography* **47(2)**, 63–74.

Little, R.L. and **Krannich, R.S.** (1988) A model for assessing the social impacts of natural resource utilization on resource dependent communities. *Impact Assessment Bulletin* **6(2)**, 21–35.

Lockhart, D.G., Drakakis-Smith, D. and **Schembri, J.** (eds) (1994) *The Development Process in Small Island States*. Routledge, New York (NY).

McCarney, W. (1996) Psychological and social impact of the trouble on young people in Northern Ireland. *Juvenile and Family Court Journal* **47(1)**, 67–75.

MacDonald, E.G. and **MacDonald, W.S.** (1979) *Fundy Tidal Power: a bibliography and guide to an assessment of its social impact*. Institute of Public Affairs, Halifax (Nova Scotia).

McElroy. J.L., Dealbuquerque, K. and **Towle, E.L.** (1987) Old problems and new directions for planning sustainable development in small islands. *Ekistics* **54(323–324)**, 93–100.

Marshall, D.W. and **Scott, P.F.** (1983) Environmental and social impact assessment of the Beaufort Sea Hydrocarbon Production Proposal. *Social Impact Assessment Newsletter* No. 85/86, 4–19.

Modell, J. and **Haggerty, T.** (1991) The social impact of war. *Annual Review of Sociology* **17**, 205–24.

Moen, E. (1981) *Women and the Social Costs of Economic Development: two Colorado case studies*. Westview, Boulder (CO).

Morash, M. (1983) The application of social impact assessment to the study of criminal and juvenile justice programs: a case-study. *Journal of Criminal Justice* **11(3)**, 229–40.

Nance, J.M., Garfield, N.H. and **Paredes, J.A.** (1994) Studying the social impact of the Texas shrimp closure. *Human Organization* **53(1)**, 88–92.

Napier, T.L. (1981) Methodologies for assessing the social impact of projects necessitating forced relocation of rural people, in K. Finsterbusch and C.P. Wolf (eds), *Methodology of Social Impact Assessment* (2nd edn). Hutchinson Ross, Stroudsburg (PA), 267–72.

Niedenthal, J. (1997) *A History of the People of Bikini Following Nuclear Weapons Testing in the Marshall Islands: with recollections and views of elders of Bikini Atoll.* Williams and Wilkins.

Nordstrom, J., Owens, N.J., Boggs, J.P. and **Socktis, J.** (1977) *The Northern Cheyenne Tribe and Energy Development in Southwestern Montana 1: social, cultural, and economic investigations.* N. Cheyenne Research Project, Lone Deer (MT).

Nottingham, I. (1990) Social impact reporting: a Maori perspective – the Taharoa case. *Environmental Impact Assessment Review* **10(1–2)**, 175–84.

O'Faircheallaigh, C. (1999) Making social impact assessment count: a negotiation-based approach for indigenous peoples. *Society and Natural Resources* **12(1)**, 63–80.

Oshin, O. (1994) The social impact of Christian missionary enterprise in the Ondo Kingdom, 1870–1940. *African Marburgensia* No. 15, 23–45.

Palinkas, L.A., Harris, B.M. and **Petterson, J.S.** (1985) *A Systems Approach to Social Impact Assessment: two Alaskan case studies.* Westview, Boulder (CO).

Palmer, G. (1974) The ecology of resettlement schemes. *Human Organization* **33(3)**, 239–50.

Panos (1992) *Forced to Move: large development projects and forced resettlement* (Panos Media Briefing No. 4). Panos Institute, London.

Payulpitack, S. (1992) Changing provinces of concern: a case-study of the social impact of the Butthadasa Movement. *Sojurn* **7(1)**, 39–66.

Prothero, R.M. (1994) Forced migration of population and health hazards in tropical Africa. *International Journal of Epidemiology* **23(4)**, 657–64.

Putt, B. and **Buchan, D.** (1987) *Project Wind-down: an experience in community consultation.* Town and Country Planning Directorate, Ministry of Works and Development, Wellington.

Rao, S., Garole, V., Walawalkar, S. and **Karandikar, N.** (1996) Gender differentials in the social impact of leprosy. *Leprosy Review* **67(3)**, 190–9.

Rosenberg, D.M., Bodaly, R.A. and **Usher, P.J.** (1995) Environmental and social impacts of large scale hydroelectric development: who is listening? *Global Environmental Change* **5(2)**, 127–45.

Ross, H. (1989) Social impact assessment and resource development: issues from the Australian experience. *Australian Geographer* **20(2)**, 153–66.

Ross, H. (1990a) Community social impact assessment: a framework for indigenous peoples. *Environmental Impact Assessment Review* **10(3)**, 185–93.

Ross, H. (1990b) Progress and prospects in Aboriginal social impact assessment. *Australian Aboriginal Studies* **1(1)**, 11–17.

Roy, A. (1999) *The Cost of Living.* Flamingo (HarperCollins), London.

Sholten, J.J. and **Post, R.A.M.** (1999) Strengthening the integrated approach to impact analysis in development cooperation. *Environmental Impact Assessment Review* **19(3)**, 233–43.

Scholtz, U. (1992) Transmigrasi – ein desaster? Problemme und chancen des indonesischen umsiedlungsprogramms. *Geograhische Rundschau* **44(1)**, 33.

Scudder, T. (1975) Resettlement, in N.F. Stanley and M.P. Alpers (eds), *Man-made Lakes and Human Health.* Academic Press, London, 453–71.

Scudder, T. (1993) Development-induced relocation and refugee studies: 37 years of change and continuity among Zambia's Gwembe Tonga. *Journal of Refugee Studies* **6(2)**, 123–52.

Seyfrit, C.L and Sadlerhammer, N.C. (1988) The social impact of rapid energy development on rural youth: a statewide comparison. *Society and Natural Resources* **1(1)**, 57–67.

Shami, S. (1993) The social implications of population displacement and resettlement: an overview with a focus on the Arab Middle East. *International Migration Review* XXVII(1), 4–33.

Smith, D. (1998) *Transforming the World?: the social impact of British evangelicalism.* Paternoster, Carlisle (UK).

Steel, T. (1975) *The Life and Death of St Kilda.* HarperCollins, London.

Taylor, B.W. (1973) People in a rapidly changing environment: the first six years of the Volta Lake, in W.C. Ackermann, G.F. White and E.B. Worthington (eds), *Man-made Lakes: their problems and environmental effects.* Monograph No. 17, American Geophysical Union, Washington (DC), 99–107.

Tisdell, C. (1993) Project appraisal, the environment and sustainability for small islands. *World Development* **21(2)**, 213–19.

Treece, D. (1987) *Bound in Misery and Iron: the impact of the Grande Carajas Programme on the Indians of Brazil.* Survival International, London.

Unruh, J.D. (1993) Refugee resettlement in the Horn of Africa: the integration of host and refugee landuse patterns. *Land Use Policy* **10(1)**, 49–66.

VandenBerg, T.M. (1999) 'We are not compensating rocks': resettlement and traditional religious systems. *World Development* **27(2)**, 271–83.

Vargas, J.R., Montes, S., Arene, A., Buenrostro, J. and **Nieto, D.** (1995) El impacto economico y social des las migraciones en Centroamerica (1980–1989). *Anuario de Estudios Centroamricanos* **21(1–2)**, 19–82.

Waldram, J.B. (1984) Native people and social impact assessment in Canada. *Environmental Impact Assessment Bulletin* **3(2)**, 56–62.

Walton, J.R., Nuttall, R.L. and **Nuttall, E.V.** (1997) The impact of war on the mental health of children: a Salvadoran study. *Child Abuse & Neglect* **21(8)**, 737–49.

Weber, B.A. and **Howell, R.E.** (eds) (1982) *Coping with Rapid Growth in Rural Communities.* Westview, Boulder (CO).

Wheatley, M.A. (1996) The importance of social and cultural effects of mercury on aboriginal peoples. *Neuro Toxicology* **17(1)**, 251–6.

Wien, N. (1996) Die westsibirische Erdolprovincz: von der 'Boom-Region' zum Problemgebiet. *Geograhische Rundschau* **48(6)**, 380–7.

Wilkes, A. and **Hildyard, J.** (1994) Evicted! The World Bank and forced resettlement. *The Ecologist* **24(6)**, 56–62.

Wilkinson, K.P., Reynolds, R. jnr, Thompson, J.G. and **Ostresh, L.M.** (1994) Violent crime in the western energy development region. *Sociological Perspectives* **27(2)**, 24–125.

World Bank, The (1980) *Social Issues Associated with Involuntary Resettlement in Bank-financed Projects* (Operational Manual Statement 2-33). World Bank, Washington (DC).

World Bank, The (1994) *Resettlement and Development: the Bankwide review of projects involving involuntary resettlement 1986–1993.* Environment Department, World Bank, Washington (DC).

9

SIA IN PRACTICE: URBANIZATION, INDUSTRIALIZATION, TECHNOLOGY AND COMMUNICATION (TRANSPORT)

During the last 8000 years or so, humankind has altered its distribution from scattered groups of nomadic or semi-nomadic hunter-gatherers, mainly living in tropical and warm temperate Africa and parts of Asia, to settle almost all the world's lands. Most practise sedentary livelihoods in towns or cities, and numbers have grown to reach over 6000 million today. Industry and technology have also changed drastically; in the last few thousand years there has been a transition from 'the stone age' to the capacity to mass-produce complex artefacts, manipulate genetics and, perhaps, destroy much of the world's biota, including humankind.

Torgerson (1980: 30) argued that SIA has arisen in the general context of industrialization as concern about the aesthetic, social, moral, spiritual and environmental impacts of industry has prompted many to ask 'Where are we?', 'Where are we going?' and 'Where should we go?' SIA is a valuable tool for addressing these questions.

SIA AND THE IMPACT OF URBANIZATION

The world's population has recently become more than 50 per cent urban. Some cities, especially in developing countries, have grown very fast, placing stresses on services and law and order. For example, the population of Mexico City has now grown beyond 22 million, and there are plenty of other cities in the multi-million category. Urban growth is likely to remove some of the best farmland from use because cities tend to expand on level lowlands, valley bottoms and other areas that tend to have good soils. The UK is currently considering where to develop housing for the expanding population; some support greenfield sites and dispersal, others brownfield sites and concentration, so as to damage less of the countryside and avoid potential conflicts with rural people. However, the brownfield option may cost more, involve polluted land problems and might well prove less attractive to people if not presented carefully.

With demographic forecasts, topographic maps, an idea of the current and likely transport network, and data on building trends and costs, property taxation and fashions, SIA can make predictions about the likely pattern of expansion and character of urban change; it should also be possible to identify broadly future social scenarios (Francis, 1995; Gurkaynat and LeCompte, 1979). The easiest prediction to make is as to the likely pattern of urban sprawl, and there is reasonable agreement about the effects of sprawl on areas surrounding cities; for example, some types of farming become non-viable, dormitory townships grow and rural–urban migration is likely.

Urban environments can damage human health: noise, traffic exhaust and fumes from domestic heating pollute the air, there is dust from tyres, and clutch and brake-pad wear add to pollution. With people in close proximity, many diseases are freely transmitted, especially where there is substandard housing and diets are poor. Urban water supplies may be contaminated with chemicals and harmful micro-organisms, and many city dwellers suffer from stress (Satterthwaite, 1993). These problems may reflect inadequate spending and the poor management of urban environments; cities like Singapore and Curitiba (in Brazil) demonstrate that problems with pollution, water supplies and waste disposal can be overcome to maintain reasonable living conditions, even if resources are relatively limited, as is the case with Curitiba.

Low-income groups – often the old, women and children – bear the greatest negative health impacts; the rich are able to afford property out of town, or to buy modern air-conditioned apartments high above much of the pollution, and can use cars to avoid street crime. This has long been the case; indeed, in the UK, poor districts tend to be to the east of cities, reflecting the prevailing westerly winds and a history of coal-based industry and domestic heating – the rich moved west and upwind.

There is interest in the UK, Europe and the USA in assessing the socio-economic impact of various means for restricting the use of cars, which are choking city streets (Sheldon and Brandwein, 1973). SIA can be used to help establish effective urban public transport systems (Llewellyn, 1981). Where city areas have become run-down the solution may be urban renewal. This often happens spontaneously, an area becoming fashionable and attracting investment which in turn leads to rising property values, 'gentrification' and further improvements in property prices. Authorities could seek to prompt and control urban renewal, with planned inputs, or simply to encourage the activities of NGOs, housing associations, etc. There is more chance of doing this if the social dynamics are known. Crook and Moroney (1995) have explored the impacts of government policy on housing associations and the effect on inner cities and urban renewal.

SIA AND THE IMPACT OF INDUSTRIALIZATION

A few thousand years ago most people could practice many of the available 'industrial' techniques themselves, or at least understand the basics of technology; nowadays, even trained specialists have difficulty keeping abreast of new developments in their own limited field, and the average person has little understanding of (and often limited curiosity about) how the services and artefacts they enjoy work. Not all people benefit from industrial 'progress' – millions of poor people are bypassed, their lives blighted by lack of food or clean drinking water, inadequate housing and poor access to public transport, with little chance to live with dignity, and suffering crushing boredom; industry often means little to these people. Sometimes those who enjoy few benefits from modern technology and industry actually suffer its negative side-effects, such as pollution. And, often, those who do enjoy greater material riches are made miserable by stress and health problems associated with modern urban life and industrial activity. There is clearly a need for careful assessment of the likely benefits and unwanted impacts of technological and industrial development.

There have been studies in a number of countries to establish the social impact of industrial and resource development (including facilities like power stations and highways) on local communities. There are plenty of retrospective assessments of technological innovation (e.g. ArroyoPichardo, 1996; Barras and Swan, 1983; Komin, 1991; Michaelis, 1994), these help establish a core of hindsight knowledge that predictive social impact assessment can draw upon in order to adopt a proactive role. Armstrong and Wearing (1981), and later Newton and Parin (1983), explored the social impact of large-scale mining and associated power stations in the Latrobe Valley (Victoria, Australia), making use of the analysis of residents' social perceptions about the changing local environment and their well-being. In New Zealand, the social impacts of large (thermal) electricity generation facilities have been under study for decades (Cocklin and Kelly, 1992; Fookes, 1980 and 1984) (*see* Box 9.1). These studies show that local resident perceptions about the development of the power stations changed between 1974 and 1981. Some of this was due to adverse environmental impacts, but rapid population increase and altered access to social services also played a part. In Canada, Torgerson (1980) has applied SIA to industrialization.

SIA of industrial change and decline

Boomtowns, and the impact of extractive industry are discussed in Chapters 8 and 11. Many industries are in a constant state of change as demand for

Box 9.1 The Huntley Project: North Island, New Zealand

Construction of the Huntley coal-fired electricity generation plant (1000 MW) was started in 1973 on the Waikato River (North Island) close to an urban area (Whangarei, population 40,000). From the late 1970s a number of large industrial developments were initiated near the power station. The sheer scale of the developments in relation to the local communities caused considerable impact, and hence interest from those developing SIA. In the late 1970s the Huntley Monitoring Project was started, mainly involving academics from Waikato University, to collect data, monitor and systematically document the social impacts. The SIA explored 10 parameters, using over 100 variables to do this. Among the parameters studied were:

- what would be the effects of the development on the existing settlement of 5300 persons
- what would happen to local incomes
- what would be the employment impacts
- what would happen to manpower availability
- what would be the effect on material resources
- what would happen to provision of services (healthcare, education, welfare provision, etc.)
- what would happen to community cohesion
- what would happen to local administration and decision-making.

The findings included the following:

- the social impacts extended far beyond the area expected
- unforeseen impacts take place and upset expected development results
- there is a need to establish and address local fears
- those advocating development tend to play down expected unwanted impacts and exaggerate expected beneficial impacts
- there is a need to inform and involve public policy-makers early on in a development
- developers should use local avenues to communicate with the public as much as possible
- social attitudes and values change – development supporters may shift rapidly to opposition, and vice versa.

The Huntley Monitoring Project was New Zealand's first comprehensive assessment of social impacts from proposal to the construction phase (Buchan and Rivers, 1990; Conland, 1985; Rivers and Buchan, 1995). It has been criticized for being too Eurocentric, and so missing Maori needs, and for failing to emphasize public participation sufficiently; nevertheless, it has provided valuable input into other New Zealand development projects.

products alters. Innovation also affects production processes, and raw materials may be replaced by new substitutes. Established industry can expand, change its character or decline. A good deal of SIA effort has focused on the latter; much of this is retrospective. Increasingly, large companies or government bodies are trying to predict the impacts of change, especially closures, so that re-employment services and retraining programmes can be put in place and problems avoided, or at least prepared for (Grady *et al.*, 1987). The impacts of industrial loss are especially pronounced where settlements have grown up mainly to service the activity that is in decline. If there is no replacement industry or alternative employment, townships suffer, degenerate and may ultimately be abandoned. Many mining settlements have become ghost towns after the market declined or production shifted to using cheaper ore from elsewhere.

SIA and energy provision

SIA has been applied to energy provision planning and, retrospectively, to establishing the effects of such measures (particularly to find out whether rural electrification yields the claimed benefits). Faced with rising fuel costs, the need to avoid air pollution, possible carbon taxes (i.e. taxation designed to discourage pollution leading to greenhouse warming) and demands for sustainable development, those charged with reviewing company, settlement or state energy policies have frequently used SIA. People can alter their attitudes to energy provision drastically; for example, in the 1950s there was much support for, and little opposition to, nuclear power generation in the UK, the USA, Sweden, the former USSR and elsewhere. Today, after decades of costly investment, the public in most of these countries would show little favour to atomic power stations and, in the case of Sweden, a referendum led to phased abandonment and decommissioning.

SIA is especially useful for comparative studies to see how people are likely to respond to various energy provision options (Capata *et al.*, 1996) and new approaches like wind turbines (Wolsink, 1988). Ideally, energy solutions should be fitted to economic situations, culture, welfare needs, social habits and environmental management goals (Glasson and Porter, 1980).

SIA AND TECHNOLOGICAL INNOVATION

Worries about industrial technology were being voiced by the middle of the nineteenth century, and were confirmed by the second half of the twentieth century by pollution disasters and environmental contamination. Accidents like Seveso (northern Italy); Love Canal (USA), Chernobyl (USSR) and, above all, Three Mile Island (*see* Box 9.2) have helped promote interest in impact assessment, including SIA (Kuhn, 1970; Moss and Sills, 1981; Pijawka and Chalmers, 1983). The socio-economic impacts of the 1984 Bhopal disaster (India) continue today: victims have recently started a group court action against Union Carbide (the company that part-owned the chemical plant) for the settlement of damages. One of the questions the debate about the Bhopal disaster has helped to raise is whether the health and welfare of poor people in developing countries are valued anywhere near as much as that of citizens in richer countries.

Pharmaceutical tragedies (like thalidomide) and more recently the BSE and CJD (*see* Glossary) problems in the UK have also prompted demands for much more stringent and widespread impact assessment. Even several years after Chernobyl the socio-economic impacts have not been thoroughly explored, yet over 24,000 people were evacuated (Marples, 1988). Not only has the assessment of impacts been relatively slow, it has also tended to focus on physical issues. Again referring to Chernobyl, in spite of serious socio-economic effects felt as far away as Scandinavia and Wales, and across the Ukraine and other parts of the former USSR, it has been difficult to get social impact information, even in retrospect, and there has been little study of related issues such as the loss of public confidence in nuclear power throughout Europe and further afield.

Throughout the last two centuries there has been huge technological innovation, and at the start of the twenty-first century it is probably accelerating, yet there is still little effort to predict social and cultural impacts before, or early on in, the process of innovation (Freudenburg and Gramling, 1992). Huge changes are being caused by new transport methods, computers, telecommunications and biotechnology; all are well under way, yet there has been poor proactive social impact assessment. Recently, people in the West have started to become more concerned about the impact of new technology, but SIA still has too low a public profile.

One of the first social impacts of technological innovation was to generate fear of unemployment as a consequence of automation. In the UK the introduction of spinning and weaving machinery led to the Luddite riots of the nineteenth century, during which gangs of fearful workers raided mills to

Box 9.2 The three mile island accident

In 1979 one of two nuclear power stations in the Harrisburg area came close to a full meltdown; considerable unrest ensued, with partial evacuation of the surrounding areas and some public concern and flight. The incident at Three Mile Island on the Shenandoah River (Pennsylvania, USA) helped focus planners and decision-makers on establishing whether there should be compulsory 'social' impact assessment.

A series of legal battles followed the accident, between the reactor owners and a local citizens' group – People Against Nuclear Energy (PANE) – for which the US Supreme Court ruled that the US Nuclear Regulatory Commission was not required to issue an environmental impact statement before restarting the undamaged reactor. PANE had argued that the severe psychological stress suffered by those living near the reactors demanded careful SIA to be passed before restarting power generation. Whatever the outcome of the legal actions, the Three Mile Island incident has helped ensure (albeit years later) that there has been careful consideration of the need for legal requirements for SIA in America, and to make sure that they are enforced (Llewellyn and Freudenburg, 1986).

smash the new innovations they worried would render them unemployed and destitute. The move to automation accelerated following Henry Ford's car manufacturing innovations in the early twentieth century; and, before long, production lines were commonplace and had prompted protest from various union and non-union sources, including anti-automation films.

Before the 1970s, automation took the form of mechanization; production processes were automated, but there was still a demand for skilled controllers, finishers, designers, etc. However, with the improvement in electronic systems since the 1970s, there has been a real impact in terms of reduced demand for semi-skilled and some skilled workers. Electronic automation reduces the need for human measurement, checking, assembly, testing, design and so on; it also makes it possible for a manufacturer to move production away from areas with a pool of skilled workers to somewhere with a limited pool of cheap and adaptable labour as well as other advantages, such as good communications, a site close to a market and so on. It also makes it important for a manufacturer to keep up to date with current techniques and to purchase the latest equipment. The changing demands on workforces and the tendency for industry to relocate have had considerable socio-economic impacts on the workforces of developed and developing countries (Filho and Luna, 1982). If anything, automation has improved safety and reduced the drudge and boredom to which workers were previously exposed.

There are communities where new technology and industry have become rapidly established, needing only a short time to train local people. For example, electronic components factories established in Malaysia, Indonesia, mainland China and peripheral areas of Europe (Sagasti, 1986). These communities have quickly to come to terms with new working practices, dependency on overseas management and markets, and possibly upset to established culture and norms of behaviour (Anon., 1993; ICPE, 1993). In a number of western countries (and some developing countries), Japanese, Korean and Taiwanese companies have established factories and promote 'eastern' approaches to production to maintain productivity and product quality. This may involve considerable adaptation of attitudes to employment, quality control, leisure time, shouldering of responsibility and so on; it has also had positive impacts – for example, on moribund or ailing elements of the UK car and electronics industries (Hwang, 1995). In many cases new, more flexible and less strike-ridden practices have been developed, with a culture of better product quality control, and government hopes that this effect may spread.

A science park, innovation centre and technopolis are basically the same thing: an association of institutional and applied commercial research & development, that initiates or supports industrial development. Such set-ups have been promoted in North America and Europe for over 30 years and help diversify economies, attract further investment, create jobs and promote innovation. They were first tried in the USA in the early 1950s and typically consist of a group of companies and institutes, mostly working at the leading edge of applied technology, and usually closely associated with a university or universities and an international airport (e.g. at Cambridge in the UK, or Shannon in the Republic of Ireland). These organizations have the capacity to promote rapid economic development and technological change. Sometimes they are established with the aim of replacing lost employment and earnings from 'old' industry that is in decline. Alternatively, the intent is to start manufacturing in a new unindustrialized area. If successful, these centres may revitalize a city or even a region, raising property values and encouraging infrastructural development (Gibb, 1985). For science parks or innovation centres to work requires: a desirable living environment to attract staff; a major technological university; good institutional research facilities; and a skilled labour force. Typically, development will follow an institutional phase and then an entrepreneurial phase.

The forward-looking assessment of technology largely began in the USA in 1970 with the establishment of the Office of Technology Assessment, charged to conduct technology assessment (TA). In North America, EIA and TA evolved to improve the social management of technology, and the two strands have largely developed along parallel paths. One of the developments has been that TA increasingly helps shape new technologies (Van den Ende *et al.*, 1998). Other fields that share much in common with EIA and TA are risk and hazard assessment – all seek to forecast future impacts or scenarios, and all could draw useful lessons from each other (Porter, 1995). TA is more concerned with the generic impacts of technology; EIA, SIA, risk and hazard assessment have, in the main, been applied to specific projects, programmes or policies.

Fear of the unknown

The public may interpret the siting of a factory, power station, waste disposal facility, or whatever, as an opportunity or benefit when they are unaware of any associated risks. This attitude can shift quite suddenly if there is an accident somewhere or the media stirs up mistrust; after such eventualities, people will probably regard such developments with hostility, even if the risks are limited. There needs to be dialogue, and SIA can play an important part in this. Much of the public concern, which in western countries has helped lead to environmentalism and green NGOs, has been triggered by fears about the disposal or escape of waste from modern technology and industry; some blame must be laid at the feet of governments, which have handled accidents so badly that people now lack trust. Fear is generated by known threats such as explosion risks, which are broadly understood by the public. There is also, however, fear of the unknown. For example, the threat from toxic or carcinogenic compounds (like asbestos or PCBs), nuclear materials, electromagnetic emissions from equipment like portable telephones, biotechnology, and even debris re-entering the atmosphere from space flights (Levine, 1983; Yoshida and Araki, 1994).

Fear of unknown effects may be coupled with the suspicion (sometimes well founded) that the authorities are withholding information; examples of these threats include extra-low-frequency transmissions, like those generated by the stations built to communicate over a long distance with submarines (Klessig and Strite, 1980). At its most extreme, this sort of concern is exemplified by recent widespread 'X Files'-type accusations that governments are concealing important issues, such as contact with aliens. Indeed, considerable numbers of even apparently quite well-educated people adopt such 'conspiracy theories'. For rational people to adopt irrational ideas is nothing new; for example, during the Second World War the inhabitants of several Pacific islands and parts of New Guinea developed 'cargo cults' as a response to sudden exposure to new technology and human contacts, and genuinely felt that the right prayers would allow them to tap the same 'supernatural' source of wealth to which the Europeans seemed to have access. Decision-makers must not assume that they can reliably guess how people will react to a development – SIA can help (Bauer, 1995).

Dangerous waste

Today, any authority or company contemplating the establishment of a chemical incinerator or nuclear power station, waste storage or reprocessing facility, or even a factory, must take great care to provoke as little opposition as possible. Nuclear power generation, atomic waste storage and treatment has especially worried the public in several western countries since the 1950s. Such fears are not irrational – there have been serious accidents and leakages in several countries, including the former USSR, Japan, the USA (*see* the discussion of the Three Mile Island accident in Box 9.2), UK (Windscale/ Sellafield) and Germany, and people now have sufficient perception of threat to greet any attempt to site facilities near them with opposition (the NIMBY response) (Milbrath and Kamieniecki, 1982; Murdock, *et al.*, 1983; Slovic *et al.*, 1991). In Sweden, in 1980, a referendum shifted government policy away from nuclear power and towards other methods of generation.

Biotechnology

Large companies, research institutes and universities in developed countries, have developed and largely control biotechnology. Public interest and much of the impact assessment focused on the field so far have concentrated on the possible physical impacts. There has been less effort to assess social and economic impacts. Such impacts could be huge; biotechnology, for example, could permit the substitution of some important developing country export products; make it possible for companies to control key agricultural, manufacturing and healthcare inputs; lead to new energy supply systems; better pollution control; more efficient, diverse and adaptive industrial processes; and make possible terrifying and highly selective biological weapons. Most countries, including developing countries, are therefore keen to get adequate access to biotechnology, and the latter seek controls to ensure that they are not disadvantaged. Costs can be high, and much of the research and development can only be afforded by large commercial bodies and research institutes in developed countries (these naturally want to make profits to repay development costs).

Biotechnology impacts will certainly be far-reaching and are likely to grow considerably and play an increasingly important role in relations between nations and in economic development (George, 1988). There have been attempts to make some assessment of the likely future socio-economic impacts of biotechnology; for example, by Yoxen (1986). Galhardi (1995 and 1996) explored the future trade implications of biotechnology in developing countries, and has also tried to assess how employment in Latin America would be affected. Efforts have also been made to assess the social impacts of biotechnology in Europe (European Foundation for the Improvement of Living and Working Conditions, 1986).

There are clearly risks that biotechnology could lead to the substitution of cash crops, the production of which is depended upon by many farmers. Even use of biotechnology to improve crops in developing countries might lead to overproduction and price falls. However, if biotechnology can improve salt-tolerance, drought-resistance and disease-tolerance, and can improve nitrogen fixation, it has the potential to help a wide range of farmers diversify, improve and maintain crop yields, expand agriculture into unfarmed areas, and possibly cut the use of agrochemicals (reducing dependency, outgoings and pollution). It is clear that there is a need for an increased application of SIA to biotechnology innovation in order to try to enhance benefits and reduce problems. Unfortunately, biotechnology is big business, and is mainly in the hands of powerful MNCs and TNCs (as discussed in Chapter 7). So, there is a risk that SIA will not to be applied in a way which ensures that its recommendations are sufficiently well acted upon (Hindmarsh, 1990).

Genetic testing to determine people's susceptibility to diseases, illnesses, psychological disorders and so on, has considerable potential impact, and raises serious ethical issues. For example, recently in the UK many patients who have had blood samples taken for routine reasons, have been tested for HIV/AIDS, without their knowledge or permission. This provided valuable evidence of higher-than-expected rates of infection, but also raises serious ethical questions. Similar tests could be adopted in order to screen potential employees or insurance customers; in the latter case, this could lead to loadings for those who test positive for a risk, with increased premiums or even rejection. People with a disease which has a long incubation period (e.g. CJD), or who have an inherited disposition to developing a problem, could experience difficulty in obtaining health or life insurance, and might be rejected by employers or pension agencies. Balanced against these negative impacts are the possibilities of identifying those at risk, allowing preventative treatment, immunization, focused check-ups, etc. A state may be tempted to prevent those carrying certain genes from breeding, or may seek to pursue eugenic goals. There is a need to focus SIA on such problems (Davidson *et al.*, 1994).

In recent months, in the developed countries, the public have become aware of the problem (less perhaps of the value and potential) of biotechnology and genetic engineering. The latter has caused most controversy; it is the deliberate transfer of recombinant-DNA (r-DNA). There has been much protest at experimental trials of genetically modified (GM) crops in the UK and concern that GM foodstuffs are already widespread. It has been difficult to identify and control the use of GM sources by the food industry and some people have lost trust in suppliers and their governments (Barling, *et al.*, 1999; Martin, 1991). GM soya, for example, is already used in many processed foods. There is also worry about the use of growth-promoting or lactation-enhancing hormones such as bovine somatotrophine (BST). Perhaps the main social impact so far has been the blow to public trust and complacency towards agricultural research (already damaged in the UK and Europe by the BSE problem). This could be difficult to soothe, and could hinder valuable and safe applications of genetic engineering (for example, in pollution control, pharmaceuticals and in the crucial sustainable supply of cheap food for a growing world population). There is also a risk that fears about biotechnology and genetic engineering could hold back the future development of a country.

Biotechnology and property rights

As mentioned earlier, research can be costly, so companies seek to protect their findings in order to ensure that profits at least pay for their development costs. This has increasingly become a contentious issue, with arguments over the ethics and legality of attempts to patent parts of living things or material taken from one country and altered in another (Stahler, 1994) and then marketed under patent-like laws (Ahmed, 1989; Baker, 1991; Moy, 1997). Extremists accuse biotechnology developers of plundering the biodiversity of poor countries for raw materials – a form of bio-imperialism. There are also problems with trying to control intellectual property rights. The arguments are often between developed and developing countries, or between corporations and countries (Ghosh, 1995).

SIA OF ENERGY DEVELOPMENT

Energy development may impact in various ways:

- some generating plant, heating systems or vehicles may affect people and the environment (pollution, noise, traffic accidents, etc.)
- due to the provision of fuel for some types of generation or transport (oil wells, coal mines, dams) (*see* Chapter 12 for a discussion of mining impacts)
- via the distribution of power (power-lines may enable people to gain

access to an area to poach game, house prices are likely to be higher in areas served with electricity, gas, etc.)
- the availability of electricity, domestic gas or petrol.

The widespread availability of electricity to domestic households is a relatively recent development and still something largely restricted to developed countries, although change is taking place rapidly in some developing countries. Even in North America, the UK and Europe, more remote areas have only gained access within the last few decades. New forms of electricity generation may renew interest in local, rather than regional or national, power generation.

In many developed countries there has been a shift from coal gas to natural gas, delivered by a network of pipes or by road tanker to local holding tanks. In developing countries gas is more likely to be supplied commercially in small pressure cylinders (bottled gas). There is presently a rapid spread of photovoltaic electricity generation and small combustion-engine generator sets (Honda generators) in many developing countries; little is known about the likely socio-economic impact, not least that it may open opportunities for education (through better home lighting) and lead to the adoption of satellite TV even in remote areas.

Ideally, all countries should have a long-term energy policy, and should use SIA to plan for the best energy supply to each social situation (Capata *et al.*, 1996). Unfortunately, many countries have not assessed energy policies for environmental and social impact, and some (including a number of developed countries) have little if any long-term strategy. If appropriate and sustainable development is going to be achieved the use of tools like SIA is crucial to ensure that the best practicable environmental options 'fit' social situations, and that there are social institutions established to support implementation and management (or a good possibility of their establishment).

Many developing countries have a severe and growing problem with supply of fuel wood for domestic heating and cooking. In the short term, charcoal production may expand to meet the cooking needs of cities and rural areas, but that may be difficult to maintain and production easily degrades the environment. Alternatives to charcoal, fuel wood, dung and peat must be developed; at present the main alternatives are bottled gas and kerosene, which can be difficult to supply on a regular basis and is a costly option for poor people. Solar heating for water is reasonably developed; and in terms of cooking, biogas and solar-concentrator (parabolic reflector) methods are spreading slowly; but these are too expensive, and perhaps impractical, for poor people.

Provision of limited amounts of electricity, even for quite remote, poor and scattered communities is beginning to improve, either through rural electrification programmes using conventional networks of power-lines or village generator sets, or through household photovoltaic panels. This is unlikely to have much impact on cooking or heating, but it is starting to enable people to get access to TV, telecommunications and a little electric lighting. As photovoltaic cells fall in price and improve in terms of their effectiveness and working life, this is likely to have a considerable social and cultural impact worldwide. Some governments and companies may be prepared to supply villages with cheap, or even free, photovoltaic units, making available lighting, healthcare use (district storage of vaccines), and TV for entertainment and educational programmes. The downside is that the people are suddenly exposed to TV, often direct satellite broadcasting, which is difficult for local people or the state to control. This exposure may mean commercial pressures through advertising, 'cultural erosion' through the screening of foreign and indigenous soap operas and other unsuitable programmes, such as, perhaps, pornography, propaganda and inappropriate lifestyle images. These may cause false hopes, degrade local customs and social capital (e.g. the youth may be more tempted to migrate to cities to seek their fortune), and may encourage people to give in to commercial pressures and buy items they do not need, and which may actually prove to be harmful. Access to public service, educational and traditional culture TV programmes should also be possible, but may get less funding than commercial programming.

Communities may be capable of controlling new technology; for example, during 1998 I visited the High Atlas Mountains in Morocco, where many households and local cafes, even in remote villages had photovoltaic panels to power satellite TV. In some village cafes the cultural intrusion was being relatively well managed by one or two of the viewers being delegated as 'censors' – a quick press of the remote control at the first sight of an undesirable scene limited social and cultural impact; although the more subtle commercialism and lifestyle messages still got through. In remote areas of Brazil it is common to find a cafe TV set powered by a village generator. These provide valuable entertainment and an opportunity for the government to cement community cohesion, law-abiding attitudes and so forth, through 'soft' TV propaganda.

In many countries, high hopes are held for TV and radio to provide a means of education, and to distribute programmes on agricultural improvement and healthcare. Household photovoltaic units can have a considerable beneficial impact where families install lights and allow children to study beyond sunset, or at any time in poorly lit housing. However, all these goals are only likely to be achieved where the state has provided adequate media education and parents realize its value. There is a risk that electricity will be used only for entertainment TV, which may relieve a family's boredom, but may hinder rather than help education and could degrade culture. One might argue that this is what has happened for close on 50 years across the UK, the USA and Europe (and possibly in the West as a whole); what is needed is more SIA to assess just what has happened. There have been retrospective impact assessments of rural electrification in several countries, but relatively little application of SIA seems to be under way as yet into the likely impacts, so that governments and other responsible bodies can assess and possibly better control change.

SIA AND THE IMPACT OF TRANSPORT COMMUNICATION DEVELOPMENTS

Highways, urban metro systems, bridges, tunnels, railways and airports all generate annoying, or even health-threatening, levels of noise, vibration and, sometimes, air pollution. Usually the nuisance is restricted to a belt on either side of the routeway, although with air traffic the pattern may be more 'egg-shaped' (the broad end centred on the airport and the 'tail' pointing away from the end of the main runway(s)). In recent years the trend in air travel has been towards better noise suppression, although flights from major airports have become more frequent. The socio-economic impacts of noise and the fear of air crashes range from disturbed sleep, to driving certain sensitive activities and employment away from the noise source; often the main effect is to devalue domestic property prices (Tomkins, *et al.*, 1998). Enough is known about the way noise is propagated and how it can be controlled for specialists to assess in advance the pattern and likely levels; the effects are less easy to predict, however, and SIA might help determine these.

Airports have other socio-economic impacts on communities nearby (Stratford, 1974) and, in the case of islands and isolated areas, on wider groups and the economy. Small islands may become heavily dependent on air transport for supplies and tourism access; nevertheless, in many cases the construction of airport facilities has been vital in reversing economic decline and out-migration. A recent, somewhat hyped-up, problem of air travel has been 'air rage'. While alcohol and weak personality plays a part in this, other factors too may be responsible for increased on-board violence. The risks associated with the problem merit impact assessment to see what triggers it so that it can be better avoided, and so that the risk it poses can be reduced.

Transport improvements can have profound health impacts; the positive side is the ability to transport food, commodities, medicines, etc. more effectively. The negative side is the risk of transferring communicable diseases and pests to new areas where local people and biota may have little immunity, leading to severe outbreaks. In some developing countries the transmission of HIV/AIDS closely correlates with the pattern of road transport.

Technology can radically alter transportation; the aircraft supplanted ship travel for passenger traffic mainly after the 1950s, and especially after the introduction of jet-engined aircraft; numbers of passengers carried rose again following the introduction of the Boeing 747 and similar jumbo jets in the early 1970s. In snow-bound regions, the snow-mobile has had considerable physical and socio-economic impact in the last few decades (Bernard and Pertti, 1972).

Future technological innovations can be difficult to forecast: the spread of supersonic air travel has been on nothing like the scale expected in the early 1970s; high-speed shipping, coupled with improved telecommunications, may lead to a come-back for transatlantic and other sea travel. One might embark on speculation about the possible impacts if there was a room-temperature superconductivity breakthrough; this might lead to fast, long-distance trains as a cheaper, and almost as swift, alternative to medium-distance air travel (it would also have a huge impact on computing and electricity transmission). However, fears about the adverse health effects of the electro-magnetic fields involved may preclude such developments.

Bridges, tunnels and new highways that link previously remote areas can have considerable socio-economic impacts; for example, in the UK the Humber Bridge permitted much more direct links between Humberside and eastern England south of the River Humber, although usage was slow to develop. Prior to the completion of the Channel Tunnel between the UK and France there were efforts to assess the physical and socio-economic impacts of the link (Economic Consultants Ltd, 1973). Proposals have recently been mooted for a UK–Dublin rail tunnel; although over 60 km long this seems technically and economically feasible and would have marked impacts on the economy and outlook of the UK, especially north-west Wales, Eire and Europe. The Channel Tunnel has affected the way companies transport their goods and raw materials, has had some impact on employment practices (mainly for higher-level white-collar workers) (Goodenough and Page, 1994) and has promoted growth in 'railhead' communities such as Ashford and Folkestone.

Political change can have huge effects on transport and, consequently, on trade, political economy, culture and so on (and vice versa): a single German nation was created in the nineteenth century, and greatly aided the formation of a customs union and railway system; in the Americas, highways built since the 1950s have had as much a political effect as they have on trade (the Pan-Am Highway is seen as a means of improving co-operation between states); Brazil's Amazon roads are intended to underpin national territory and encourage resource exploitation. In Asia there are the beginnings of a new 'Silk Road' – the Asian Highway from Saigon (Vietnam) to Ankara (Turkey) – which many hope will boost international and inter-regional trade. In central and eastern Europe, the post-perestroika period has seen more freedom of travel and, with it, social and economic change (Lijewski, 1996).

There has been considerable application of EIA, and rather less SIA, to highway development (Finsterbusch, 1976). It makes sense to subdivide coverage into the following areas:

- urban road development
- motorway (i.e. major autoroute, trunk road, inter-city road) and railway development (e.g. Snow, 1984)
- rural road and local track network development (Howe and Richards, 1984).

As the road network has expanded and private car ownership has grown in many countries there has been considerable socio-economic impact on those without access to a car. This is most marked in countries like the USA, Canada and the UK where there is a trend towards the closure and relocation of high-street stores to out-of-town shopping malls. Some of these new shopping centres have cheap, or even free, public transport provision, but are still likely to be less easy to reach, especially for the poor and elderly. Recently, the UK Government expressed concern that this trend meant that some city areas and other settlements had virtually lost reasonable access to shops selling food, and other vital commodities and services. In some US states the combination of mall formation and the greying population has led to a relaxation of car driving regulations at certain times of day for those with slower reactions and poorer eyesight to retain access to shops and services.

References

Ahmed, I. (1989) Advanced agricultural biotechnologies. Some empirical findings on their social impact. *International Labour Review* **128(5)**, 533–70.

Anon. (1993) Social impact assessment/acquisition of technology projects in developing countries, with particular reference to the position of women. *Public Enterprise* **13(3–4)**, 239–56.

Armstrong, A.F. and **Wearing, A.J.** (1981) Social impact assessment and its application to the assessment of energy policy impacts in the Latrobe Valley. *Australian Psychologist* **16(2)**, 298.

ArroyoPichardo, G. (1996) El impacto cultural del cambio technologico: una problematica. *Relaciones Internacionales* No. 71, 73–80.

Baker, K.R. (1991) Biotechnology: a strategic opportunity for agriculture. *Outlook on Agriculture* **20(2)**, 79–82.

Barling, D., DeVriend, H., Cornelse, J.A., Ekstrand, B., Hecker, E.F.F., Howlett, J., Jensen, J.H., Lang, T., Mayer, S., Staer, K.B. and **Top, R.** (1999) The social aspects of food biotechnology: a European view. *Environmental Toxicology and Pharmacology* **7(2)**, 85–93.

Barras, R. and **Swan, J.** (1983) *The Adoption and Impact of Information Technology in the UK Insurance Industry*. Technical Change Centre, London.

Bauer, M. (ed.) (1995) *Resistance to New Technology*. Cambridge University Press, Cambridge.

Bernard, H.R. and **Pertti, J.P.** (eds) (1972) *Technology and Social Change*. Macmillan, New York (NY).

Buchan, D. and **Rivers, M.J.** (1990) Social impact assessment development and application in New Zealand. *Impact Assessment Bulletin* **8(4)**, 97–105.

Capata, R., Naso, V. and **Orecchini, F.** (1996) Social impact of energy systems. *Renewable Energy* **9(1–4)**, 1291–4.

Cocklin, C. and **Kelly, B.** (1992) Large-scale energy projects in New Zealand: whither social impact assessment? *GeoForum* **23(1)**, 41–60.

Conland, J. (ed.) (1985) *Social Impact Assessment in New Zealand – a Practical Approach*. Town and Country Planning Directorate, Ministry of Works and Development, Wellington.

Crook, A.D.H. and **Moroney, M.** (1995) Housing associations, private finance and risk avoidance: the impact on urban renewal and inner cities. *Environment and Planning A* **27(11)**, 1695–712.

Davidson, C., Macintyre, S. and **Smith, S.** (1994) The potential social impact of predictive genetic testing for susceptibility to common chronic diseases: a review and proposed research agenda. *Sociology of Health & Illness* **16(3)**, 340–71.

Economic Consultants Ltd (1973) *The Channel Tunnel: its economic and social impact on Kent* (report). HMSO, London.

European Foundation for the Improvement of Living and Working Conditions (1986) *The Social Impact of Biotechnology*. European Communities, Luxembourg.

Filho, W.D.P. and **Luna, H.P.L.** (1982) Social impact of automation: some specific problems of LDCs. *Human Systems Management* **3(4)**, 311–16.

Finsterbusch, K. (1976) *A Methodology for Social Impact Assessment of Highway Locations*. Bureau of Research, Maryland State Highway Administration, Brooklandville (MD 20402).

Fookes, T.W. (1980) Monitoring social and economic impacts (a New Zealand case study). *Environmental Impact Assessment Review* **1(1)**, 72–6.

Fookes, T.W. (1984) *Social Monitoring: the Huntley Monitoring Project in retrospect*. PhD thesis, University of Waikato, Hamilton.

Francis, M. (1995) Urban social impact assessment and community involvement. *Environment and Behavior* **7(3)**, 373–404.

Freudenburg, W.R. and **Gramling, R.** (1992) Community impacts of technological change: toward a Longitudinal perspective. *Social Forces* **70(4)**, 937–55.

Galhardi, R.M.A.A. (1995) The impact of biotechnology on North–South Trade: implications for employment in Latin America. *Futures* **27(6)**, 641–56.

Galhardi, R.M.A.A. (1996) Trade implications of biotechnology in developing countries: a quantitative assessment. *Technology in Society* **18(1)**, 17–40.

George, S. (1988) Biotechnology and the Third World. *Chain Reaction* **54(1)**, 40–1.

Ghosh, P.K. (1995) Impact of industrial policy and trade related intellectual property rights on biotech industries in India. *Journal of Scientific & Industrial Research* **54(4)**, 217–30.

Gibb, J.M. (1985) *Science Parks and Innovation Centers: their economic and social impact*. Elsevier, Amsterdam.

Glasson, J. and **Porter, J.** (1980) Power Stations: their local socio-economic effects. *Town and Country Planning* **49(3)**, 84–7.

Goodenough, R.A. and **Page, S.J.** (1994) Evaluating the environmental impact of a major transport infrastructure project: the Channel Tunnel High-Speed Rail Link. *Applied Geography* **14(1)**, 26–50.

Grady, S., Braid, R., Bradbury, J. and **Kerley, C.** (1987) Socioeconomic assessment of plant closure: three case studies of large manufacturing facilities. *Environmental Impact Assessment review* **7(2)**, 151–65.

Gurkaynak, M.R. and **LeCompte, W.A.** (eds) (1979) *Human Consequences of Crowding*. Plenum, New York (NY).

Hindmarsh, R. (1990) The need for effective assessment: sustainable development and social impacts of biotechnology in the Third World. *Environmental Impact Assessment Review* **10(1–2)**, 195–208.

Howe, J. and **Richards, P.** (eds) (1984) *Rural Roads and Poverty Alleviation*. Intermediate Technology Publications, London.

Hwang, K.K. (ed.) (1995) *Easternization: socio-cultural impact on productivity*. Asian Productivity Organization, Tokyo.

ICPE (1993) Social impact assessment of investment/acquisition of technology projects in developing countries with particular reference to the position of women. *Public Enterprise* **13(3–4)**, 239.

Klessig, L.L. and **Strite, V.L.** (eds) (1980) *The ELF Odyssey: national security versus environmental protection*. Westview, Boulder (CO).

Komin, S. (1991) Social dimensions of industrialization in Thailand. *Regional Development Dialogue* **12(1)**, 115–38.

Kuhn, T.S. (1970) *The Study of Scientific Revolutions* (2nd edn). University of Chicago, Chicago (IL).

Levine, A. (1983) Psycho-social impact of toxic chemical waste dumps. *Environmental Health Perspectives* **48(Feb.)**, 15–17.

Lijewski, T. (1996) The impact of political changes in Central and Eastern Europe. *Transport Reviews* **16(1)**, 37–53.

Llewellyn, L.G. (1981) The social cost of urban transportation, in I. Altman., J.F. Wholwill and P. Everett (eds) Transportation and Behavior. Plenum, New York, 169–202.

Llewellyn, L.G. and **Freudenburg, W.R.** (1986) Legal requirements for social impact assessment: assessing the social-science fallout from Three Mile Island. *Society and Natural Resources* **2(3)**, 193–208.

Marples, D.R. (1988) *The Social Impact of the Chernobyl Disaster*. Macmillan, Basingstoke.

Martin, M.A. (1991) Socioeconomic aspects of agricultural biotechnology. *Phytopathology* **81(3)**, 356–60.

Michaelis, A.R. (1994) 100 years of the diesel-engine: economic and social impact. *Interdisciplinary Science Reviews* **19(3)**, 177–80.

Milbrath, L.W. and **Kamieniecki, S.** (1982) A social impact assessment of the nuclear fuel services facility at West Valley, New York. *International Journal of Public Administration* **4(2)**, 113–34.

Moss, T.H. and **Sills, D.L.** (eds) (1981) *The Three Mile Island Nuclear Accident: lessons and implications* (Annals of the New York Academy of Sciences Vol. 365). New York Academy of Sciences, New York (NY).

Moy, R.C. (1997) International dimensions of patent law as it pertains to animal and agricultural biotechnology. *Animal Biotechnology* **8(1)**, 81–9.

Murdock, S.H., Leistritz, J.L. and **Hamm, R.R.** (1983) *Nuclear Waste: socioeconomic dimensions of long-term storage*. Boulder, Westview.

Newton, P.W. and **Parin, J.** (1983) The social impact of industrial and resource development on local communities: a survey of residents' views. *Australian Journal of Social Issues* **18(4)**, 245–58.

Pijawka, D. and **Chalmers, J.A.** (1983) Impact of nuclear generating plants on local areas. *Economic Geography* **59(1)**, 66–80.

Porter, A.L. (1995) Technology assessment. *Impact Assessment* **13(2)**, 135–51.

Rivers, M.J. and **Buchan, D.** (1995) Social assessment and consultation: New Zealand cases. *Project Appraisal* **10(3)**, 181–8.

Sagasti, F.R. (1986) The technological transformation of China and its social impact: an agenda for policy research. *Interciencia* **11(1)**, 36–39.

Satterthwaite, D. (1993) The impact on health of urban environments. *Environment and Urbanization* **5(2)**, 87–111.

Sheldon, N.W. and **Brandwein, R.** (1973) *The Economic and Social Impact of Investments in Public Transit*. Lexington Books, Lexington (MA).

Slovic, P. Layman, M., Kraus, N., Flynn, J., Chalmers, J. and **Gesell, G.** (1991) Perceived risk, stigma, and potential economic impacts of a high-level nuclear waste repositry in Nevada. *Risk Analysis* **11(4)**, 683–96.

Snow, R.T. (1984) Pastoral nomads, aid agencies, and international highways: the

Turkana and the Kenya–Sudan road link. *Social Impact Assessment Newsletter* No. 93–95, 11–15.

Stahler, F. (1994) Biological diversity: the international management of genetic resources and its impact on biotechnology. *Ecological Economics* **11(3)**, 227–36.

Stratford, A.H. (1974) *Airports and the Environment: a study of air transport development and its impact upon the social and economic well-being of the community*. Macmillan, London.

Tomkins, J., Topham, N., Twomey, J. and **Ward, R.** (1998) Noise versus access: the impact of an airport on an urban property market. *Urban Studies* **35(2)**, 243–58.

Torgerson, D. (1980) *Industrialization and Assessment: social impact assessment as a social phenomenon*. York University Publications in Northern Studies, Toronto.

Van den Ende, J., Mulder, K., Knot, M., Moors, E. and **Vergragt, P.** (1998) Traditional and modern technology assessment: toward a toolkit – a research methodology and learning strategy for social impact assessment. *Technological Forecasting and Social Change* **58(1)**, 5–21.

Wolsink, M. (1988) The social impact of a large wind turbine. *Environmental Impact Assessmewnt Review* **8(4)**, 323–34.

Yoshida, H. and **Araki, M.** (1994) Social impact of space debris: study of economic and political aspects. *Acta Astronautica* **34**, 345–55.

Yoxen, E. (1986) The social impact of biotechnology. *Trends in Biotechnology* **4(4)**, 86–8.

10

SIA IN PRACTICE: TELECOMMUNICATIONS AND HEALTH

For some problems there may be laws or ethics that can guide impact avoidance or mitigation, but others may be so novel that there is little available help. SIA can assist by forewarning planners and others in authority of the risk of new impacts, so that law-making, formulation of ethics and mitigation practices can be developed in time. The fields discussed in this chapter have seen rapid development, often with considerable social impact, partly because proactive SIA has been too seldom attempted.

Improved communications

Communications developments have had huge social impact: writing has allowed the inter-generational and spatial transmission of records, ideas and opinions; the development of the printing press – and, more recently, cheap paperback books – further extended the transmission of ideas and knowledge. There are signs at present of the development of something probably at least as powerful as printing: the IT revolution. Information technology (IT) is supporting an increasingly global culture, with virtually instant global transmission of information which, although it might be eavesdropped upon, is not yet controllable by states to anywhere near the extent printing has been. Some 200 years ago, a hand-written letter might have taken months, or even years, to convey a message between countries; only the literate and rich had easy access to such measures, and interception and censorship was quite easy. Today a much wider range of people can post and receive letters, use a public phone or access the World Wide Web via their own personal computer (PC), or by using one in an internet cafe; communication has become more accessible, much faster and less easy to intercept and control.

The impacts of this are enormous and diverse. Local 'minority' languages and cultures may come under pressure from global culture. NGOs and individuals can tell the world of a problem before they are silenced. Even quite small groups can afford to prepare and distribute written or voice broadcasts. There may also, however, be risks from improved communications: those who control some elements of the media may be able to, openly or covertly, propagandize; the power of commercial advertisers has grown; and governments or concerned bodies may find it difficult to prevent the spread of adverts, dangerous ideas and damaging information.

Jared Diamond (1991) pointed out that modern communications may kill off some minority languages and vulnerable cultures, and reduce other local cultural elements. But that may be a reasonable price to pay, given that modern weapons technology can kill millions; at least with a global culture there might be a reduced chance that our dangerously improved weaponry will be used to destroy whole countries or even the world, rather than a tribe. Some have hesitated to promote the modern world's lingua franca (English) because this could increase domination by better-educated richer classes and the dependency on English-speaking developed countries. However, there may be risks that by promoting only an indigenous language there will be problems with conducting research and acquiring technology.

Clearly, the telecommunications developments currently under way are having diverse and far-reaching effects. Better use could be made of SIA to improve understanding of these and to help reduce future problems. Something to which SIA must be sensitive (TA assessors are familiar with the phenomenon) is 'leap-frogging': the pattern of technology innovation where a developed country may invest heavily and take time to develop and adopt a system, and yet a few years after it is perfected and sold commercially, other companies and countries install something equivalent or better at a much reduced cost. This has certainly been the case with modern telecommunications technology, with even remote areas now getting access to satellite phones and cyber-cafes (Domatob *et al.*, 1996). Another impact of the spread of modern telecommunications and computing was highlighted by the Y2K, or millennium bug, scare: a body or country, once it becomes dependent on technology, may be more vulnerable to disruption. An organization or country with record-keeping based on written (duplicate copy) ledgers and index cards is less likely to be brought to a halt by a natural disaster, computer virus or nuclear detonation radiation than one with sophisticated IT systems.

Media

Countries like the UK, USA and many European nations have now had over 50 years during which TV has impacted on most of their public (longer for radio broadcasting and sound recording equipment). Precisely what the social, economic and cultural impacts of this have been has been much debated (Inamasu, 1987; Ito, 1987; Okabe, 1987). By the time of the Second World War, broadcasting services were a major influence on morale and public order in the UK, USA and Germany. Although there have been studies of the impact on values, family cohesion and behaviour, focusing especially on the impacts of violence and sex in TV programmes; the real effects still seem to be only vaguely identified. In various countries there serious worries have long been expressed about the effect of TV, especially on children. Recently in the UK concerned groups have called for much stricter control over children's exposure to TV (*see* http://www.users.globalnet.co.uk/~mcdwest/index2.htm). There has been less study of the effects on the adult population, including the elderly, who often spend much time viewing. Given the probably significant effects of broadcasting on western societies since the 1950s, it is surprising how little SIA has been conducted to establish impacts so far and those likely in the future.

Whether broadcast media have had an overall beneficial, as opposed to damaging, effect is still not clear for any country. This debate is unlikely to reach a conclusion in the foreseeable future for the following reasons: the content of broadcasting is constantly changing; those who do assess it have very different standpoints; and most assessments are commissioned by broadcasting bodies and are, therefore, unlikely to criticize. Study is complicated by a series of media technology shifts: the 1950s saw the spread of monochrome TV; the 1960s colour TV; the 1990s direct satellite TV broadcasting and digital TV; and throughout the last three decades there has been a trend toward much cheaper and improved receivers, and the multiplication and commercialization of TV channels. Also, in western countries since the 1980s there has generally been a relaxation of controls over the content of broadcasts. One may guess that the coming decades will see as much change as the last few, probably much more (given the possibility of the establishment of digital TV, interactive TV and subject-specialist TV channels).

Certain social groups come to depend a great deal on TV: children, the elderly and the poor. Broadcasters should be familiar with the social impacts of their programming and act in a responsible way to try to avoid damage, and to help and 'improve' people. In practice there is seldom objective SIA of broadcasting – there are more likely to be estimations of ratings, which prompt offerings in order to boost future ratings. Damaging programming can attract viewers: commerce pays for much broadcasting and is likely to support whatever boosts ratings, rather than what might help or improve the lot of individuals or society. In those countries that have public service-type broadcasting there may be cut-backs, greater support for more popular entertainment, or an attempt to cater too much for the growing number of elderly viewers at the expense of other age groups. Some would argue that the potential of broadcasting for education and public service has not been sufficiently realized, although a few countries have established distance learning ('open university'-type) broadcasting, agricultural extension and healthcare programmes. In some countries banks and other services are starting to shift to the internet or interactive TV; within a few years this may have a considerable impact on available services and people's banking and shopping habits.

In many countries the arrival of satellite TV (direct satellite broadcasting) has made it difficult for government to control what the public can watch. This may lead to the formation of a TV global village with at least a veneer of universal culture, language and shared values. However, it might also erode traditions, values and cultures. As the technology for the broadcast of a greater number of TV channels appears, there will be increased opportunity to offer both global channels and local services which could be in minority languages and cater for regional needs.

Telecommunications

One cannot help but notice the rapid spread of mobile telephones in Europe and the USA, and increasingly among the affluent classes in developing countries. Slick marketing and media role models mean that a rapidly growing number of people acquire mobile (cellular or portable phones), and some run up serious debts with little real benefit; there are also, as yet unsubstantiated, fears that the handsets may emit enough radiation – via their electromagnetic fields (EMFs) – to cause cancer or affect the mental abilities of users (Freude *et al.*, 2000). Business has been greatly affected by improved telecommunications, e-mail, voice-mail, greater choice of fixed lines, and mobile phones. Mobile phones mean much greater flexibility for some service industries (Bogdanowicz, 1997; Perugini, 1996). The negative impacts of mobile phones have been highlighted by the media, but there are also many positive impacts; for example, improved responses to road accidents because bystanders can immediately call for help (Chapman and Schofield, 1998; Santini, 1999). There may also, however, be an increased incidence of false alarm calls to police, medical and rescue services.

Portable phones have spread so fast that the rules and etiquette controlling their use has not yet evolved sufficiently. There may be other risks, such as phone transmissions affecting electronic controls – most airlines restrict mobile phone use for this reason (the phones may also affect car engines and brakes); social habits may also change as people find they have better communication (Davis, 1993). In North America and Europe the use of portable phones by relatively poor groups of people takes up a fairly large proportion of their total income. So far, there has been little assessment of the clearly important role portable phones play for youth culture, for crime, small business or the general public.

The spread and considerable improvement of the world's fixed telephone network has attracted less attention, yet it has reached the state where there are few places where it is not possible to find a public or a private phone within a few kilometres, from which almost anywhere on in the world can be contacted instantly. The telephone has undoubtedly had a huge impact on commerce, with some forms of retailing now heavily dependent on it.

In recent years a number of new technological innovations have been added to phones: fax, voice-mail, caller identification, phone-based e-mail, etc. These may intrude on privacy, cause alterations of people's habits and have other social impacts (Dutton, 1992). In France the telecommunications system has offered many householders something like the internet through Mintel for some years. Assessment of such telecommunication developments would help to predict use scenarios and impacts elsewhere in the future.

INFORMATION TECHNOLOGY

Larger computers and cybernetics have been in use in business, the military and various institutions since the 1960s. The overall impact has been for increased storage of more diverse data, and for faster processing of that information. This has affected banking, control systems for public utilities, police and security service monitoring, aircraft and ship navigation, weather forecasting and many other fields (Lucky, 1984; Rosenberg, 1997; Schumann, 1984). These impacts have had a considerable effect on some societies (Dechert, 1966; Silver, 1979; Szyperski *et al.*, 1983).

In the 1990s there were widespread fears that 'computerization' would reduce opportunities for clerical employment. However, as user-friendly, icon-based software systems have spread, there seems to have been less impact on semi-skilled workers than was expected. There have also been impacts on the communities that produce electronic components and computers: there are now new computer- and IT-related industries, which have generated employment, regional economic growth and spin-off activities for Silicon Valley (California), Japan, Taiwan, Korea, and other countries or areas. Attempts to predict future developments in this sector (Rossini *et al.*, 1986) have been made difficult by the rapid evolution of hardware and software, and commercial secrecy.

The spread of personal or home computers (PCs) has had both positive and negative effects; it would be interesting if an assessment could confirm which is the greater, especially given the messianic fervour with which some decision-makers treat their promotion. Certainly there has been a marked impact on the recreational habits of youth in the West, a significant number of whom now make heavy use of computer games and the internet, which in turn might adversely affect health (e.g. damaged eyesight, electromagnetic radiation emission risks, repetitive strain injury (RSI), impaired physical fitness, and an altered capacity to mix and form normal social relationships).

The information technology skills, so often called for by modern governments, cost a lot to impart, and demand expensive, often delicate, and rapidly obsolescent equipment, as opposed to pencil and paper. There is also some doubt as to whether these 'skills' are a real substitute for the ability to read, write fluently and perform mental arithmetic, rather than rely on a word-processor or calculator. If IT training means young people alone in their bedrooms playing intellectually unchallenging computer games or surfing the net to acquire unreliable or even harmful information, at the expense of developing analytical or other more traditional skills or pursuing hobbies, then it is a false investment. These fears may be exaggerated, because a study by Robinson *et al.* (1997) suggested that increased PC use led to greater reference to printed media and less of a reduction in other activities than might be expected.

The potential of the PC and the internet for older age groups has been little-studied. Access to these facilities might help reduce the isolation suffered by the housebound and elderly. Another issue that needs investigation is the failure of some sectors of society to gain IT skills and access to facilities, so that they are increasingly disadvantaged as opportunities and services shift to IT. The problem is that the social impacts of IT have not yet been anything like adequately assessed, yet governments are promoting it, apparently blindly.

Many countries are investing heavily in PCs for schools and universities, but there has been little serious assessment of the value of this expenditure in the long term, especially given that the funds may have been diverted from other uses such as library book purchases. At college level in the USA, and increasingly in Europe, there may already be a shift from use of printed sources to more reliance on the internet. While this shift could be positive in the sense of giving rapid access to information, it is less than beneficial where students download material that has generally not been subject to the peer review of traditional publishing with little discrimination or even reworking. Some UK schools are trying to return students to mental arithmetic without the aid of computers or pocket calculators, and there have been problems with plagiarism from the web for university student assessment essays in the USA, UK and elsewhere.

Worldwide, the PC has been of tremendous benefit to professionals, small businesses and researchers. It is possible to store and process data and manipulate and print information to levels beyond what were almost everyone's dreams in the 1970s. But, it would make sense to assess more accurately what sort of IT education or training is needed to enhance a given user's abilities and likely future needs. Too often money is being spent on software designed for commercial users in California, or the mass leisure market, rather than on good, appropriate packages. The practice of 'bundling' a free, but possibly poor-quality, selection of software with some PCs means that some users start, and may stay, with inappropriate programmes.

In North America, Japan and Europe, and in a growing number of other countries, the PC has allowed people to work from home (telecommuting). It would be interesting to determine what social impacts this is having and will have: might it, perhaps, help cut traffic and public transport congestion, and associated pollution? One assessment suggested that, by 2010, telecommuting will cut mass transit congestion in Tokyo by as much as 10.9 per cent (Mitomo and Jitsuzumi, 1999). There have been similar studies, particularly in California (Olszewski and Mokhtarian, 1994; US Dept of Transportation,

1993). But has telecommuting improved family relationships, job satisfaction and incomes? Or has there been a blurring of distinction between 'home' and 'work' (Ellison, 1999), with negative social impacts?

In the space of a few years the World Wide Web (internet) has had a tremendous impact (Kraut *et al.*, 1998; Schwab, 1995). It is possible to transmit large amounts of information instantly and at very low cost as e-mail attachments; and there are specialist services providing the public with various types of information or conducting commissioned searches. The main impact has been on the more affluent, intellectuals, academics, NGOs and financial services. New opportunities for the study and exchange of ideas have begun to open up: NGOs have a greater opportunity to pass on messages than ever before – which means that misconduct and oppression have become more difficult to conceal; it has also enabled lobby groups and protesters to share information and keep in better contact, with mixed results for society. Criminals have already grasped the opportunities, and this problem will probably grow as more people conduct their financial affairs and shopping using IT.

What the future socio-economic impacts of the World Wide Web will be is difficult to assess. Tonn (1996) argued that social scientists should become more actively involved in developing IT, and better aware of its social impacts. Governments or commerce may manage to cut back the current availability of free, largely uncontrolled access. Some claim that there is a growing and desirable freedom of information 'like the agora in ancient Greece', and that the impact of the World Wide Web is at least on a par with Guttenburg's invention of the printing press; and it is widely claimed that, at the turn of a new century, we are beginning a new Information Age. The development of IT could be seen as part of a social movement towards post-modernity, offering the potential for decentralization without isolation, 'empowering' the individual and NGOs, opening access to an information superhighway (Bhatnagar and Odedra, 1992; Kenway, 1996). (For information on recent internet use trends and statistics on its growth *see* http://www.internetcenter.state.mn.us/Itn-a.htm.)

If the indecipherable encryption of internet messages becomes established, then higher earners will almost certainly conduct their finances to hide their real income. Encrypted investment and business transactions on the internet could quickly rob governments of much of their tax revenue, and the role of the state would alter drastically worldwide. Given the difficulty of policing the internet or breaking such encryption, it seems a distinct possibility that the power and nature of government will change, and with it the provision of social services, defence, etc. A new 'global free economy' might well emerge within a decade, yet few seem to have investigated the likely impacts (Berry, 1999).

In addition to marked cultural and social impacts, IT is having significant economic effects – for example, offering employment and foreign exchange earning opportunities for developing countries if they can exploit the trend for commerce to 'follow the sun'. This is the situation where a multinational company or large organization sends its computer tasks to a series of facilities in countries that combine cheaper IT services and 24 hour staffing without expensive shiftwork. For example, various developed countries' tax offices send their data-processing, and a number of airlines send their ticketing business, to India (especially Bombay) where skilled computer personnel can undertake the work quickly and cheaply.

Publishing

It is easy to overlook the huge impact that the availability of books has (and has had) upon societies. The invention of printed books made the spread of ideas and the expansion of libraries possible; in Victorian times, lending libraries (fee charging) and then public libraries (non-fee charging) appeared in the UK, Europe and the USA. Assessing the impact of these facilities on society is not easy, but it must have been considerable (Kerslake and Kinnell, 1998). Since the 1930s there has been a huge expansion of relatively cheap paperback books, further facilitating access to literature and information. Some might argue that the last few years have seen increasing globalization and commercial pressures acting to reduce the range of book titles on sale.

Along with cheaper editions, there has been a trend (at least in the West) towards reduced censorship and increased freedom of information (the release of information in the past was much restricted by governments, companies and organizations). This freedom of information trend makes it possible for SIA to gain access to more information than was once the case, and strengthens public demand for consultation and participation in policy-making, planning and development.

Other marked changes, that have had a social impact, have affected publishing over the last few decades: the spread of colour supplements to newspapers, giving advertisers a new and powerful medium; the relaxation of pornography and blasphemy laws in the West; increasing control of newspapers and other news media by multinational and transnational companies; the beginnings of paper-free and rapid electronic publishing. There has been little or no attempt to assess the current or future social impacts of such developments.

Health

The relationship between disease transmission or incidence of an illness, social behaviour, sense of well-being and physical environment can be complex; but enough is now known to make forecasting reasonably reliable for the future occurrence of diseases like malaria, many other mosquito-borne diseases, and also schistosomiasis, Chagas disease, and infections spread by rodents. Other illnesses, especially those resulting at least in part from stress or pollution can be more difficult to predict. As diseases mutate, new habitats are disturbed, pollution occurs and human behaviour shifts, there will always be surprises. Some health impacts are difficult to measure and there may be a long delay between causation and the manifestation of symptoms of ill-health; for example, asbestos contamination may not cause obvious illness for decades.

Some effort is being directed towards establishing the social and economic impacts of ill-health; there have been a number of studies on asthma, migraine, heart disease, cancer, HIV/AIDS and TB (Clarke *et al.*, 1996; Stewart and Lipton, 1994). There has also been the application of impact assessment other than SIA, especially EIA, to health issues (Cooper-Weil *et al.*, 1990; Scott-Samuel, 1996; BMA, 1998). There has been limited use of SIA to help shape health programmes (Birley, 1995; Lerer, 1999; Mitchell and Mitchell, 1979). Recently, health impact assessment seems to be separating out from EIA and SIA as a discrete field.

Another aspect of healthcare is innovation. As new techniques, technology and funding become available there are social and economic impacts. Taxation may have to be increased in order to pay for sophisticated new medical care; people may be reluctant to settle in areas with relatively poor healthcare; there may be rising expectation of increasingly expensive treatment (Maloney, 1989). Health care clients are also changing. In western countries the last decade has seen a growing trend towards litigation by those dissatisfied with treatment, together with a greater mistrust of, and lack of respect for, medical personnel. Changes like these can have a huge impact on how healthcare services operate, as well as on costs, so any forecasting would be welcome.

Epidemics

Some of the earliest 'social impact studies' focus on the effects of serious disease outbreaks. There are Roman accounts of people's reaction to the plague, and Defoe's detailed account of the physical, social, psychological and economic effects of the plague on London in 1665 should be compulsory reading for all urban epidemiologists or health planners (Defoe, 1986).

Ageing

Ageing, or 'greying' (as the media often term it) is a global trend that has become especially obvious in certain countries and regions. The NGO HelpAge International published a report on the issues involved (Anon., 1999a and 1999b), and there have been calls for a world summit meeting to address ageing. The percentage of over-65s (predominantly women) is growing in most developed countries; and, in some developing countries, there is now increasing survival of the elderly. In developed countries many of the aged have made little provision for pensions and most developing countries have little funding for the elderly, who seldom have income other than from their families. There are increasingly signs of a breakdown of once-supportive family traditions and respect for the aged. The situation is worrying in a number of developed countries, both in relation to the plight of the elderly and the burden on the rest of the population.

In developed countries, with the decline in labour force numbers, and greatly increased demands on public expenditure for healthcare and state pensions (Crimmins, 1986; Krivo and Chaatsmith, 1990; Peters, 1991; Restrepo and Rozental, 1994), the working-age cohort is having to pay progressively more for those currently drawing state support. They will increasingly be called upon to do so, and if inflation eats into what they can put aside, the consequence will be that they have less to save for themselves. (There is a widespread misunderstanding in the UK that current tax payers are investing for their future, in reality they are paying for current pensioners, and there are unlikely to be sufficient people of working age to pay for them in the future.) As there will be progressively fewer people of working age, this cohort will probably, then, receive less support when its turn comes – the 'intergenerational bargain' is effectively breaking down. Recently a UK Government spokesperson proposed raising the retirement age from 65 to 70 to try to ease the burden of large numbers of retired people on the national budget; those paying for the current cohort of pensioners may have to wait longer for their own retirement (and many may not live to enjoy it).

While care must be taken to avoid anti-aged bias, there are predictions that wage earners will experience a relative decline in income, and that greying may cause the standard of living in western countries (and Japan) to decrease (Dewulf and Becker, 1993: 227). Greying demands careful SIA to try to minimize any negative impacts and to maximize possible positive impacts. However, assessment has to cope with uncertainties: while mortality forecasts are considered relatively reliable, fertility and migration forecasts are less accurate; there may also be medical innovations, such as an effective treatment for Alzheimer's disease, that reduce elderly people's healthcare problems and costs, so the impact of greying is not easy to forecast.

There may well be more subtle and far-reaching impacts of greying. Governments, the media and commerce increasingly cater for, and play the tune favoured by, grey voters and consumers; a possible consequence is resistance to crucial long-term investments in education, infrastructure, environmental protection and defence, through conscious or unconscious inertia (Restrepo and Rozental, 1994).

Mental health

Social conditions play a significant role in mental health. Stress leads to more breakdowns, suicides, antisocial behaviour, and probably to reduced resistance to physical illness. In the West the response to mental illness and stress has often been to prescribe drugs. In countries like the USA and UK medication is being used to control disruptive primary school children, and the use of anti-depressants by adults has become a cause for concern. Some of these treatments seem to have spread faster than the ability or willingness to assess the impacts. The same is true of some social changes; for example, the restriction of freedom of certain social groups, such as children prevented from playing outside due to parental fear of traffic or paedophiles.

Urbanization and health

The growth of cities has some positive and many negative impacts. The urban concentration of people can make it possible to have sophisticated hospitals, along with their support services and research institutes for the study of health problems. Provided that the many forms of pollution associated with urban living are adequately countered, a city can be a relatively healthy environment; however, rapid population growth, especially in poor countries, means that this is not always possible. In too many urban areas, the air is polluted, the available domestic water supply is contaminated, sewage and vermin may be difficult to avoid, refuse disposal is unsatisfactory, and noise and overcrowding are rife. People who are unemployed, under-employed or poorly paid, and many city folk, fall into these categories and cannot afford a sufficiently healthy lifestyle. The health problems of urbanization are thus often related to poverty and rapid, poorly planned, city growth, rather than urbanization *per se* (Stephens, 1996).

HIV/AIDS

One of the growing problems of the late twentieth and early twenty-first centuries is human immuno-deficiency virus (HIV), precursor to acquired immuno-deficiency syndrome (AIDS) (known as SIDA in Francophone and Spanish-, Portuguese- and Italian-speaking countries). In excess of 33 million worldwide people are already affected. In a number of countries there are huge numbers of people debilitated by the disease, and this, in turn, affects labour availability, results in loss of family livelihood as breadwinners fall ill, causes increased numbers of orphans, and diverts money from other uses in the health services, education and environmental care (Armstrong, 1991; Barnett and Blaikie, 1992; Danziger, 1994; Fitzsimons *et al.*, 1997; Walraven *et al.*, 1996).

During the last decade there has been a great deal of research on the impacts of HIV/AIDS, much of which is retrospective or 'stock-taking'. One estimate was that, by AD 2000, more than 13 million children would have been orphaned by AIDS in sub-Saharan Africa (*The Times* (UK), 2/12/99: 21). In some developing countries the prevalence of HIV infection is worryingly high; for example, in Rwanda by 1994 over 30 per cent of urban adults had the disease. Rwanda is by no means unique, so clearly the social and economic impact is substantial and growing (Keogh *et al.*, 1994).

There is a large and expanding literature on the psychological (Tolley *et al.*, 1995; VandeWalle, 1990), social and economic impacts of AIDS (Johnson, 1989). SIA can be used to assess the impact of HIV/AIDS on societies and economies, and to establish the mental health and other important characteristics of patients in order to help improve their chances of survival and quality of life. (This sort of information enables the more efficient provision of treatment and support.) In some countries HIV/AIDS has led (and may still lead) to discrimination against homosexuals in reaction to what was perceived as an affliction largely restricted to that group. Worldwide, the disease is impacting upon immigration controls (with sufferers and intravenous drug users unlikely to be admitted by countries fearful of their spreading the infection and becoming a burden on health and welfare services), on insurance company procedures and premium charges, and to a varying extent on moral behaviour and usage of barrier methods of contraception.

HIV testing is spreading, and studies show how different practices and policies yielding similar test results can have very different social impacts (Danziger, 1999); there has been some attempt to assess future HIV/AIDS social impact scenarios (Jager and Ruitenberg, 1992). Recent controversial studies of some African populations suggest that there are strong social controls of HIV/AIDS transmission, notably the possibility that circumcision may reduce the risk of infection.

Reproduction issues

In recent years, western media have published many articles on technological innovations and new habits that affect human reproduction. The greatest impact since the 1960s has been the spread of oral contraception in many countries; this has affected relations between the sexes and career development for women, to the extent that there have been claims that it represents one of the most significant developments of the twentieth century. There have been intermittent scares following media release of research reports on the side-effects of 'the pill', and more recently implanted forms of hormonal contraceptives. There is a vital need to establish more effectively why some 'at risk' groups, notably teenagers, fail to make use of available contraception and means of reducing AIDS transmission. Japan recently lifted a ban on the widespread use of oral contraception; if this results in a decline in the use of barrier methods there may be implications for HIV/AIDS transmission. It would be useful to conduct SIA to establish the likely effects of such changes in legislation.

Biotechnology can already facilitate easy prediction of the sex of a foetus soon after conception, or even make it possible for this to be reliably 'engineered'; such activity could have enormous social and economic impacts. The same could be said of the introduction of genetic testing for inherited traits and susceptibility to diseases (Davidson *et al.*, 1994), and the possibility of cloning and other gene manipulation. SIA could be applied to these issues to predict likely trends and prompt the development of controls, laws and ethics, before problems become too serious.

Another potential problem is that water and food in many countries appears to have been contaminated by chemicals that can accumulate in wildlife and humans and have a 'gender-bending' effect. Put crudely, insidious background pollution – possibly from butyltins and pharmaceutical hormones used on livestock, polychlorinatedbiphenyls (PCBs) and sewage contaminated with oral contraceptives, plastic manufacture, plastic food wrappers, PVC pipes, paint and possibly pesticide contamination – is leading to lower human sperm counts, or to fewer male births, and may be difficult to reverse. Lower sperm counts may also reflect other modern developments, such as clothing fashions, diet, rising alcohol consumption and so on. There have been signs, too, that wildlife in several countries has suffered gender-bending effects, and several nations have average human sperm counts today that are a fraction of those in the 1950s.

Environmental change and health

There are examples from the past of climatic change appearing to have a serious effect on human well-being. The extinction of the Greenland Viking settlements between the ninth and eleventh centuries AD is an example that has been well researched. Poor harvest of vital winter animal feed, resulting from cold summer conditions, gradually killed off the Greenland settlers, who had failed to adapt as well as the Inuit peoples. Environmental impacts on health are often more subtle and difficult to recognize until they are well under way. One may divide environmental change into that caused by wholly natural factors, and that triggered by human activity. The latter includes global warming and reduction of stratospheric ozone, which present potentially serious challenges to human health. Separating natural and human causes is often difficult: the Greenlanders probably met their demise because of cultural factors which hindered adaptation, rather than simply extreme climate; in dry lands, drought may be blamed on a decline in precipitation, when it has more to do with poor land husbandry. The literature on the health impacts of global environmental change is expanding fast; for an introduction *see* the 1990 special issue of *Environmental Impact Assessment Review* **10(4)** which offers a review of 'Environmental change and public health in the next fifty years'.

Serious health impacts have been associated with land development, especially through the degradation of forest cover and the spread of irrigation; e.g. outbreaks of malaria, yellow fever or schistosomiasis. Another cause of health problems has been the intentional and inadvertent transport of organisms that cause, spread or harbour disease.

Major diseases outbreaks – for example, schistosomiasis and malaria – are often triggered by irrigation, hydroelectric development or the use of agrochemicals that alter the alkalinity of water bodies or destroy the predators that control disease vectors. Given the huge sums spent on large dams and irrigation schemes over the last few decades, the associated health problems have attracted less impact assessment than one might expect (Renshaw *et al.*, 1998). This possibly reflects the fact that it is mainly impoverished people that are affected, and they are unlikely to be able to pay much for medication, so pharmaceutical companies, state health authorities and health research institutes can see little chance of a return on any research investment. Nevertheless, the socio-economic impact of environmental change, and of natural resources exploitation and land development, is huge: people and economies are debilitated, land husbandry is damaged, food production is held back, and the misery generated is considerable (Farooq, 1963; Stanley and Alpers, 1975). It may take social assessment to show that the gains to be had from the government subsidy of medication justify intervention.

Effective immunization against smallpox has had enormous social impact. What is often overlooked is that smallpox was easy to overcome compared with many of the diseases that are currently causing misery. There are signs that polio can be controlled, and the treatment of river blindness (onchocerciasis), a disease often made more prevalent by environmental disturbance, will improve in the next decade – developments that could have considerable socio-economic impacts.

Global environmental change is likely to affect health and alter demands for healthcare in the future (McMichael *et al.*, 1998). The most far-reaching impacts of environmental change are likely to be through global warming. Malaria incidence could well shift, as could other mosquito and fly-borne diseases (e.g. dengue). For example, in Africa sleeping sickness could spread to new areas even if there is only slight warming as tsetse flies alter their range. The patterns of these shifts should be predictable from known distributions of disease vectors, human populations and forecasts of climate change; what the likely socio-economic effects could be is something that deserves better research.

Healthcare provision

A crucial factor in improving public well-being is health education; eating habits, hygiene, childcare and many other things can be improved through this if problems are adequately assessed and suitable measures tailored to needs. Considerable advances have been made thanks to the wide adoption of immunization and other public health measures; between the 1940s and 1970s the UK and USA went a good way towards controlling and even eliminating diseases such as TB, polio, measles, diphtheria, and several others that only a few decades earlier had taken a huge toll. But now, in the twenty-first century, TB and a number of other conquered diseases have returned to cities in Europe and the USA, in some cases in a virulent and drug-resistant form. The reasons for this are diverse: drug-resistant bacteria, patients failing to complete treatment, migration, poor and overcrowded living conditions. Those infected or at risk may have inadequate diets or AIDS, are often using narcotics or are alcoholic, and thus have depressed immunity. SIA could help health authorities track down and ensure the treatment of carriers, and raise the rate of immunization of vulnerable groups.

Reports of cases of adverse reaction to vaccines against measles, whooping cough, chickenpox and the like have led some parents to avoid immunizing their children; others may be too feckless to seek available vaccination. This is making it difficult for health authorities to achieve satisfactory control or eradication even though effective vaccines are available. To develop the best strategies to tackle these diseases, it is important to understand how the target groups behave and react to healthcare; SIA is a tool that can help.

Without careful social impact assessment it can be difficult to judge the effectiveness of past, let alone future, healthcare developments. Some problems may be under-rated without impact assessment. What socio-economic impacts do illnesses like migraine, rheumatic diseases, epilepsy, backache, or asthma have on individuals, society and institutions (for instance, in terms of lost labour)?

Some aspects of healthcare are affected by fashion, employment practices and political ideology. There may be marked changes in the administration of treatments: for instance, caesarean deliveries (Chu, 1990); hospital, rather than home births; an increase or decline in breast-feeding; smoking; drinking alcohol or coffee. SIA can assist in the prediction of healthcare demands, the design of health education, shaping public relations programmes, policy formulation and healthcare targeting, deciding the way in which future immunization and other healthcare will be delivered, and predicting the impact of changed healthcare provision (Wong and Chiu, 1997). In particular, for problems like fighting AIDS, a prediction of the responses of various cultures and social groups can be extremely important. Given the frequent changes in public attitudes, and the appearance of new technology and health problems, SIA must be used for healthcare in a dynamic and adaptive manner.

Hospital closures and other health service changes

Health services have been cut in a number of countries as a consequence of debt, or economies required as part of structural adjustment measures (*see* Chapter 11). In the UK, USA and Europe, and increasingly in other countries, there has also been a move to privatize public utilities and introduce management practices that seek economies and 'rationalization'. The UK moved some years ago to closure of some of its mental health care institutions and long-stay hospitals, in favour of a policy of care in the community. It was hoped that this would result in as good or better access to healthcare at lower costs; and, because it is provided locally, the patients would be relatively free to mix with the community and become less 'institutionalized'. In practice some of those who would have been reasonably cared for in institutions become unhappy, fail to seek or get aid, cease necessary medication, and may even become a danger to themselves and others (Barr and Huxley, 1999). The public may become worried by what is seen as a threat from people they are used to seeing institutionalized, and there has been strong resistance to the relocation of sex offenders, mental health patients, and those undergoing alcohol or narcotics rehabilitation. Those resettled from institutions to which they have become attached may suffer serious physical and mental trauma, even if the new care offered is good. The relocation of elderly patients may result in increased illness and mortality rates.

Large projects and health

The dislocation of people by large developments is considered in Chapter 8, the effects of natural resources development is covered in Chapter 11. The impacts of large dams and irrigation schemes has generated a significant proportion of all SIAs (Brinkmann *et al.*, 1988; Cooper-Weil *et al.*, 1990; Lerer and Scudder, 1999; Myaux *et al.*, 1997; N'Goran *et al.*, 1997). These developments share much in common with other, often hurriedly executed, poorly planned, expensive and inflexible developments.

Gambling

Gambling can adversely affect health, law and order, and welfare. It can also be harnessed to support tourism, healthcare provision and tax revenue generation. Gambling is big business for many countries, and governments often support and encourage its development to attract tourists and generate tax revenue. Its impact on health and social behaviour can be marked and is seldom adequately assessed. In the UK the National Lottery has had both good and bad effects (McKee and Sassi, 1995), but there seems to have been little effort to assess these or predict future effects.

References

Anon. (1999a) *Ageing & Development Newsletter* (Help the Aged, issue No. 3). HelpAge, London.

Anon. (1999b) *The Ageing & Development Report: poverty, interdependence and the world's older people* (a report produced by HelpAge International). Earthscan, London.

Armstrong, J. (1991) Socioeconomic implications of AIDS in developing countries. *Finance and Development* **28(4)**, 14–17.

Barnett, T. and **Blaikie, P.** (1992) *AIDS in Africa: its present and future impact*. Belhaven, London.

Barr, W. and **Huxley, P.** (1999) The impact of community health reform on service users: a cohort study. *Health & Social Care in the Community* **7(2)**, 129–39.

Berry, A. (1999) *The Great Leap: mankind heads for the stars*. Headline (Hodder), London.

Bhatnagar, S.C. and **Odedra, M.** (eds) (1992) *Social Implications of Computers in Developing Countries*. Tata McGraw-Hill Publishing, New Delhi.

Birley, M.H. (1995) *The Health Impact Assessment of Development Projects* (Liverpool School of Tropical Medicine, Health Impact Programme Monograph). HMSO, London.

BMA (1998) *Health and Environmental Impact Assessment*. Earthscan, London.

Bogdanowicz, M. (1997) The social impacts of telecom liberalisation in Europe. The productivity gains hypothesis: how do corporate users react? *Telematics and Informatics* **14(4)**, 357–63.

Brinkmann, U.K., Korte, R. and **Schmidt-Ehry, B.** (1988) The distribution and spread of schistosomiasis in relation to water resources development in Mali. *Tropical Medicine and Parasitology* **39(2)**, 182–5.

Chapman, S. and **Schofield, W.N.** (1998) Lifesavers and samaritans: emergency use of cellular (mobile) phones in Australia. *Accident Analysis & Prevention* **30(6)**, 815–19.

Chu, C.M. (1990) The need for social impact assessment of reproductive technology: the case of caesarean birth in Taipei. *Environmental Impact Assessment Review* **19(1–2)**, 16–174.

Clarke, C.E., MacMillan, L., Sondhi, S. and **Wells, N.E.J.** (1996) Economic and social impact of migraine. *QJM – Monthly Journal of the Association of Physicians* **89(1)**, 77–84.

Cooper-Weil, D.E., Alicbusan, A.P., Wilson, J.F., Reich, M.R. and **Bradley, D.J.** (1990) *The Impact of Development Policies on Human Health: a review of the literature.* World Health Organization, Geneva.

Crimmins, E.M. (1986) The social impact of recent and prospective mortality declines among older Americans. *Sociology and Social Research* **70(3)**, 192–9.

Danziger, R. (1994) The social impact of AIDS in developing countries. *Social Science and Medicine* **39(7)**, 905–17.

Danziger, R. (1999) The social impact of HIV testing: a comparative analysis of Britain and Sweden. *Social Science and Medicine* **48(3)**, 293–300.

Davidson, C., Macintyre, S. and **Smith, G.D.** (1994) The potential social impact of predictive genetic testing for susceptibility to common chronic diseases: a review and proposed research agenda. *Sociology of Health & Illness* **16(3)**, 340–71.

Davis, D.M. (1993) Social impact of cellular telephone usage in Hawaii, in J.G. Savage and D.J. Wedemeyer (eds), *Proceedings of the Pacific Telecommunications Council Fifteenth Annual Conference* (Vols 1 and 2). PTC, Honolulu (HI), 641–8.

Dechert, C.R. (ed.) (1966) *The Social Impact of Cybernetics.* University of Notra Dame Press, London (IN).

Defoe, D. (1986) *A Journal of the Plague Year* (Penguin Classics edn). Penguin, Harmondsworth.

Dewulf, G. and **Becker, H.A.** (1993) Cohort replacement in industrialised and developing countries: a social impact assessment. *Project Appraisal* **8(4)**, 225–30.

Diamond, J. (1991) *The Rise and Fall of the Third Chimpanzee: how our animal heritage affects the way we live.* Radius Books, London.

Domatob, J.K., Ausmus, W.A. and **Butler, J.M.** (1996) New communications in tropical Africa. *Development in Practice* **6(3)**, 228–39.

Dutton, W.H. (1992) The social impact of emerging telephone services, *Telecommunications Policy* **16(5)**, 377–87.

Ellison, N.B. (1999) Social impacts – new perspectives on telework. *Social Science Computer Review* **17(3)**, 338–56.

Farooq, M. (1963) A possible approach to the evaluation of the economic burden imposed on a community by shistosomiasis. *Annals of Tropical Medicine and Parasitology* **57(4)**, 323–31.

Fitzsimons, D., Hardy, V. and **Tolley, K.** (1997) The economic and social impact of AIDS in Europe. *Journal of Biological Science* **29(1)**, 123–4.

Freude, G., Ullsperger, P., Eggert, S. and **Ruppe, I.** (2000) Microwaves emitted by cellular telephones affect human slow brain potentials. *European Journal of Applied Physiology and Occupational Physiology* **81(1–2)**, 18–27.

Inamasu, T. (1987) Radio cultural impact. *East Asian Cultural Studies* **26(1–4)**, 22–30.

Ito, Si (1987) Cassette and video tape recorders' cultural impact. *East Asian Cultural Studies* **26(1–4)**, 31–42.

Jager, J.C. and **Ruitenberg, E.J.** (1992) *AIDS Impact Assessment*. Elsevier Science, New York (NY).

Johnson, S.S. (1989) AIDS economic, social impact heighten concern. *Journal of the American Medical Association* **261(1)**, 17.

Kenway, J. (1996) The information superhighway and post-modernity: the social promise and the social price. *Comparative Education* **32(2)**, 217–31.

Keogh, P., Allen, S., Almedal, C. and **Temahagili, B.** (1994) The social impact of HIV infection on women in Kigale, Rwanda: a prospective study. *Social Science and Medicine* **38(8)**, 1047–53.

Kerslake, E. and **Kinnell, M.** (1998) Public libraries, public interest and the information society: theoretical issues in the social impact of public libraries. *Journal of Librarianship and Information Science* **30(3)**, 159–67.

Kraut, R., Kiesler, S., Mukhopadhyay, T., Schlerlis, W. and **Patterson, M.** (1998) Social impact assessment of the internet. What does it mean? *Communications of the ACM* **41(12)**, 21–22.

Krivo, L.J. and **Chaatsmith, M.L.** (1990) Social services impact on elderly independent living. *Social Science Quarterly* **71(3)**, 474–91.

Lerer, L.B. (1999) Health impact assessment. *Health Policy and Planning* **14(2)**, 198–203.

Lerer, L.B. and **Scudder, T.** (1999) Health impacts of large dams. *Environmental Impact Assessment Review* **19(2)**, 113–23.

Lucky, R.W. (1984) The social impact of the computer. *Annals of the New York Academy of Sciences* **426(November)**, 1–10.

McKee, M. and **Sassi, F.** (1995) Gambling with the nation's health? The social impact of the National Lottery needs to be researched. *British Medical Journal* **3111(7004)**, 521–2.

McMichael, A.J., Patz, J. and **Kovats, R.S.** (1998) Impacts of global environmental change on future health and health care in tropical countries. *British Medical Bulletin* **54(2)**, 475–88.

Maloney, J.V. (1989) Technology in health care: the social impact and economic cost. *Medical Progress Through Technology* **14(3–4)**, 109–14.

Mitchell, F.H. and **Mitchell, C.C.** (1979) Social impact assessment for healthcare programmes: steps toward a research protocol. *Social Impact Assessment Newsletter* Nos 40–1, 20–9.

Mitomo, H. and **Jitsuzumi, T.** (1999) Impact of telecommuting on mass traffic congestion: the Tokyo case. *Telecommunications Policy* **23(10–11)**, 741–51.

Myaux, J.A., Ali, M., Chakraborty, J. and **de Francisco, A.** (1997) Flood control embankments contribute to the improvement of the health status of children in rural Bangladesh. *Bulletin of the World Health Organization* **75(6)**, 533–9.

N'Goran, E.K., Diabate, S., Utzinger, J. and **Sellin, B.** (1997) Changes in human schistosomiasis levels after the construction of two large hydroelectric dams in Central Cote d'Ivoire. *Bulletin of the World Health Organization* **75(6)**, 541–5.

Okabe, K. (1987) Television cultural impact. *East Asian Cultural Studies* **26(1–4)**, 11–21.

Olszewski, P. and **Mokhtarian, P.** (1994) Telecommuting frequency and impacts for State of California employees. *Technological Forecasting and Social Change* **45(3)**, 275–86.

Perugini, V. (1996) Anytime, anywhere: the social impact of emerging communication technology. *IEEE Transactions on Professional Communication* **39(1)**, 4–15.

Peters, A. (1991) Altere menschen als problemgruppe des arbeitsmarkts. Ein neues phanomen und dessen regionale dimension. *Informationen zur Raumentwiklung* Nos 3–4, 211–20.

Renshaw, M., Birley, M.H., Sang, D.K. and **Silver, J.B.** (1998) A rapid health impact assessment of the Turkwell Gorge hydroelectric dam and proposed irrigation project. *Impact Assessment and Project Appraisal* **16(3)**, 215–26.

Restrepo, H.E. and **Rozental, M.** (1994) The social impact of aging populations: some major issues. *Social Science and Medicine* **39(9)**, 1323–38.

Robinson, J.P., Barth, K. and **Kohut, A.** (1997) Social impact research: personal computers, mass media, and use of time. *Social Science Computer Review* **15(1)**, 65–82.

Rosenberg, R.S. (1997) *The Social Impact of Computers*. Academic Press, San Diego (CA).

Rossini, F.A. and **Porter, A.L.** (1986) A forecast of office automation technology through 2000. *Impact Assessment Bulletin* **4(3–4)**, 81–98.

Santini, R. (1999) Les telephones cellulaires et leurs stations relais: risques pour la sante? *Presse Medicale* **28(34)**, 1884–6.

Schumann, G. (1984) The macroeconomic and microeconomic social impact of advanced computer technology. *Futures* **16(3)**, 260–85.

Schwab, U. (1995) The information highway and its social impact. *Nachrichten für Documentation* **45(5)**, 293–301.

Scott-Samuel, H. (1996) Health impact assessment (editorial). *British Medical Journal* **313(7051)**, 183–4.

Silver, G.A. (1979) *The Social Impact of Computers*. Harcourt, Brace Jovanovich, New York (NY).

Stanley, N.F. and **Alpers, M.P.** (eds) (1975) *Man-made Lakes and Human Health*. Academic Press, London.

Stephens, C. (1996) Healthy cities or unhealthy islands? The health and social implications of urban inequality. *Environment and Urbanization* **8(2)**, 9–30.

Stewart, W.F. and **Lipton, R.B.** (1994) The economic and social impact of migraine. *European Neurology* **34(5)**, 12–17.

Szyperski, N.E.G., Richter, U. and **Weitz, W.P.** (eds) (1983) *Assessing the Impacts of Information Technology: hope to escape the negative effects of an information society by research*. International Publishing Services Inc., New York (NY).

Tolley, K., Hardy, V. and **Fitzsimons, D.W.** (eds) (1995) *The Economic and Social Impact of AIDS in Europe*. Cassell, London.

Tonn, B.E. (1996) Global society and information technology: social science challenges in the 21st century. *Social Science Computer Review* **14(1)**, 78–80.

US Dept of Transportation (1993) *Transportation Implications of Telecommuting*. US Government Printing Office, Washington (DC).

VandeWalle, E. (1990) The social impact of AIDS in sub-Saharan Afirica. *Milbank Quarterly* **68(1)**, 10–32.

Walraven, G., Nicholl, A., Njau, M. and **Timaeus, I.** (1996) The impact of HIV–1 infection on child health in sub-Saharan Africa: the burden on the health services. *Tropical Medicine and International Health* **1(1)**, 3–14.

Wong, V.C.W. and **Chiu, S.W.S.** (1997) Health-care reforms in the People's Republic of China: strategies and social implications. *International Journal of Public Sector Management* **10(1–2)**, 76–92.

11

SIA IN PRACTICE: ECONOMIC AND POLITICAL CHANGE

Economists and politicians have long been interested in retrospective impact studies of policies such as fiscal policy tax reform, trade agreements and economic reform. Economic disasters such as the Great Depression, and more recent stock market crashes, have also attracted attention. Better understanding of past changes aids forecasting. Obviously, an economist or politician who can avoid unpopular and damaging policies and accidents is in a very advantageous position. Being a little less cynical, most governments and businesses want to serve their supporters and/or shareholders as best they can, and so seek to understand how economic impacts develop and what the social consequences may be. Economists have tried to predict economic developments using tools like export base theory, location theory and central place theory (Leistritz and Murdock, 1981: 19–61). Booth (1999) has tried to assess the social impact of the Asian economic crisis of 1997–8, including its effects on employment, social welfare, social security, poverty and so on.

There have been repeated calls for established or modified forms of cost–benefit analysis (CBA) to be used to aid impact assessment (Conopask and Reynolds, 1981; Hundloe *et al.*, 1990). Another approach is to adopt a regional focus for assessment of social and economic impacts (Bell and Hazell, 1980; Bell and Slade, 1982). It is important not only to assess the immediate (on-site) socio-economic impacts of development – say an irrigation scheme – but also to explore its impact on the surrounding region (off-site) and over a longer period. The assessment of socio-economic and economic impacts has been examined by Cantor *et al.* (1985), Halstead *et al.* (1984), Murdock *et al.* (1986), Scholten and Post (1999), and Tassey (1999).

A point made by Cooper (1983: 84–8) is that information available for predictive economic assessment is seldom complete or reliable. There may be an absolute or a relative lack of information, the former when something is new or not understood fully by science. Any assessment of what people are willing to pay to support or oppose a proposal reflects their perception; for example, if they are not aware there is likely to be a toxic emission from a site they may not invest much in protest. With poor public dissemination of information, traditional welfare economics based on the concept of 'pareto optimality' is difficult. Given the uncertainties involved in seeking to assess economic impacts in advance, approaches like the Delphi technique (*see* Chapters 6 and 4) may be the best option.

Johnston (1999) explored the social impact assessment of micro-economic policy reform in Australia, including the privatization of public utilities, and presented notes on how to test policy proposals for their economic impact. One aspect that emerged from Johnston's studies was the need to ensure that assessment includes consideration of 'access equity' (i.e. that those affected by reforms vary in their ability to pay for things). Micro-finance programmes and institutions are increasingly important in development but knowledge about their impact is partial and debated; Hulme (1999) has tried to address this gap.

A research method known as generational accounting has been developed with the aim of enhancing SIA and demographic impact assessment. This involves estimating net tax payments for typical members of each generation: past, present and future (at current rates). These estimates may then be used by those seeking sustainable development or interested in equity issues between various sections of society (Auerbach *et al.*, 1998).

SIA AND BUSINESS

Clearly there are several ways in which business can adopt SIA:

- use it as a tool to reduce public opposition, and reassure governments and NGOs without seriously considering modification, let alone abandonment, of goals
- genuine use of SIA as a way of guiding development, to suggest improvements and to identify problems in advance
- as a way of assessing the likely cost of a proposal or accident, e.g. establishing the 'social' cost of something like the *Exxon Valdez* oil spill.

There has been a growing interest in corporate social responsibility and SIA (D'Amore, 1978; McPhail and Davy, 1998), and corporate use of SIA has been examined by Sawyer (1979). The concept of 'corporate social responsibility' has been aired since the mid-nineteenth century; some Victorian industrialists in the UK undertook 'social engineering', in part to ensure a more content, healthy, placid and controllable workforce; this was achieved via the establishment of company housing, education, healthcare, pensions and insurance (e.g. the creation of Bournville or Port Sunlight). Similarly, Krupp in Germany had made similar moves in the 1840s.

Simply providing employee benefits may, however, ultimately increase dependency; at worst this may mean reliance on company housing, welfare and leisure facilities which tend to be withdrawn if employees are made redundant or retire, or the business fails or cuts back. Since the 1970s there has been a growing acceptance that business has a responsibility to society as a whole, not just to shareholders and employees. Some companies are now corporate sponsors of various charities, via college endowments, prizes for environmental or literary activity, sports activities, research and so on.

In a free-enterprise society many would argue that business cannot operate in isolation and must seek to benefit all; so, interest in SIA is not just prompted by an interest in avoiding litigation, if unwanted impacts arise, or a desire to cultivate good public relations. If this is the case, concern for social costs must be incorporated into business obligations; as Adlai Stevenson said: 'Like it or not, the business of the modern corporation is society' (Stevenson, 1960: 156). There are various ways in which corporate social responsibility can be encouraged and supported: members of the public can be represented on a company's management board; a company can be prompted or required by a government to undertake social accounting or social auditing (*see* Chapter 1); government on behalf of society can encourage or force business to conduct its affairs in a socially responsible way through regulation, taxation and licensing. The process is two-way – society makes the rules and business must respond – but business is often powerful enough to lobby government, and can use advertising and public relations to shift and manipulate public opinion.

SIA can provide business and society with a proactive view, so that regulations can be developed or adjusted in good time, and opportunities researched and followed up. Nowadays, business is often transnational – company policies affect many countries and the global stage, although the impacts may well not be the same everywhere. SIA could be applied to this issue more frequently than at present.

Changes in retailing

In North America and Europe in particular there has been a marked shift in retailing, away from small specialist urban high-street shops to out-of-town supermarkets and mail-order shopping. During the last decade, in the USA and UK, there has been a massive investment in grouping supermarkets and chain-store outlets, often under one roof (known in the USA as a mall). This has had considerable impact on shopping and recreational habits, with shopping becoming more of a hobby than a chore. Spending habits have been altered and large stores have increased control of the market. Unfortunately, for those without cars, access to these new shopping facilities may be problematic and access to alternative shopping may be difficult. Urban areas may decline and become run-down as spending shifts to these shopping centres.

There is clearly a need for greater application of SIA to retail decentralization and its related changes.

The promotion of new livelihoods

The promotion of small industries, improvement of agriculture and so on attracts considerable funding and effort from aid agencies, governments and NGOs. When things take off, this sort of investment can grow and promote wider regional development (Pernia and Pernia, 1986). An example of the successful promotion of innovation has been the spread in West Africa of stone-lines as an appropriate technology to facilitate improved agricultural production, security of harvest and better soil conservation. Initially promoted by a few NGOs, this approach has subsequently spread spontaneously and is improving agriculture even in remote areas where aid agencies have had limited contact (Atampugre, 1993). It would be very useful if SIA and TA could identify the factors that help an innovation succeed and spread, and were used more widely for this purpose.

An innovation or approach that can have considerable impact is the formation of a co-operative; in rural areas this may prove to be crucial for supporting the transport and marketing of produce, giving access to equipment, seeds and other inputs, and providing supportive agricultural research (Mishra, 1994). Often, a co-operative provides sufficient cohesion for a group of farmers or workers in other fields to survive and prosper. A co-operative may be needed to allow small producers to standardize their product, maintain reasonable quality control and compete with other, possibly larger, producers (Mishra, 1994). The socio-economic impacts can be enormous, something realized by even the earliest pioneers (like Robert Owen), some of whom felt that a radically new social order and much improved livelihoods could be achieved through co-operatives. A co-operative approach to lifestyle and livelihood has been widely adopted in Israel through the kibbutz system. Alas, as Owen discovered when his early nineteenth-century co-operative communities failed, establishing a successful co-operative may not be easy; SIA might be used to assist.

SIA AND INFLATION, DEBT, RETRENCHMENT, SECTOR REFORM AND STRUCTURAL ADJUSTMENT

Anyone who collects stamps sooner or later comes across German postage stamps issued during the inter-war years whose face value has been altered from a few pfennig to millions of marks; there can be few more impressive indicators of the impact of sustained monetary inflation, and it is easy to imagine from this the misery and chaos people must have suffered. A number of countries have suffered ongoing, often 'super'-inflation, since the 1960s with a marked impact on their societies (Ryan, 1982). One example has been Brazil, where a banknote that would pay for room and board in a good hotel in 1981 only sufficed for a couple of coffees by 1985. People try to adapt to this sort of inflation, spending and investment habits alter, many live by their wits and the black market is likely to flourish; there may even be a return to unofficial forms of trade that circumvent the national currency. Those on low and fixed incomes find inflation it difficult – in the former USSR pensioners and many others are now in dire straits. In the long term, such inflation can undermine social cohesion, trigger political unrest and generally destabilize things – it is worth noting that many of the over-printed (i.e. re-priced to match inflation) 1930s German postage stamps bore the image of Adolph Hitler.

Since the 1970s a number of countries have run into serious debt repayment problems. This has serious implications both for debtor country, regional economies and possibly the world economy (Bultena and Stewart, 1990; Ghai and DeAlcantara, 1990; Marshall, 1992; Potts and Mutambirwa, 1998). There have been attempts to assess the social impacts of retrenchment policies (Seley and Wolpert, 1985), one approach used has been SEA (*see* the discussion of strategic environmental assessment in Chapter 3).

One response to debt has been the promotion of structural adjustment. Since the early 1980s there have been numerous studies of the impact of structural adjustment on the economies, and on the working and lower-middle classes in developing countries, most of these retrospective (Please, 1996). Some of these studies have moved on to suggest responses that might reduce future problems (Gutierrez-Santos, 1995). The main impact of structural adjustment has been the contraction of public spending (through reduction of public services, privatization of public-owned institutions and a shift from controlled to free market), 'austerity measures' which include the ending of subsidies for agricultural inputs and extension services, cuts to health and social services provision, reduction of employment opportunities and promotion, and frequently stagnant or even reduced wages. Such impacts result in the failure to meet traditional family commitments, which may mean that the poor and elderly suffer, farming may be neglected, school drop-out rates rise, and prostitution and crime rates increase. Structural adjustment has helped trigger rural–urban migration in a number of countries, swelling the ranks of the squatter settlements, and causing environmental degradation and misery in the countryside (Bijlmakers *et al.*, 1996; Meagher, 1997).

Predicting the socio-economic impacts of policy measures like structural adjustment is not easy, although it has been tried at the regional level (using input–output analysis techniques such as the Leontieff matrix) (McDonald, 1990; Miller and Blair, 1985). There are indications that adjustment has had more beneficial social impact where the country has preserved budgetary allocations for priority social expenditure, such as primary education and basic healthcare (World Bank, 1995). However, if sustainable development is to be achieved, the impacts of policies like structural adjustment must be assessed and suitable measures taken as early as possible (Abaza, 1996). The EU is keen to establish what pattern future rural–urban migration will have in eastern Europe, the Balkans, and parts of Africa and southern Asia, in order to assess to what extent it will result in immigration into Europe, and whether there would be socio-economic impacts. Structural adjustment is seen by some to be a serious threat to environmental quality as well as livelihoods, and hence a hindrance to any hope of sustainable development, unless it is carefully managed.

In the EU, changes in agricultural subsidies can have a huge socio-economic impact. Recently in the UK small dairy farmers and those working landholdings in upland areas have found their incomes falling as subsidies have altered, and as a consequence of BSE. There should be better assessment of such changes to help the agricultural sector adjust, and to identify the best choice of aid in order to implement it before things get too bad.

Political and economic changes

For many practitioners, SIA is a political process, or one very much influenced by politicians (*see* Chapter 3). While some assessments focus on the impacts of political change, many more are subtly, and even sometimes blatantly, affected by politics (Craig, 1990).

Since the mid-1980s a number of former socialist centralized economies have been transformed (and as a consequence there has been marked political and social change), or are in the process of transforming, in most cases adopting types of free market economy; these countries include Poland, Bulgaria, Slovakia, Hungary, the former USSR and the People's Republic of China. There have been marked socio-economic impacts associated with these changes for the bulk of the populations, unfortunately many of them negative (Adam, 1996; Clark and Soulsby, 1998; Gumpel, 1996; Stoyanov, 1997; Toth, 1992; Zagorsky, 1993). Xing (1999) examined the impact of transformation in China from Mao's socialism to Deng's economic marketization, not surprisingly concluding that an ideological system is important in determining the outcome of social welfare policy. Other countries have suffered serious disruption from warfare or disasters and, although they are not transforming their political and economic systems, have to undergo considerable change as they struggle to reconstruct (Do Duc Dinh, 1995).

The ongoing formation of the EU has had socio-economic impacts; it has also shaped the way in which SIA has developed in Europe and how it has been implemented (Bennington, 1991). During the Second World War and the Cold War it was not uncommon for psychologists to be commissioned to assess the character of key people in opposing camps and try to predict their likely future actions; in all probability this sort of activity continues.

SIA and tax changes

Governments made little real effort in the past to forecast the impacts of tax changes (increases and relaxations), other than making crude efforts to weed out what might cause unpopularity and loss of votes; those studies that have been undertaken have mainly been retrospective (Hamnett, 1997). Measures like the introduction of poll tax in some African colonies in the 1940s and 1950s caused considerable ill-feeling, yet in the UK during the Thatcher Administration (early to mid-1980s) there was a shift from household rates to a poll tax. This proved far more unpopular than most government ministers had expected, a fact that could probably have been predicted. Today, greater efforts are made to assess in advance the likely impacts of legislative and taxation changes, using focus groups, public forum discussion and referenda (Hamnett, 1997). Much of this is covered by the subfield of fiscal impact assessment (Burchell and Listockin, 1978).

SIA and the privatization of public services and utilities

Since the mid-1980s there has been a marked trend towards the privatization of those services and utilities that, in the past, were offered by local authorities or state governments. This has been driven by various political and ideological motives, including a desire for less 'state control' or reduction of public expenditure. The World Bank has promoted privatization, and even the eastern bloc has been affected – essentially, privatization has been a global phenomenon. The services affected vary from country to country, but include water, gas and electricity supplies, postal services, telecommunications, healthcare, care of the elderly, railways, social services, pension provision, agricultural research and extension, prisons, and many other things.

The UK has progressed a good way down this path with privatization of part or all of the aforementioned sectors, and there have been considerable social impacts (Ernst, 1996). Other countries, even strongly socialist states like the former USSR and its satellites, are moving towards some degree of privatization. In the UK there has been considerable controversy over the performance of privatized railway systems; telecommunications were privatized in 1984 as, between 1986 and 1991, were the gas and electricity services. Ernst (1994: 3) expressed surprise at how little effort there had been to attempt SIA of privatization, or even retrospective assessment of impacts, although many of the activities play an important part in social welfare.

Some of the negative impacts of privatization include: risk of loss of government control over vital utilities (water, electricity, etc.); a likelihood that the new owner of a utility will pursue profits and possibly offer less of a service for more money; public feeling that something 'they' owned and paid for in taxes has been 'hijacked' by private speculators; confusion as to who provides various services; and difficulties of communication and co-ordination between utility providers (Australian Consumers' Council, 1995; Engler, 1996; Ernst, 1994). The positive impacts may include: better access to funds for development; possible reduced inefficiencies; sale of shares to the public (which aids investment); benefits perceived to come from market competition; and, of course, profits for shareholders and executives. Ernst (1994) cautioned that the full impacts of privatization may take some years to be felt.

There are potential disadvantages in the privatization of research in universities and institutes; it is likely to result in a focus on applied studies and the neglect of pure, 'blue sky' research. Without the latter, long-term progress is unlikely and new opportunities may be missed because they are not seen to have commercial value. Another problem is that academic neutrality may be compromised by the need to reach conclusions that ensure satisfied customers and employers (or funding will be cut) (Pray, 1995). The latter is also a problem when SIA is conducted by non-academic or non-accredited consultants who lack the will or independence to offer unpopular advice. There is also a risk that young researchers will tend to enter only the obviously in-demand (applied) fields, and without security will be reluctant to specialize in potentially 'dead-end' new fields. Demands for relevant college education may mean a shift to key skills and other training, and cut-backs in the sort of education that develops analytical skills, inquisitiveness and initiative. More traditional education may appear to give little immediate benefit, and so loses resources to training. The policy changes focused on these complex issues can swiftly do tremendous good or harm; can SIA forewarn of the pitfalls and highlight desirable outcomes?

SIA AND UNEMPLOYMENT

There have been relatively few predictive SIAs focused on unemployment, although plenty of studies of the impact of unemployment on various groups should make it easier to assess future scenarios (Lovejoy, 1983; Ramsay and Ryman, 1982) (*see* Chapter 8 for a further discussion of unemployment). The effects of unemployment are reasonably well known: the individuals without work suffer deprivation, stress and ill-health; the community may suffer a reduction in services as spending declines; crime and delinquency often increase; and whole communities may lose confidence and hope (Krahn *et al.*, 1985; Walker, 1981). There are situations where a community has abandoned established livelihoods for new, only to have the latter fail. When this takes place the people may have little on which to fall back – for example, where an extractive industry has replaced farming or small-scale fishing (Nance *et al.*, 1994). In some countries, like the USA, Canada and the UK, large-scale (town- or regional-scale) loss of employment, such as the closure of a mine or petrochemical plant, has prompted predictive SIA to try to optimize re-employment, retraining, relocation and so on (Neil *et al.*, 1992) (*see* the discussion of boomtowns in Chapter 8).

Trade agreements

There have been attempts to assess the likely future impacts of trade agreements; for example, the General Agreement of Tariffs and Trade (GATT), the North American Free Trade Agreement (NAFTA) (Wirth, 1992) and the New Zealand and Australian Free Trade Agreement (Flores, 1992). Generally, these agreements are under negotiation, and often well advanced before there is any in-depth assessment, so SIA can neither really shape the discussion nor determine what is agreed.

References

Abaza, H. (1996) Integration of sustainability objectives in structural adjustment programmes using strategic environmental management. *Project Appraisal* **11(4)**, 217–28.

Adam, J. (1996) Social costs of transformation in the Czech Republic. *MOCT-MOST: Economic Policy in Transitional Economies* **6(2)**, 163–83.

Atampugre, N. (1993) *Behind the Lines of Stone: the social impact of a soil and water conservation project in the Sahel*. Oxfam, Oxford.

Auerbach, A.J., Gokhale, J. and **Kilikoff, L.J.** (1998) Generational accounting: a meaningful way to evaluate fiscal policy. *Journal of Economic Perspectives* **8(1)**, 73–4.

Australian Consumers' Council (1995) *Issues Paper: privatization of utilities. How are consumers affected?* Australian Government Printing Service (AGPS), Canberra.

Bell, C. and **Hazell, P.** (1980) Measuring the indirect effects of an agricultural investment project in the surrounding region. *American Journal of Agricultural Economics* **62(1)**, 75–86.

Bell, C. and **Slade, R.** (1982) *Project Evaluation in Regional Perspective*. Johns Hopkins University Press, Baltimore (MD).

Bennington, J. (1991) The social impact of the single European market: the challenges facing voluntary and community organizations. *Community Development Journal* **26(2)**, 85–95.

Bijlmakers, L.A., Basset, M.T. and **Sanders, D.M.** (1996) *Health and Structural Adjustment in Rural and Urban Zimbabwe* (Uppsala Research Report No. 101). The Scandinavian Institute for African Studies, Uppsala.

Booth, A. (1999) The social impact of the Asian crisis: what do we know two years on? *Asian-Pacific Economic Literature* **13(2)**, 16–29.

Bultena, G.L. and **Stewart, R.** (1990) Impacts of national economic reforms upon urban households in an African society. *Environmental Impact Assessment Review* **10(1–2)**, 209–18.

Burchell, R.W. and **Listockin, D.** (1978) *The Fiscal Impact Handbook*. Center for Urban Policy Research, Rutgers University, New Brunswick (NJ).

Cantor, L.W., Athinston, S.F. and **Leistritz, F.L.** (1985) *Impact of Growth: a guide for socioeconomic impact assessment and planning*. Lewis Publishers, Chelsea (MI).

Clark, E. and **Soulsby, A.** (1998) Organization-community embeddedness: the social impact of enterprise restructuring in the post-communist Czech Republic. *Human Relations* **51(1)**, 25–50.

Conopask, J.V. and **Reynolds, R.R.** (1981) Using cost–benefit analysis in social impact assessment, in K. Finsterbusch and C.P. Wolf (eds), *Methodology of Social Impact Assessment* (2nd edn). Hutchinson Ross, Stroudsburg (PA), 100–7.

Cooper, C. (1983) *Economic Evaluation and the Environment*. Hodder and Stoughton, London.

Craig, D. (1990) Social impact assessment: politically oriented approaches and applications. *Environmental Impact Asessment Review* **10(1)**, 37–55.

D'Amore, L.J. (1978) An executive guide to social impact assessment. *The Business Quarterly* summer 1978, 35–44.

Do Duc Dinh (1995) *The Social Impact of Economic Reconstruction in Vietnam: a selected review.* International Institute for Labour Studies, ILO, Geneva.

Engler, U. (1996) The impact of privatization and change of social security systems upon living conditions of East German households. *Innovation: European Journal of Social Sciences* **9(3)**, 279–314.

Ernst, J. (1994) *Whose Utility? The Social Impact of Public Utility Privatization and Regulation in Britain*. Open University Press, Buckingham.

Flores, M.D. (1992) The social impact: a Mexican commentary, in J.A. McKinney and M.R. Sharpless (eds), *Implications of a North American Free Trade Region: multi-disciplinary perspectives*. Baylor University Program for Regional Studies, Waco (TX), 181–6.

Ghai, D. and **DeAlcantara, C.H.** (1990) The crisis of the 1980s in sub-Saharan Africa, Latin America and the Caribbean: economic impact, social change and political implications. *Development and Change* **21(3)**, 389–426.

Gumpel, W. (1996) Social impact of the economic decline of Russia. *Osteuropa* **46(1)**, 3–12.

Gutierrez-Santos, L.E. (1995) How to deal with the social impact of sector reform. *Pacific and Asian Journal of Energy* **5(2)**, 197–210.

Halstead, J.M., Chase, R.A., Murdock, S.H. and **Leistritz, F.L.** (1984) *Socioeconomic Impact Management: design and implementation*. Westview, Boulder.

Hamnett, C. (1997) A stroke of the Chancellor's pen: the social and regional impact of the Conservatives' 1988 higher rate tax cuts. *Environment and Planning A* **29(1)**, 129–47.

Hulme, D. (1999) *Impact Assessment Methodologies for Microfinance: theory, experience and better practice*. Institute for Development Policy and Management, Manchester University, Manchester (UK).

Hundloe, T., McDonald, G.T., Ware, J. and **Wilks, L.** (1990) Cost-benefit analysis and environmental impact assessment. *Environmental Impact Assessment Review* **10(1–2)**, 55–68.

Johnston, C. (1999) Social impact assessment of microeconomic reform. *Impact Assessment and Project Appraisal* **17(1)**, 9–20.

Krahn, H., Lowe, G.S. and **Tanner, J.** (1985) The social-psychological impact of unemployment in Edmonton. *Canadian Journal of Public Health – Revue Canadienne de Sante Publique* **76(2)**, 88–92.

Leistritz, F.L. and **Murdock, S.H.** (1981) *The Socioeconomic Impact of Resource Development: methods for assessment*. Westview, Boulder.

Lovejoy, S.B. (1983) Employment predictions in social impact assessment: an analysis of some unexplored variables. *Socio-Economic Planning Sciences* **17(2)**, 87–93.

McDonald, G.T. (1990) Regional economic and social impact assessment. *Environmental Impact Assessment Review* **10(1–2)**, 25–36.

McPhail, K. and **Davy, A.** (1998) *Integrating Social Concerns into Private Sector Decisionmaking*. The World Bank, Washington (DC).

Marshall, J. (1992) *War, Debt and Structural Adjustment in Mozambique: the social impact*. North-South Institute, Ottawa.

Meagher, K. (1997) Shifting the imbalance: the impact of structural adjustment on rural-urban population movements in northern Nigeria. *Journal of Asian and African Studies* **32(1–2)**, 81–92.

Miller, R.E. and **Blair, P.** (1985) *Input – Output Analysis: foundations and extensions*. Prentice-Hall, Englewood Cliffs (NJ).

Mishra, A.K. (1994) Social impact of handloom cooperatives on weavers in western Orissa: an empirical study. *Journal of Rural Development* **13(2)**, 259–67.

Murdock, S.H., Leistritz, F.L. and **Hamm, R.R.** (1986) The state of socio-economic impact analysis in the United States: an examination of existing evidence, limitations and opportunities for alternative futures. *Impact Assessment Bulletin* **4(3–4)**, 101–32.

Nance, J.M., Garfield, N.H. and **Paredes, J.A.** (1994) Studying the social impacts of the Texas shrimp closure. *Human Organization* **53(1)**, 88–92.

Neil, C., Tykklainen, M. and **Bradbury, J.** (1992) *Coping with Closure: an international comparison of mine town experiences*. Routledge, London.

Pernia, E.M. and **Pernia, J.M.** (1986) An economic and social impact analysis of small industry promotion: a Philippine experience. *World Development* **14(5)**, 637–51.

Please, S. (1996) The social impact of adjustment operations. *Development Policy Review* **14(2)**, 185–202.

Potts, D. and **Mutambirwa, C.** (1998) 'Basics are now a luxury': perceptions of structural adjustment's impact on rural and urban areas in Zimbabwe. *Environment and Urbanization* **10(1)**, 55–75.

Pray, C.E. (1995) The impact of privatizing agricultural research in Great Britain: an interim report on PBI and ADAS. *Food Policy* **21(3)**, 305–18.

Ramsay, L. and **Ryman, P.** (1982) Health and social costs of unemployment: research and policy considerations. *American Psychologist* **37(10)**, 1116–23.

Ryan, A. (1982) The social impact of year-after-year inflation. *New Society* **59(1008)**, 383–5.

Sawyer, G.C. (1979) *Business and Society: managing corporate social impact assessment*. Houghton Mifflin Co., Boston (NJ).

Sholten, J.J. and **Post, R.A.M.** (1999) Strengthening the integrated approach to impact assessments in development cooperation. *Environmental Impact Assessment Review* **19(3)**, 233–43.

Seley, J.E. and **Wolpert, J.** (1985) The savings harm tableau for social impact assessment of retrenchment policies. *Economic Geography* **61(2)**, 158–71.

Stevenson, A.E. (1960) Businessmen who think greatly, in D.H. Fenn jnr (ed.), *Business Responsibility in Action*. McGraw-Hill, New York (NY), 156.

Stoyanov, A. (1997) Social impact of economic transition in Bulgaria. *Sudosteuropa Aktuell* No. 24, 37–55.

Tassey, G. (1999) Lessons learned about the methodology of economic impact studies: the NIST experience. *Evaluation and Program Planning* **22(1)**, 113–19.

Toth, A. (1992) The social impact of restructuring in rural areas of Hungary: disruption of security or the end of the rural socialist middle class society? *Soviet Studies* **44(6)**, 1039–43.

Walker, A. (1981) South Yorkshire: the economic and social impact of unemployment. *Political Quarterly* **52(1)**, 74–87.

Wirth, J.D. (1992) The cultural impact of a North American Free Trade Agreement: an American perspective, in J.A. McKinney and M.R. Sharpless (eds), *Implications of a North American Free Trade Region: multidisciplinary perspectives*. Baylor University Program for Regional Studies, Waco (TX), 187–94.

World Bank, The (1995) *Social Dimensions of Adjustment: World Bank Experience, 1980–1993*. Operations Evaluation Division, World Bank, Washington (DC).

Xing, L. (1999) The transformation of ideology from Mao to Deng: impact on China's social welfare outcome. *International Journal of Social Welfare* **8(2)**, 86–96.

Zagorsky, A.V. (1993) Cultural impact of the post-perestroika period on Russian economic reforms, in M. Maruyama (ed.), *Management Reform in Eastern and Central Europe: use of pre-communist cultures*. Dartmouth, Aldershot, 3–12.

12

SIA IN PRACTICE: RURAL DEVELOPMENT, LAND DEVELOPMENT, AGRICULTURAL CHANGE AND CONSERVATION, TOURISM AND NATURAL RESOURCES DEVELOPMENT

Rural development

Most countries have a ministry or department responsible for rural development and there is often overlap of its activities with regional planning, natural resources development, forestry, and irrigation and drainage bodies. Rural resource exploitation tends to affect various groups differently – often it is the locals that suffer – although some alert and united communities have managed to control things (e.g. the Shetland Islands, Falkland Islands and several North American Indian Tribes), and affluent outsiders that profit when development takes place (Elkind-Savatsky and Kaufman, 1986). The 'precautionary principle' is becoming increasingly important for development planning and environmental management: whatever the body involved, and regardless of the approach adopted, natural resources exploitation, conservation, agricultural improvement and land development should make more use of impact assessment, including SIA (Campbell, 1990; Christiansen, 1976; De'Ath, 1982; Healing, 1984).

Land development at one extreme can be real estate management in a developed country and, at the other, the implementation of large schemes to settle or relocate developing-country peasant farmers on plots cleared from the forest. There have been efforts to apply SIA to land development since the 1970s (Christiansen, 1976). In practice, it is not easy to apply SIA effectively to land development and agricultural development, because the two are so diverse and are usually affected by complex environmental influences, national socio-economic changes and world economic factors. Accurate forecasting is difficult even for production of a single commodity. The linkages can also be complex and subtle; for example, there is still argument about the causes of famine, which most would have attributed to food availability decline prior to the championing by Sen (1981) of the entitlement theory.

For agricultural development, perhaps more than any other application, SIA must integrate with physical impact assessment (e.g. EIA), economic appraisals and other impact assessments (Hansen and Erbaugh, 1983). The need for such integration with other impact assessment arises because agriculture succeeds only if a complex of factors are right; if just one is inadequate, production falters and may well fail. However, in practice, this can be a challenge; social scientists working with interdisciplinary teams frequently complain of failure to define their role and of communications problems, and conflict with natural scientists and economists (Rickson and Rickson, 1990: 109). It may be that the SIA team will need to define its roles, data needs, clarify what it has to offer, and establish what others expect of it.

Land development

Land and real estate development generate physical, social and economic impacts. When either necessitate the relocation of people, there may be trauma of the kind discussed in Chapter 8. Modern media developments – coupled with the fact that remote settlements are less likely as unsettled land becomes rare – mean that there is probably less likelihood of there being a problem of real isolation than was once the case.

Great quantities of money are involved in real estate development, and profits can quickly be affected by adverse impacts. Consequently, SIA may be attractive as a way of forecasting and countering problems. Housing values often vary a great deal from locality to locality without much obvious reason to casual observers; impact assessment can help investors identify the best investments, and perhaps even enable them to manipulate fashion as it unfolds.

Agricultural change

Crop introductions, new techniques and tools can have a huge social and economic impact, affecting the sustainability and quality of livelihoods (Chamala, 1990). Many of the social impact studies of agricultural change are retrospective and focused at village level, the latter reflecting the preference many assessors have for a community approach (Tamari and Giacaman, 1997). Agricultural development (or 'modernization') may ultimately provide the foundation for industrial development, and specialized services and activities. A new tool, crop or technique might rapidly open up new opportunities; in the past, new wheat varieties (like Red Fife) made it possible for the Canadian prairies to produce grain for the world; the transfer of rubber (*Hevea brasiliensis*) and oil palm (*Elaaeus guinensis*) from Brazil and Africa to Malaya played a significant part in the development of the Malaysian economy; Africa has acquired maize since the sixteenth century; and, the green revolution has helped the world avoid widespread famine in spite of its growing population.

The world depends on agriculture for food and many commodities; faced with growing human populations, the risk of global climate change, pollution, natural disasters, worsening environmental degradation and people's increasing expectations, the sector must still give secure yields that increase year after year. That challenge is difficult enough even if hindrances and mistakes can be identified and quickly avoided or mitigated. Monitoring and impact assessment (especially SIA) are thus increasingly vital because social institutions are so involved in successful agricultural management and innovation.

Research and farming decisions are very much affected by personal values. The ability to predict what will happen over, say, the next 25 years is valuable but a challenge (Francis and King, 1997). Innovations may not be especially beneficial to society as a whole in the long term, or environmentally wise, but they take place because individual farmers or agribusinesses benefit in the short term. If SIA can predict where things are leading it may be possible to make precautionary course changes and promote better ways.

Many involved in agricultural development seek innovations that will boost food and commodity production without leading to environmental damage or dependency; ideally, things that actually improve the environment and livelihoods and that can be adopted by relatively poor and unassisted farmers. One such innovation has been stone-lines, an alternative technology technique used to halt soil degradation, improve yields and offer security and sustainability of production; Atampugre (1993) has explored the social impact of these.

Since the late 1980s, in a number of developing countries, structural adjustment programmes have led to cut-backs in the provision of agricultural subsidies and extension services, often making it difficult for small farmers to earn an adequate living, and making it less likely that they will modernize and improve production with any degree of success. In some cases, people have been driven from their farms, encouraged to over-graze common land or to practise shifting cultivation in order to boost their food supplies or income.

Villagization and transmigration

Villagization is the concentration of scattered hamlets and homesteads to form larger villages that can better be provided with services and that can be taxed and policed more easily. This approach has recently characterized rural development policy in a number of developing countries. In the former USSR, nationalization of land to form collective farms, together with a policy of villagization, formed a key part of rural development between the 1920s and 1930s, and had huge impacts, often in ways not expected by the administration. In South Africa during the Boer War, the British concentrated villagers and scattered householders to more effectively control their contact with opposing forces; similar approaches were adopted in Malaya in the 1960s and during the Vietnam War. Villagization may also occur after disasters or may be encouraged by aid agencies (Tafessa, 1995).

Several countries have undertaken large-scale land development, and in some cases population relocation. These include: Indonesia (there is a brief discussion of transmigration in Chapter 8), Malaysia, Bolivia, Brazil, the former USSR and the People's Republic of China. The Indonesian Transmigration Programme has probably generated the greatest number of impact studies (for a recent English-language review of the environmental and social impacts *see* Fearnside, 1997).

Agro-technology innovation impacts

At a number of points in history, seemingly minor agricultural technology (agro-technology) innovations have had enormous impacts on agricultural production and the landscape. For example, in early Medieval times, new types of plough opened up Europe's heavier clay soils facilitating the spread of settlements and the expansion of food production; introduction of the horse-collar also had considerable impact, by increasing the efficiency of available animal power. Technological innovation has been the main way of ensuring that food and commodities continue to be available. This has tended to show a step-like progression: adoption of new technology or crops, followed by a 'plateau' phase and then another innovation (it is to be hoped that this pattern will continue). However, in the late eighteenth and early nineteenth centuries, Thomas Malthus warned that population increases geometrically, whereas agricultural improvement follows a more arithmetic stepped curve. The risk is that crop improving breakthroughs, even using biotechnology, may plateau before population growth slows.

Since the Second World War, the scale and pace of the spread of new agro-technology (especially mechanization), and the use of chemical fertilizers, artificial pesticides, herbicides and improved crop varieties has been impressive. Before the 1930s, tractors and combine-harvesters had barely begun to spread even in agriculturally advanced countries such as the UK (which already had steam traction engines for threshing and some ploughing). Those driven off the land by mechanization had some hope of industrial or other urban employment, even during the Depression of the 1920s and 1930s. Nowadays, the spread of mechanization can mean loss of rural employment and dependency on foreign countries for spare parts and fuel, and alternative jobs may be hard to come by (Campbell, 1990). Realization of these impacts prompted the development and promotion of what has come to be known as 'appropriate technology' by bodies like the UK Appropriate Technology Development Group. Appropriate technology seeks to improve outputs without increasing dependency, to ensure equity of access, and minimize unwanted environmental social and economic impacts. So, efforts to assess the impacts of agricultural change have grown since the early 1980s (Berardi and Geisler, 1984), but much could be done to improve the frequency with which SIA is used for agriculture, and to make its use more proactive.

New seeds

A large part of agricultural modernization since the 1940s has been centred on the adoption of new varieties ('new seeds', although some improved crops may be vegetatively propagated). Modern varieties can boost crops markedly, and may also open up new areas to cultivation by offering drought, frost or salt tolerance. In the future, there may also be improved security of harvest and less dependency on chemical fertilizers and pesticides. So far, these innovations have tended to increase dependency (especially on a few large seed merchants) and even reduce security. The new varieties and their accompanying support packages (fertilizers, pesticides, irrigation, etc.) have to be fully adopted and carefully managed, and much can go wrong. The social and economic impacts of agricultural innovation have attracted a great deal of study, much of it under the general heading of 'green revolution research' (Lipton and Longhurst, 1989). Some of these studies have helped to prompt multidisciplinary study approaches and participatory approaches that have spread to impact assessment.

Biotechnology

The world population is growing, and the environment may be about to undergo considerable change through global warming and various other forms of pollution. Somehow, food and commodity production must face these challenges and meet growing demand. Biotechnology may be the only realistic way to do this. Yet, there are growing worries about the social, economic and physical impacts of biotechnology (some of these issues have been covered in Chapter 9). There is a risk that dissenters will slow or halt biotechnology development, denying opportunities to increase food and commodity production and to cut the use of polluting agro-chemicals. There is also a danger that some biotechnology innovation might get out of control. If the pace of biotechnology application to agriculture is to increase without the risk that people will reject it, there is a need to assess carefully its impacts so far and its likely impacts in the future (Ahmed, 1989; Ruivenkamp, 1987). The application of SIA to biotechnology innovation may thus be one of the most crucial of its uses.

Worries have been voiced by Hindmarsh (1990) that the application of SIA to biotechnology in developing countries may be inhibited by corporate control (biotechnology is very big business). SIA may be used to approve innovations that profit commercial interests and larger landowners, rather than developments that might better feed the poor or protect the environment (but with little profit for business). The important questions posed by Hindmarsh are: 'How can SIA control innovation of the magnitude of commercial biotechnology?' and 'How can it better be focused on developing-country priorities?'

There are plenty of retrospective and stock-taking assessments of the social impact of agricultural developments – some conducted by agricultural scientists, some by social researchers and some valuable studies by archaeologists. Many of these focus on the green revolution, seeking to trace how it is progressing and how it should, perhaps, be steered in the future (Ayri and Furtan, 1989; Conway, 1997). From this ever-expanding literature it is clear that agricultural modernization must be culturally compatible with the society adopting it, should whenever possible provide employment, and should be environmentally sustainable if it is to adequately serve the long-term needs of the world (Glaeser, 1987); precautionary SIA is vital to ensure such developments.

Archaeological research has uncovered a number of techniques and strategies that have worked well in the past, even in remote and harsh environments, yet people have ceased to practice them, often because of identifiable social changes. For example, vast areas of terraced agriculture in Latin America, and huge areas of intensive floodland agriculture in Central and South America were abandoned after the social upheaval of the Conquest; rainfall harvesting in the drylands of the Negev Desert, Israel, were abandoned probably because of successive invasions and changing trade routes. If these techniques and strategies can be revived – and, ideally, modernized and improved – and are supported by appropriate social organizations, they could fill the gaps in modern agricultural improvement or offer a base from which to develop new strategies. Success will depend on careful social assessment before and during restoration/innovation.

One of the features of the last hundred years or so has been the penetration of capitalism into subsistence agriculture communities. Farmers have increasingly shifted, either partly or wholly, towards producing cash crops (i.e. crops for sale, rather than for subsistence use by the family group or local community) and, while they may now have funds to spend on various items, they are also exposed to national and international market forces. This may mean a less secure livelihood or, at its most extreme, a farmer may have exchanged adequate non-cash crop subsistence for cash cropping that gives only a precarious and poor return (this is because the crop sold hardly buys enough food, usually because market prices have fallen in relation to the costs of farming inputs). There are even situations where a farmer may produce a nutritious crop for sale (such as groundnuts) and uses the profits to buy other, less dependable food of poorer nutritional quality (e.g. imported grain) (Rennie, 1991). Before an agency promotes a shift to cash cropping it should assess the risks of dependency, loss of traditional crops and employment, vulnerability to market price shifts, and the risk of substitution or loss of demand.

An agricultural problem that has had a very serious social, economic and political impact, especially in the UK, has been the outbreak of BSE. This has affected farming and retail livelihoods, UK trade with Europe and other countries, farming practices, human health, eating habits, international relations and food retail regulations. The costs due to this unexpected problem have been so high that the expense of impact assessment, even if it had only part-avoided the spread of BSE, would have been more than justified. The BSE disaster might, one hopes, serve to stress to administrators the vital need for anticipatory impact assessment.

Contract farming

Contract farming is a form of vertically integrated production, whereby the farmers are contracted to food processing and marketing companies to deliver agreed quantities of a specified crop, usually grown according to the wishes of the contractor. Farmers agreeing to undertake contract farming can expect a guaranteed price for produce, and so can plan ahead and enjoy some security – provided they supply produce of a good enough quality on time. The contract protects from depressed market prices but means that, when prices are high, the farmer does not benefit in terms of increased profit; it may also allow agriculture to expand, which will generate employment and foreign exchange. There are other benefits in the form of advice, marketing, access to markets and so on. Produce must meet set standards, which may be a good way of improving practices. The consumer may benefit from better, possibly cheaper, produce and less risk of fluctuating prices.

The disadvantage of contract agriculture is that there is a risk that standardization will reduce genetic diversity of crops; so a state may shift from numerous potato varieties to just one variety demanded by a food conglomerate, and this may mean that producers are more vulnerable to large-scale crop failure and ruination of livelihood. Contract farming is likely to lead to greater dependency, for inputs and know-how, and for transport and marketing. It integrates farmers and their dependants with the national and global economy, and reduces the land user's power to make decisions about what to grow and how; the farmer effectively becomes an agribusiness employee (Burch *et al.*, 1990; Watts, 1994). There is also a risk that land and water supplies for locally consumed foods will be converted to commercial production for export or city consumption, which could have serious impacts on the ability of rural poor people to get access to food.

There has been considerable growth of contract farming in developed and developing countries, often comprising a significant proportion of total output. For some crops virtually the whole market is controlled by contract agriculture.

Industrial crops

In a few years California will insist on all new road vehicles having zero emissions; given time, the rest of the world will probably follow suit. The most likely replacements for petrol and diesel engines are electric motors powered by batteries or fuel cells, together with clean combustion engines burning hydrogen or methanol. The hydrogen may be obtained by catalytic conversion of methanol, rather than fitting hydrogen tanks to road vehicles. Methanol is already being widely used in Brazil for relatively low-emission combustion engines (as it is mixed with petrol there is some pollution), so it is possible to see what sort of socio-economic impacts might result if methanol use spreads elsewhere. Brazilian methanol production may have made sense when oil import costs were high and export prices for crops like sugar were low, but at other times it is not especially beneficial to the economy, the environment or rural employment. Methanol production did help to stabilize the economy and save foreign exchange when Brazil had no indigenous petroleum production (Moreira and Goldemberg, 1999). However, the production of alcohol fuel causes serious river pollution, contaminating water supplies, hitting poor fishermen and decimating aquatic wildlife. The use of land for producing alcohol feedstock has forced many small farmers to relocate, often to poorer-quality land. While large alcohol production companies have benefited, the impact on the poor has included reduced and more precarious livelihoods, natural vegetation clearance and loss of biodiversity, land conflict and land degradation (Rask, 1995). If the spread of industrial feedstock crops (including alcohol production) grows, especially if expansion takes place in the USA and Europe, this could result in reduced food surpluses. This would mean less food security, fluctuating food prices and even increased famine risk if care is not taken.

Biodiversity conservation

Using SIA for improving conservation planning and management is a two-way challenge: to make biologists, ecologists and environmental managers more aware of the value of social studies; and to get social researchers involved in conservation.

Various environmental managers have reviewed the value of biodiversity conservation. The following list is fairly typical.

- Source of future food and commodity crops: vital to provide genetic material to counter the constant challenges of environmental change, diseases, pollution and other presently unforeseen problems. A rising human population also demands new, more productive, crops which will have to draw upon genetic resources.
- Degraded biodiversity is widely held to lead to a reduction in ecosystem stability.

- Source of future pharmaceuticals and other new materials.
- Biodiversity might be exploitable for future livelihoods (e.g. eco-tourism, or raw material for bioengineering).
- Inspiration for research, literature, the arts.
- Moral questions: such as 'Should humans have the right to destroy biodiversity?'

Even though conservation of biodiversity can, clearly, improve human well-being, these values were little explored by economists and social scientists until recently (Posey, 1999).

There are basically two modes of conservation: in-situ and ex-situ. The former includes areas solely or partly for biodiversity survival: forest reserves, nature reserves, game parks, on-farm conservation areas (woodland patches, hedgerows, ponds, etc.), highway and railway verges, public parks, military training zones (all of which offer opportunities for activities other than conservation). Increasing efforts are being taken to understand and predict people's attitudes to conservation initiatives, and the role that the social sciences can play in ecosystem management. Without knowledge of how people manage and get access to resources it is difficult to plan conservation, tourism or natural resources development. Ecosystem management must consider socio-economic issues (EndterWada *et al.*, 1998; Flood *et al.*, 1993). Kamppinen and Walls (1999) have explored the problem of integrating biodiversity issues into social and economic decision-making (Place, 1988; Tsai, 1987).

Ex-situ conservation includes zoos, botanic gardens, arboreta, seed collections and gene banks. These forms of conservation can have considerable social benefits, offering recreational and educational opportunities, and a chance for people to feel that they are participating in the protection of biota. However, there are questions of access to the stored material; ideally there should be open access to developing countries and all companies, rather than a selected few.

Conservation areas, and the way they are managed, affect the surrounding district. The formation of protected areas can have a considerable impact on people living in their vicinity which, in turn, can determine whether the conservation efforts are viable in the long term (Hough, 1991; Olwig, 1980; Peters, 1994; Rao and Geisler, 1990; West, 1994). If the people living near parks or reserves are ignored, they may fail to support, or might even oppose and undermine, conservation (e.g. by poaching and deforestation). Where people are so poor that they cannot afford alternative fuel, no amount of public education or warning notices will prevent wood-cutting from reserves. Assessment can warn of such problems and would prompt conservation planners to establish alternatives, such as appropriate and accessible sustainable wood lots, in good time. A significant proportion of those involved in conservation planning and management, and many agencies, support a community development approach to conservation. One could almost go as far as to suggest that, today, 'mainstream' conservation and sustainable development supports the integration of economic development with environmental management and biodiversity protection. However, a growing number of conservationists and environmental managers see such a utilitarian approach as misguided. For example, even as early as the 1960s, Hill (1963) criticized such approaches in Ghana. More recently, Oates (1999: *xv*) noted that '. . . there are serious flaws in the theory that wildlife can be conserved through providing human economic development . . . especially if the local people are recent settlers'. Careful study of impacts is vital to ensure that misguided dogmatic approaches do not cause serious damage.

It is valuable to conduct an SIA early in the process of planning conservation (Fortin and Gagnon, 1999). How the conservation area is demarcated, policed and managed can be crucial. SIA should be used to ensure that optimal choices are made (Williams *et al.*, 1992); it is also necessary because local and national attitudes to conservation can change, sometimes quickly and unexpectedly.

Renewable natural resources conservation

Retrospective SIA can be invaluable for improving resource exploitation and conservation strategies; an assessment can give a clearer idea of how exactly the process of damage proceeds, so that decision-makers – rather than make do with vague ideas about encroachment on reserves, illegal logging, etc. – can formulate policies that work (Wilkie and Carpenter, 1999). For example, if it is clear that poaching or illegal forest product extraction follows controlled logging, the logging company must be told that its responsibility does not cease after removal of timber – it (or some other authority) must fell sufficient trees that are not of timber or conservation value across the logging roads to deny easy access (some may oppose this, arguing that new tracks are useful).

Since the early 1990s in north-western USA and Canada there has been controversy over forest management to ensure the survival of native plant and animal species. Companies that provide much of the employment in these regions wish to pursue clear felling to save costs, while conservation groups and the government are keen to see selective logging or other forms of forest management that better protect biodiversity. The northern spotted owl, in particular, has become a notorious subject of controversy (Levi and Kocher, 1995; Waters *et al.*, 1994; Yaffee, 1995). Because conservation needs conflict with current livelihood strategies, arguments have been acrimonious, and those seeking to conserve enough 'old growth' forest to ensure the survival of this owl have had to assess the opportunity costs and compare these with the likelihood that restrictions would ensure species recovery.

The northern spotted owl controversy has generated much resentment – the front of T-shirts worn by some locals in the affected region read 'Earth First!' (implying support for one of the NGOs opposing logging), but on the back appeared the legend 'Then we log the other planets!'. Elsewhere, biodiversity conservation is often compatible with, or can even enhance, livelihoods. For example, in Amazonia there is growing interest in tolerant forest management (TFM) for providing better livelihoods and ensuring that some wildlife is conserved. It may also offer opportunities for tourism. TFM involves the land users encouraging various forest products without excessive disturbance, so that some areas are virtually untouched. There are studies which suggest that this offers a better and more sustainable livelihood than available alternatives for smallholders and it seems to be welcomed by many local people.

Eco-tourism

There are situations where tourism and biodiversity conservation are mutually supportive, and where eco-tourism can beneficially be established. There are also situations where powerful tourism interests are only too keen to develop profitable tourism which exploits biodiversity or landscape, but which fails to do more than a token amount to support these – this is pseudo-eco-tourism (and is unfortunately becoming quite common). SIA should be applied in order to check whether tourism and ecology are compatible and, if they are, to identify how best to optimize the interrelationship. SIA can also show how the development can best help local people, and be supported by them (Mercer and Thompson, 1993). Without support and sustainable institutions there is unlikely to be successful ongoing eco-tourism. This is not an isolated challenge; multifaceted sustainable development objectives are increasingly being pursued and involve human–environment–biota interactions. In this, the following environmental management dilemmas often surface: whether human welfare is to be put before conservation and environmental quality or vice-versa and, whichever is chosen, how the two should be traded off.

Around the world a number of ocean and freshwater fisheries have come under stress through over-fishing, pollution and periodic environmental change such as the El Niño effect off the southern Pacific coast of South America. As fisheries are damaged there are impacts on the fishing community: reduced earnings, unemployment, the need to change tactics or fishing areas (which may mean more distant operations and higher risks). There are impacts on consumers: rising food prices, decline in dietary quality, consumption of poorer-quality fish, the possibility of contamination through pollution and so on. There are also impacts on the environment: for instance, fishing efforts may damage other organisms such as dolphins, turtles or coral. SIA can provide some forewarning of likely socio-economic impacts (Vanderpool, 1987).

In the 1970s declining fish stocks led the UK and Iceland into a 'cod war', and there have since been a number of disagreements and conflicts over access to ocean fisheries (Weber, 1995). On the positive side, as competition for wild fish stocks has grown, more interest has been shown in developing aquaculture. Potentially vastly more productive than fishing, indeed similar to the terrestrial shift from hunter-gathering to agriculture, fish farming and aquaculture are, however, not without the risk of negative environmental and socio-economic impacts. In tropical coastlands the development of ponds for producing tiger prawns and fish has had a marked socio-economic impact, in several countries. This aquaculture is now a major source of foreign exchange and employment, but also destroys the mangroves on which many poor people may depend for fuel wood and other commodities, and hits traditional inshore fisheries and shellfish gathering.

On-farm conservation may be encouraged simply for biodiversity conservation, relying a good deal on farmer support in lieu of attractive subsidies. There are also situations where conservation has been encouraged as an alternative to agriculture in order to try to control water pollution, meet national carbon emission quotas, or as a way of reducing foreign debts. The first of these includes set-aside in Europe. In the USA, a rough equivalent to set-aside is the Conservation Reserve Program; this too has had significant socio-economic impacts (Mortenson *et al.*, 1990).

SIA AND TOURISM

Tourism development is a field that has attracted a great deal of socio-economic impact studies into actual and perceived impacts, although only a proportion of it is predictive, rather than retrospective, SIA (Archer and Fletcher, 1996; Dai Fan and Bao Jigang, 1996; Dunkel, 1984; Keogh, 1982; Lindberg and Johnson, 1997; Mathieson, 1982). Tourism development on islands has generated a growing number of SIAs because administrators and funding bodies are generally aware of the potentially serious effects on relatively small and isolated communities (for example, the Caribbean islands, Hawaii, the Greek islands and the Scottish islands) (Beekhuis, 1981; Brougham, 1977; Gilder, 1995; Lockhart, 1996; Matsuoka, 1991; Patullo, 1996; Shera and Matsuoka, 1992; Sutton *et al.*, 1992). The cultural impacts of tourism have been studied in many countries and effective cultural impacts-focused SIA is now possible (Teo, 1994).

One field that has grown is the prediction of likely tourism usage problems, such as crowding and environmental degradation (particularly erosion of paths and vegetation damage). Enough is known of the psychology of tourists to make reasonably accurate assessments of where people will congregate, what numbers will attend, etc. If a tourist attraction becomes too crowded it may decline in popularity and fail to repay infrastructure investments, so the study of crowding is important. Fashion may suddenly affect how people behave: for instance, the growing popularity of surfing has led to the crowding of some UK West Country beaches (in Devon, Cornwall and Somerset) that had formerly failed to attract people; the spread of mountain biking is leading to highland path erosion; and, in Europe, the shift towards snowboarding is having unexpected social impacts on many ski resorts.

A body of tourism SIA has been concerned with how the host population is affected, but there has been less focus on assessing the impacts of tourism on tourists or the regional society and economy or the tourists' home country (Gilbert and Clark, 1997; King *et al.*, 1993). Yet, tourism is probably the world's largest single 'industry' and has been growing strongly. Some forecasters predict that tourism may fund a large part of future space exploration and development; tourism has already become a significant force in biodiversity and landscape conservation; and it is a driving force in the development of new transportation technology. These aspects of tourism merit more SIA.

In recent years there has been a growing interest in eco-tourism, the development of which can affect local peoples. SIA can be valuable for helping to protect local peoples and cultures and in assessing what they might contribute to conservation (King and Stewart, 1996).

SIA AND NATURAL RESOURCES DEVELOPMENT

Large natural resource development schemes (e.g. Alaskan oil exploitation, Canadian tar sands, large open-cast mines) were one of the driving forces behind the development of SIA from the 1970s. Natural resource development often happens in areas previously little exposed to commercial activity; it can be on a large scale and may trigger boomtown conditions (*see* Chapter 8), noise, pollution and new communications developments. From its earliest days SIA has been applied to natural resource development projects and, more recently, to programmes and policies (Freeman and Frey, 1986). SIA could, however, be more widely used to establish how and why people use nature and resources (Rickson *et al.*, 1995: 149). However, the disruption or change of resource-dependent communities has been a focus of SIA.

Natural resource exploitation can mean advantages for some people and disadvantages for others: the positive impacts are often felt by urban, middle-class entrepreneurs or city dwellers (in the case of hydroelectricity), and the negative impacts tend to hit local people, especially the poor (Baviskar and Singh, 1994; Geisler *et al.*, 1982; Goldsmith and Hildyard, 1984; McCully, 1996). (The health impacts of natural resources development are discussed in Chapter 10.) The exploitation of natural resources may damage traditional food sources and disrupt the lifestyle of indigenous peoples. For example, mining may ruin fisheries, timber extraction may drive away game and remove plants that provide food or supplementary incomes. While some may profit, others far downstream or downwind from a mineral processing facility may suffer. There may also be problems because one settlement, valley or area benefits and others fail to experience anything positive, leading to regional disparities and disputes (Burch and DeLuca, 1984; Elkind-Savatsky and Kaufman 1986). A country may become dependent on a natural resource, and then find that it become exhausted or demand for it falls. Even worse, exploitation may damage the environment.

Since the Second World War a number of countries have acquired considerable wealth from mineral exploitation, notably petroleum, and SIA has frequently been called upon to help shape project development (Leistritz and Murdock, 1981). This can mean the relatively sudden arrival of funds where there were few before, and those involved may need reminding that it may be a short-lived boom, likely to dwindle after a few decades of plenty. The impact of a powerful 'alien' industry on local communities can be marked, and can lead to considerable dependency, inflation, the influx of migrant workers, and the transformation of the existing economic environment. In Scotland, 'docile' non-unionized local labour increasingly came into contact with 'experienced' and unionized migrant labour, leading to considerable social change. There were also delays before opportunities were realized, or they were missed altogether. SIA could have helped warn of these risks (Francis and Swan, 1973).

Richer countries such as The Netherlands and the UK have made little effort to convert oil revenue into long-term investments like improved infrastructure or alternative sources of revenue and power. The profits have largely been fed into national economies, and are helping to fund today's social services and state pensions. In the Gulf States, some groups of people have shifted rapidly from rags to riches, generating tremendous social, political and cultural impacts; elsewhere the change has been much slower (Ibrahim, 1983; Moore, 1982; Parsler and Shapiro, 1983; Seyfrit, 1988; Stangeland, 1984). Ideally, any community or country undergoing an oil or other natural resource-based boom should draw on the hindsight now available, conduct SIA and use it to plan a sensible strategy that ensures minimum negative impacts, maximum social welfare and long-term plans that will take over when the resource is exhausted, based on the wise investment of revenue (Muth and Lee, 1986).

SIA AND MINING IMPACTS

Mining has had a marked impact on people and the environment when practised both on a major scale by big companies, and on a minor scale by small bands of, often illegal, miners. The impacts of the latter are all too apparent in Amazonia, where alluvial gold extraction frequently results in damaging contact between miners (*garimpeiros*) and indigenous peoples, in mercury pollution of rivers, and in civil unrest associated with money-laundering and widespread lawlessness. Bands of diamond miners cause similar problems in Ghana; in Columbia it is groups of emerald miners; in parts of south-east Asia small-scale tin mining; and in Mongolia gangs of gold miners have caused serious cyanide poisoning around the Gobi Desert. These physical impacts obviously disrupt health and livelihoods, but mines also attract migrants, prompt the formation of boomtowns, and may make use of essentially indentured labour (or even slaves). Large mines – for example those exploiting copper and other minerals in Papua New Guinea, iron in northeast Brazil or diamonds in Southern Africa, have caused serious socio-economic problems and this has encouraged companies and governments to adopt SIA. Large-scale strip (open-cast) mining has prompted a considerable number of SIAs in North America and elsewhere (Albrecht, 1978; Filer, 1994; Gold, 1974; Holden and O'Faircheallaigh, 1995; Krutilla *et al.*, 1978; Pandy, 1998; Radford, 1982). In Papua New Guinea, the PNG Mineral Resources Development Company funded a study between 1995 and 2001 entitled 'Mining Project Social Impact Assessment and Monitoring' which may be viewed at http://www.nri.org.pg/mpsiam.html.

References

Ahmed, I. (1989) Advanced agricultural biotechnologies: some empirical findings on their social impact. *International Labour Review* **128(5)**, 553–70.

Albrecht, S. (1978) Socio-cultural factors and energy development in rural areas in the west. *Journal of Environmental Management* **7(1)**, 78–90.

Archer, B. and **Fletcher, J.** (1996) The economic impact of tourism in the Seychelles. *Annals of Tourism Research* **23(1)**, 32–47.

Atampugre, N. (1993) *Behind the Lines of Stone: the social impact of a soil and water conservation project in the Sahel*. Oxfam, Oxford.

Ayri, T.Y. and **Furtan, W.H.** (1989) The impact of new wheat technology on income distribution: a green revolution case-study, Turkey, 1960–1983. *Economic Development and Cultural Change* **38(1)**, 113–22.

Baviskar, A. and **Singh, A.K.** (1994) Malignant growth: the Sardar Sarovar Dam and its impact on public health. *Environmental Impact Assessment Review* **14(4)**, 349–58.

Beekhuis, J.V. (1981) Tourism in the Caribbean: impacts on the economic, social and natural environments. *Ambio* **X(6)**, 325–31.

Berardi, G.M. and **Geisler, C.C.** (eds) (1984) *The Social Consequences and Challenges of New Agricultural Technologies*. Westview, Boulder (CO).

Brougham, J.E. (1977) *Social Impact of Tourism: Sleat, Skye*. Unpublished report (held by the Library of the University of Wales Swansea, Swansea, UK).

Burch, W.R. and **DeLuca, D.R.** (1984) *Measuring the Social Impact of Natural Resource Policies*. University of New Mexico Press, Albuquerque (NM).

Burch, D., Rickson, R. and **Thiel, I.** (1990) Contract farming and rural social change: some implications of the Australian experience. *Impact Assessment Review* **10(1–2)**, 145–56.

Campbell, M.J. (ed.) (1990) *New Technology and Rural Development: the social impact*. Routledge, Chapman and Hall, London.

Chamala, S. (1990) Social and environmental impacts of modernization of agriculture in developing countries. *Environmental Impact Assessment Review* **10(1–2)**, 219–31.

Christiansen, K. (1976) *The Social Impacts of Land Development*. The Urban Institute, Washington (DC).

Conway, G. (1997) *The Doubly Green Revolution: food for all in the 21st century*. Penguin, Harmondsworth.

Dai Fan and **Bao Jigang** (1996) The social impacts of tourism: a case study in Yunnan Province, China. *Chinese Geographical Science* **6(2)**, 132–44.

De'Ath, C. (1982) Social impact assessment: a critical tool in land development planning. *International Social Science Journal* **34(3)**, 441–50.

Dunkel, D.R. (1984) Tourism and the environment: a review of the literature and issues. *Environmental Sociology* **37(1)**, 5–18.

Elkind-Savatsky, P.D. and **Kaufman, J.D.** (eds) (1986) *Differential Social Impacts of Rural Resource Development*. Westview, Boulder (CO).

EndterWada, J., Blahna, D., Krannich, R. and **Brunson, M.** (1998) A framework for understanding social science contributions to ecosystem management. *Ecological Applications* **8(3)**, 891–904.

Fearnside, P.M. (1997) Transmigration in Indonesia: lessons from its environmental and social impacts. *Environmental Management* **21(4)**, 553–70.

Filer, C. (1994) Socio-economic impact assessment of Tolukuma Gold Mine, Central Province, Papua New Guinea. *Research in Melanesia* **18(1)**, 1–84.

Flood, S., Cocklin, C. and **Parnell, K.** (1993) Coastal resource management conflicts and community action at Margawhai, New Zealand. *Coastal Management* **21(2)**, 91–111.

Fortin, M.J. and **Gagnon, C.** (1999) An assessment of social impacts of national parks on communities in Quebec, Canada. *Environmental Conservation* **36(3)**, 200–11.

Francis, C. and **King, J.** (1997) Impact of personal values on agricultural research. *Society and Natural Resources* **10(3)**, 273–82.

Francis, J. and **Swan, N.** (1973) *Scotland in Turmoil: a social and environmental assessment of the impact of North Sea oil and gas on communities in the north of Scotland* (Church of Scotland, Church and Nation Committee). St Andrew Press for the Church of Scotland Home Board, Edinburgh.

Freeman, D.M. and **Frey, R.S.** (1986) A method for assessing the social impacts of natural resources policies. *Journal of Environmental Management* **23(3)**, 229–45.

Geisler, C.C., Green, R., Usner, D. and **West, P.** (eds) (1982) *Indian SIA: the social impact assessment of rapid resource development of native peoples*. University of Michigan Press, Ann Arbor (MI).

Gilbert, D. and **Clark, M.** (1997) An exploratory examination of urban tourism impact with reference to residents attitudes, in the cities of Canterbury and Guilford. *Cities* **14(6)**, 343–52.

Gilder, M.M. (1995) A social impact assessment approach using the reference group as a standard of impact analysis. The case of Hana: Hawaiians and the proposed golf course. *Environmental Impact Assessment Review* **15(2)**, 179–93.

Glaeser, B. (ed.) (1987) *The Green Revolution Revisited: critique and alternatives*. Allen and Unwin, London.

Gold, R.L. (1974) Social impacts of strip-mining and other industrialisations of coal resources, in C.P. Wolf (ed.), *Social Impact Assessment: man-environment interactions*. Dowden, Hutchinson & Ross, Stroudsburg (PA).

Goldsmith, E. and **Hildyard, N.** (1984) *The Social and Environmental Impacts of Large Dams* (3 vols) Wadebridge Ecological Centre, Wadebridge (UK).

Hansen, D.O. and **Erbaugh, J.M.** (1983) Different modes of participation by sociologists in interdisciplinary team development efforts. *The Rural Sociologist* **3(1)**, 11–16.

Healing, L. (1984) A note on impact monitoring of agricultural development projects. *Journal of Agricultural Economics* **35(2)**, 279–81.

Hill, P. (1963) *The Migrant Cocoa Farmers of Southern Ghana: a study in rural capitalism*. Cambridge University Press, Cambridge.

Hindmarsh, R. (1990) The need for effective assessment: sustainable development and the social impacts of biotechnology in the Third World. *Environmental Impact Assessment Review* **10(2)**, 195–208.

Holden, A. and **O'Faircheallaigh, C.O.** (1995) *Economic and Social Impact of Silica Mining at Cape Flattery* (Centre for Australian Public Sector Management, Aboriginal Politics and Public Sector Management Research Monographs and Papers No. 1). Griffiths University, Brisbane.

Hough, J.L. (1991) Social impact assessment: its role in protected area planning and management, in P.C. West and S.R. Brechin (eds), *Resident Peoples and National Parks: social dilemmas and strategies in international conservation*. University of Arizona Press, Tucson (AZ), 274–82.

Ibrahim, S.E. (1983) *The New Arab Social Order: a study of the social impact of oil wealth*. Westview, Boulder (CO).

Kamppinen, M. and **Walls, M.** (1999) Integrating biodiversity with decision making. *Biodiversity and Conservation* **8(1)**, 7–16.

Keogh, B. (1982) The social impact of tourism: the case of Shediac, New Brunswick. *Canadian Geographer – Geographer Canadien* **26(4)**, 318–31.

King, B., Pizam, A. and **Milman, A.** (1993) Social impacts of tourism on host perceptions. *Annals of Tourism Research* **20(4)**, 650–65.

King, D.A. and **Stewart, W.P.** (1996) Ecotourism and commodification: protecting people and places. *Biodiversity and Conservation* **5(3)**, 293–305.

Krutilla, J.V., Fisher, A.C. and **Rice, R.E.** (1978) *Economic and Fiscal Impacts of Coal Development: northern Great Plains*. Johns Hopkins University Press, Baltimore (MD).

Leistritz, F.L. and **Murdock, S.H.** (1981) *The Socioeconomic Impact of Resource Development: methods for assessment*. Westview, Boulder (CO).

Levi, D and Kocher, S. (1995) The spotted owl controversy and the sustainability of rural communities in the Pacific northwest. *Environment and Behavior* **27(5)**, 631–49.

Lindberg, K. and **Johnson, R.L.** (1997) The economic values of tourism's social impacts. *Annals of Tourism Research* **24(1)**, 90–116.

Lipton, M. and **Longhurst, R.** (1989) *New Seeds and Poor People*. Unwin Hyman, London.

Lockhart, D. (1996) The impact of tourism on small islands. *The Geographical Journal* **162(1)**, 131–2.

McCully, P. (1996) *Silenced Rivers: the ecology and politics of large dams*. Zed, London.

Mathieson, A. (1982) *Tourism: economic, physical and social impacts*. Longman, London.

Matsuoka, J. (1991) Differential perceptions of the social impact of tourism development in a rural Hawaiian community. *Social Development Issues* **13(2)**, 55–65.

Mercer, E. and **Thompson, A.** (1993) Social impact assessment of ecotourism on the rural quality of life in the Blue Crow Mountains National Park in Jamaica, West Indies. Website: http://www.rtp.srs.fs.fed.us/econ/research/sia42_3htm.

Moore, R. (1982) *Social Impact of Oil: the case of Peterhead*. Routledge and Kegan Paul, Boston (MA).

Moreira, J.R. and **Goldemberg, J.** (1999) The alcohol program. *Energy Policy* **27(4)**, 229–45.

Mortensen, T.L., Leistritz, F.L., Leich, J.A., Coon, R.C. and **Ekstrom, B.L.** (1990) Socioeconomic impact of the Conservation Reserve Program in North Dakota. *Society and Natural Resource* **3(1)**, 53–61.

Muth, R.M. and **Lee, R.G.** (1986) Social impact assessment in natural resource decision making: toward a structural paradigm. *Impact Assessment Bulletin* **4(3–4)**, 168–83.

Oates, J.F. (1999) *Myth and Reality in the Rain Forest: how conservation strategies are failing in West Africa*. University of California Press, Berkeley (CA).

Olwig, K.F. (1980) National Parks, tourism and local development: a West Indian case. *Human Organization* **39(1)**, 22–31.

Pandy, B. (1998) *Displaced People: impact of open cast mining on environment*. Friedrich Ebert Stifhung, New Delhi.

Parsler, R. and **Shapiro, D.** (eds) (1983) *The Social Impact of Oil in Scotland: a contribution to the sociology of oil*. Gower, Farnborough.

Patullo, P. (1996) *Last Resorts: the cost of tourism in the Caribbean*. Cassell, London.

Peters, D. (1994) Social impact assessment of the Ranomafan National Park Project of Madagascar. *Impact Assessment* **12(4)**, 385–408.

Place, S. (1988) The impact of national parks development on Tortuguero, Costa Rica. *Journal of Cultural Geography* **9(1)**, 37–52.

Posey, D.A. (ed.) (1999) *Cultural and Spiritual Values of Biodiversity* (a complimentary contribution to the Global Biodiversity Assessment UNEP). Intermediate Technology Publications, London.

Radford, J. (1982) Stripmining and Navajo lands in the US: threats to health and heritage. *Ambio* **XI(1)**, 9–14.

Rao, K. and **Geisler, C.** (1990) The social consequences of protected area development for resident populations. *Society and Natural Resources* **3(1)**, 19–32.

Rask, K. (1995) The social costs of ethanol production in Brazil: 1978–1987. *Economic Development and Cultural Change* **43(3)**, 627–649.

Rennie, S.J. (1991) Subsistence agriculture versus cash cropping. *Journal of Rural Studies* **7(1–2)**, 5–9.

Rickson, R.E. and **Rickson, S.T.** (1990) Assessing rural development: the role of the social scientist. *Environmental Impact Assessment Review* **10(1–2)**, 103–12.

Rickson, R.E., Lane, M., Lynch-Blosse, M. and **Western, J.S.** (1995) Community, environment, and development: social impact assessment in resource-dependent communities. *Impact Assessment* **13(4)**, 347–69.

Ruivenkamp, G. (1987) Social impacts of biotechnology on agriculture and food processing. *Development* **4(1)**, 58–9.

Sen, A.K. (1981) *Poverty and Famines: an essay on entitlement and deprivation*. Clarendon Press, Oxford.

Seyfrit, C.L. (1988) A need for post-impact and policy studies: the case of the 'Shetland experience'. *Sociological Inquiry* **58(4)**, 206–15.

Shera, W. and **Matsuoka, J.** (1992) Evaluating the impact of resort development on an Hawaiian island: implications for social impact assessment policy and procedures. *Environmental Impact Assessment Review* **12(4)**, 349–62.

Stangeland, P. (1984) Getting rich slowly: the social impact of oil activities. *Acta Sociologica* **27(3)**, 215–37.

Sutton, S.T., Devlin, P.J. and **Simmons, D.G.** (1992) Kapati Island, a natural area in demand: assessing social impact. *GeoJournal* **29(3)**, 253–62.

Tafessa, T. (ed.) (1995) *Villagization in Northern Shewa, Ethiopia: impact assessment*. Government Publisher, Addis Abbaba (ISBN 382582616x).

Tamari, S. and **Giacaman, R.** (1997) *Zbeidat: the social impact of agricultural technology on the life of a peasant community in the Jordan Valley*. Birzeit University Publications, Birzeit (Jordan).

Teo, P. (1994) Assessing socio-cultural impacts: the case of Singapore. *Tourism Management* **15(2)**, 126–36.

Tsai, H.C. (1987) Socioeconomic environmental impacts of developing a national park in east region of Taiwan. *Taiwan Economic Review* **240(1)**, 12–23.

Vanderpool, C.K. (1987) Social impact assessment and fisheries. *Transactions of the American Fisheries Society* **116(3)**, 479–85.

Waters, E.C., Holland, D.W. and **Weber, B.A.** (1994) International effects of reduced timber harvests: the impact of the northern spotted owl listing in rural and urban Oregon. *Journal of Agricultural and Resource Economics* **19(1)**, 141–60.

Watts, M.J. (1994) Living under contract: the social impacts of contract farming in West Africa. *The Ecologist* **24(4)**, 130–4.

Weber, P. (1995) Facing limits in oceanic fisheries. Part II: the social consequences. *Natural Resources Forum* **19(1)**, 39–46.

West, P. (1994) Resident people and protected areas – Part III. *Society and Natural Resources* **7(4)**, 303–5.

Wilkie, D.S. and **Carpenter, J.F.** (1999) Bushmeat hunting in the Congo Basin: an assessment of impacts and options for mitigation. *Biodiversity and Conservation* **8(7)**, 927–55.

Williams, D.R., Roggenbuck, J.W., Patterson, M.E. and **Watson, A.E.** (1992) The variability of user-based social impact standards for wilderness management. *Forest Science* **38(4)**, 738–56.

Yaffee, S.L. (1995) Lessons about leadership from the history of the spotted owl controversy. *Natural Resources Journal* **35(2)**, 381–412.

13

SIA IN PRACTICE: ENVIRONMENTAL CHANGE IMPACTS

Many fields of research have shown that the earth's environment is a lot less stable than many administrators like to imagine. Palaeoecology and archaeology have uncovered marked, and possibly quite sudden, climatic shifts; there are also signs of considerable variations in sea level in the last 20,000 years, as well as other environmental changes that have, doubtless, affected human fortunes.

NATURAL CLIMATE CHANGE IMPACTS

Superimposed on longer-term climatic changes have been shorter-term oscillations; for example, in the Colorado Front Range, in the USA, during the last 3000 years there have been periods of longer-than-average snow cover that appear to have had profound effects on biota and humans (Benedict, 1999). Early this century environmental determinism focused on the effects of climate on human affairs (Huntington, 1915). However, these environmental determinists fell foul of the dangers involved in trying to predict the impacts of climate change on humans; different groups of people can vary a great deal in how they react to exactly the same challenges.

As more evidence of the effects of past climate change and human responses become available, the modelling of future scenarios should improve (although it must still be cautious). There have been attempts to do this since the 1970s (Chen *et al.*, 1983; Schneider, 1974). It is easy to overlook the more subtle effects of climate change; for example, according to Behringer (1999) the 'unnatural' climate of the fourteenth and fifteenth centuries AD (the 'Little Ice Age') was seen by some at the time as the consequence of a 'conspiracy by witches'. The tensions aroused by this led to growing persecution and scapegoat reactions; in short, climate fluctuations helped provoke Medieval witch-hunting.

Presently (at the turn of the century) there is the manifestation of the quasi-periodic El Niño event (and related El Niña and El Niño – Southern Oscillation (ENSO) changes). Appearing first off western Latin America, as shifts in ocean circulation leading initially to warming off the coasts of Chile and Peru, El Niño wreaks havoc with marine life and seabirds, and increasingly triggers storms and droughts throughout Central and South America, and then months later as far afield as Australasia. In the late 1990s it may have played a part in the outbreak of widespread forest fires in Amazonia and South-East Asia. El Niño alone shows that the environment does change markedly, and that humans should try to ensure that they can either avoid the consequences, adapt to them, or move to escape from changed environmental conditions. By and large, such responses are increasingly difficult; the capacity to adapt has diminished in recent centuries as population has grown, and societies have become more complex and dependent on trade and easily disrupted technology. At the time of writing (spring 2000), some of the relief organizations that had been dealing with the AD 2000 Mozambique flooding were trying to contact those working on climatic fluctuations such as El Niño to set up an 'early warning' network which should help prevent the same level of misery in future weather-related events. Recent advances in climatic studies and global change research need to be linked to social impact prediction; Mozambique should have had clear warning months in advance of spring 2000 enabling better preparations.

The impacts of global warming

Before social impacts can reliably be assessed it is important to have good predictions of global physical changes and their economic implications. The former are partly known, and the latter have been very roughly estimated for likely scenarios (Dermeritt and Rothman, 1999). At present, however, accurate and detailed assessments are a long way off. At the time of writing, concern was being voiced that the melting of ice in Greenland and parts of Antarctica could raise sea levels by over 6m, and possibly rapidly enough for major disruption; more accurate forecasting is, however, needed. Global warming may have marked impacts on human health, the survival of flora and fauna, and on the incidence of forest fires, drought and storms. Computer modelling should be able to draw on increasingly improving knowledge of likely environmental change in order to provide more accurate predictions (Alcamo *et al.*, 1999). In the meantime, it would be wise to assume the worst and to launch SIAs of various likely physical impacts, in order to be better prepared.

Publications on the possible impacts of global change on health have been expanding (Andrews and Clayton, 1990; McMichael *et al.*, 1996). The health effects of greenhouse warming, sea level rise and reduction of stratospheric ozone have already been subject to SIA, as have pollution, the impact of biotechnology, and urbanization. There is widespread interest in assessing the likely social and economic impacts of global environmental change, with many social research funding bodies earmarking support for these studies. Bodies like the International Panel on Climate Change (IPCC), established in 1988, have been putting considerable effort into improving impact assessment in order to assist those international negotiations intended to avoid, mitigate or adapt to global warming (Taplin and Braaf, 1995). There have been efforts to assess the socio-economic impacts of agreements and treaties aimed at coping with global environmental change; for example, Environment Canada has tried to establish the consequences of implementing the (updated) Montreal Protocol on Substances that Deplete the Ozone Layer (*see* http://www.cfgroup.ca/arc/impacts/siamp.html).

Urbanization deserves more attention because more than 50 per cent of humanity are now urbanites, and their numbers are growing fast. The result of this growth is crowding. In many countries, there are cities with disintegrating infrastructure and worsening living conditions, and increasing rates of crime, traffic congestion and poverty.

There are grounds for worry about global warming resulting from atmospheric pollution; this may well cause rising sea levels, altered weather conditions and, possibly, sudden shifts of important currents like the Gulf Stream. The latter is especially worrying. Caused by global temperature and ocean salinity changes, any alteration of the Gulf Stream would have rapid and far-reaching impacts because the current plays a crucial role in moderating the western European climate. A diversion of the Gulf Stream would cool winters and summers markedly, and would bring chaos to agriculture and transport, possibly enough to generate huge numbers of eco-refugees (eco-refugees are discussed in Chapter 8).

Modern humans have much improved technology and understanding of possible global changes. Several factors, however, conspire to make adaptation or movement more difficult than it was in the past.

- There are far more people today; in the past, smaller populations had more chance of moving on when resources were challenged, climate conditions changed or a site became polluted.
- Growing populations mean that few unclaimed areas are now available for people to move to or from which to obtain resources. Demand for water has also grown hugely.
- Development has degraded many regions, so there are fewer opportunities for new livelihoods.
- Roads, farmland and urban areas form physical barriers to wildlife migration, so the response of biota to environmental change is hindered. Conservation areas are often surrounded by developed environments so that there are few opportunities for shifting upslope or downslope, or to wherever survival opportunities might previously have been found.
- Loss of biodiversity has become a problem, and is likely to mean a reduction

in 'raw materials' for crop development, new drugs and so on, restricting future options.

- It appears that modern populations have become relatively slow to adapt, and have complex institutions and survival strategies that may be difficult to modify.

Given time, however, humans can be adaptive; unfortunately, some of the environmental impacts we may have to face might not take place at a leisurely rate. A few degrees' rise in global mean temperature or a sea-level change of a metre present few problems if they take place over a century, but if they happen over 10 years the result could be chaos. So, it makes sense to divide environmental impacts into:

1. unexpected/sudden
2. predicted/sudden
3. unexpected/gradual
4. predicted/gradual.

Categories 1 and 2 present the greatest threat. SIA, however, offers a way of stock-taking and focusing ahead (Dillman *et al.*, 1983; Erikson, 1976). It has become clear that wise environmental management seeks to monitor physical change *and* forecast possible socio-economic scenarios. Gradual change should not be ignored, because it might suddenly reach a threshold beyond which there is a drastic shift to new environmental conditions or human adaptations. Environmental monitoring should, then, watch for such thresholds and any risk that they will be exceeded. There is a need for similar monitoring and forecasting of socio-economic change. Without stable and sustainable socio-economic institutions, most livelihood strategies will falter. History is replete with examples of civilizations that sustained good livelihoods for centuries only to have these fail after socio-economic change or environmental impacts. Until recently, social scientists were reluctant to explore these issues, fearing they would be branded 'environmental determinists'. There is clearly a need for more interest in neo-environmental determinism, but it will present many challenges; it is difficult enough predicting future environmental impacts – to try to assess the social impacts too is far more difficult.

Equally, to reliably predict future socio-economic change and then the environmental impacts it may cause is not easy. A good deal of attention has been paid to resource depletion challenges that may or may not be due to environmental changes (Miller *et al.*, 1987). People may cope in very different ways when faced with essentially the same problem or opportunity: some may go to war, others might co-operate. There may be groups that are fatalistic, simply ignoring threats; others may worry about future impacts but do little, and a few actually take insurance measures.

Someone who has invested in an expensive home does not want to see it devalued suddenly by the publication of a flood risk or contaminated ground map. Hazard disclosure requires care and awareness of the vulnerability of the groups that could be affected or damage may be done by the assessment. Where disaster preparedness takes the form of structures like flood protection embankments, flood or storm refuges, or avalanche diversion structures, there is a risk that elite groups will gain more than their fair share of protection and, as a consequence, the poor may be put at even greater risk.

It is important for planners to be well informed as to how people will react to threats and to avoidance, adaptation or mitigation measures, and to whether sudden or gradual environmental impacts may cause trauma before the event (where the threat is perceived), during it and/or afterwards. The impacts may cause hardship, or force relocation, but may sometimes offer opportunities too. These opportunities may not, however, be grasped by local people unless they are helped. Retrospective SIA has often identified opportunities associated with developments, accidents, disasters, policy change and so on. It has also highlighted the risk that outsiders, speculators or certain groups will exploit opportunities. Armed with this hindsight knowledge, SIA may help the authorities dealing with change to alert people, assist with funding, licensing or other controls. A good example is provided by a number of large dams in developing countries which, although they often disrupted local people, offered benefits to the distant users of electricity or water, or to opportunist settlers. Post-disaster stress may alter the vulnerability of people to illness, social disruption and unemployment; SIA may be able to predict such problems and enable mitigation measures to be taken (Tobin and Ollenburger, 1996).

Sudden catastrophic events may be caused by nature, by human activity, or a combination of both, and may offer little opportunity for anticipatory SIA. Disasters can be equally sudden, or may develop gradually (either visibly or insidiously) until a threshold is suddenly exceeded, at which point there is catastrophic change. Assessments of past events may help those faced with recent or ongoing problems. Gradual insidious onset, leading to a threshold of change, is a pattern familiar to physical and social scientists; one may recognize so-called chemical, biological, social and socio-economic 'time bombs'. For example, years of careless farming and lack of investment helped trigger the 1930s 'dustbowl' disaster in the American Midwest. Another example, is the society that withstands stress for years, and then suddenly erupts with people running amok, as was the case with the race riots that took place in 1960s America, in the late 1970s in Malaysia, and in the late 1990s in Rwanda. In each of these cases there were warning signs; SIA could help identify these types of situation, and perhaps even establish where the threshold points lie. Even if this is too much to ask, SIA should be able to suggest likely scenarios for social behaviour following a crisis (Dynes, 1974).

Several wholly or part-natural disasters (drought, storms, poor weather, crop disease) can cause famine, together with warfare, civil unrest and economic problems. The impacts of famine have attracted attention for centuries, and SIA can draw on historical reports, and more recent observations and analyses to unravel causes and effects. Although these events may be temporary, their impacts can be long term. For example, children deprived of food may be permanently debilitated, both mentally and physically; regions may be depopulated and abandoned, so land becomes degraded or re-forested; migrants may stay elsewhere; and bitter feelings may linger for centuries as in the case of the Irish Potato Famine (the 'Great Hunger') in the 1840s. Fear of future famine may alter farming and other livelihood strategies.

EXTREME CLIMATIC EVENTS

Aid agencies, like the UK's Department for International Development (DFID) are including consideration of social issues in programmes to improve early warnings and forecasts of extreme events: storms, frosts, drought, earthquakes and so on. What *is* well established is that people respond to warnings and forecasts only if they are sure that these are accurate. Improvements in computers and meteorological knowledge mean that forecasting is now more accurate than it has been; and, in recent years, there has been research into how people react to stressful weather conditions.

Storms and hurricanes

Tropical storms and their associated flooding and landslips probably cause more deaths and economic losses than any other type of natural disaster. There is a wide and growing literature on storm impacts, some focusing on demographic and socio-economic impacts, some on psychological responses before and after (David and Mellman, 1997; McDonnell *et al.*, 1995; McGoodwin and Dyer, 1993; Rotton *et al.*, 1997; Smith and McCarthy, 1996). There has also been considerable interest in making use of the opportunity after destructive events to restructure society and seek better and more sustainable lifestyles (Berke *et al.*, 1997; Russell, 1999; West and Lenze, 1995). A number of studies have also tried to assess the effectiveness of mitigation and relief strategies (Sandner, 1999), how people adapt to the change caused by disaster (Smith and Belgrave, 1995; Zeigler *et al.*, 1996), and what their media preferences are for keeping informed during storms (Piotrowski and Armstrong, 1999). Much of this is relevant to SIA that focuses on other sudden trauma or disasters in order to help improve disaster preparedness and relief efforts.

Weather forecasting has become more accurate and forward-looking than was the case a few decades ago, so there is now usually at least a few days' warning of impending weather systems. To make use of this improvement (and the same is true for other hazards) it is vital to know the likelihood and magnitude of danger, and the probable public response to threat and warnings (Baker, 1995). Whether people will evacuate depends on a number of factors, and various population subgroups may cite different reasons for their failure to move to safety (Faupel and Styles, 1993; Riad *et al.*, 1999). Insurance companies have increasingly been reviewing past storms and assessing future scenarios (likely to be affected by global warming and rising sea levels), having in recent years suffered large claims as a result of extreme climate events (and associated bush fires, landslides, avalanches or frost damage) (Berz, 1993; Flavin, 1994).

Global climate change will, however, alter the pattern and frequency of storms, droughts and floods, so people will still face 'unexpected' impacts for which there may be little local adaptation or past history of response. There may also be storm effects as yet unknown; for example, some research has suggested that geomagnetic storms might cause depressive illnesses, or possibly reduce people's immunity to diseases (Kay, 1994).

Droughts

Drought may impact on people directly, by making it difficult to gain a livelihood, and more indirectly when people have lost or abandoned the coping strategies that were once successful. The latter situation means that conditions similar to those experienced in the past have far more impact. It is important for administrators to be aware of when this is happening, or has happened, or there may well be serious and unexpected hardships. Drought can be triggered by many things, acting alone or in combination; for example, population increase, settlement policies that restrict nomadism, veterinary improvements that cause increasing livestock numbers, gradual soil degradation, excessive collection of fuel wood (possibly by outsiders, rather than locals), structural adjustment, loss of social capital and breakdown of co-operation. Sometimes the causation is composed of a complex chain of impacts, some exogenous, that come together as cumulative impacts. There are limits to the effectiveness of SIA when applied to this sort of problem. Mainstream SIA is not very effective at identifying cumulative impacts or even some single indirect exogenous impacts (*see* the discussion of strategic environmental assessment in Chapter 4).

Responses to drought can have marked socio-economic and physical impacts. Food aid, for example, may lead to excessive concentrations of people and livestock, as can provision of new wells; the wrong sort of aid may result in dependency; and inappropriate relief projects, like large commercial irrigation schemes, may do little to help locals and a good deal to harm them.

There are currently hopes that the growing understanding of El Niño-type events may facilitate the reliable warning of drought and other adverse climate conditions, perhaps a year or more in advance. This knowledge is coming from current studies of these events and from archaeology, palaeoclimatology and palaeoecology. SIA benefits from looking well back in time in order to solve today's challenges (what may crudely be termed 'backcasting'). There are indications that El Niño-type events have altered conditions in areas presently regarded as relatively stable. The forests of Amazonia or tropical South-East Asia, for example, have charcoal layers in their soil and other evidence suggesting considerable vegetational change and the altered incidence of forest fires (Meggers, 1994).

Floods

Flood myths are widespread: at least 500 cultures claim past catastrophic floods. This may have some basis in fact, given the marked sea-level changes during the last 10,000 years and, if true, these will have played a major role in shaping human history (Oppenheimer, 1998). There are also signs of large tsunami (tidal waves) in many parts of the world, some of which may have reached hundreds of metres above present sea level.

In developed countries, good information from hazard assessment enables the insurance industry to develop restrictions on policy cover, increased premiums (fees) for high-risk areas, or to refuse the custom of those in high-risk situations. In time this should help discourage settlement or at-risk activities in flood-prone areas – provided that people value insurance cover. The adaptations people make when faced by flood hazards require greater investigation (Zaman, 1989). Even when the risk is known, people may not take out insurance or even be prepared; if SIA suggests that this is the case, efforts could be made by local authorities to promote insurance, make it compulsory, or legislate to prevent or discourage the settlement of risk areas. In North America post-flooding victim interviews have been used to gather information on how people cope with early warnings, preparation and recovery. This sort of study is valuable for reducing hardship in subsequent floodings. An example of such a study is the International Joint Commission, Red River Basin Task Force (1997) 'Assessment of the Social Impact of Flooding for Use in Flood Management in the Red River Basin', which can be viewed at http://www.ijc.org/boards/rrb/assess.html.

A number of factors can make flood risk greater and are easily overlooked by people and planners, so impact assessment is vital. For example, mining, oil exploitation or groundwater drawdown may cause subsidence which, in turn, alters the areas likely to flood; the removal of mangrove vegetation for land development, timber or aquaculture is also likely to increase exposure to flooding. Housing fashions and behaviour change and affect factors such as flood impact. In the past, for example, houses had no electrical equipment, carpets or other vulnerable and costly furnishing, so a flood caused less trauma and damage; antisocial behaviour (such as fly-tipping into storm channels and streams) may obstruct flows and choke drains, altering risk even though there has been no change in physical conditions or infrastructure; successive flooding may have an increasingly disruptive effect, though the problem has not grown in magnitude. Citizens may grow to expect the state to come to their aid with compensation, when in the past they accepted that they themselves should take precautions such as investing in insurance. SIA should be able to identify many such developments.

In Bangladesh a large and growing population live at risk of flood in low-lying lands, through which flood-prone rivers discharge. If, as seems likely, global warming takes place, sea levels will rise and there is a chance that storms will become more severe and frequent, so the threat of floods grows. Many people settle risky areas in the absence of alternative land and livelihood. Well-intentioned, but possibly ill-thought-out, flood protection schemes may focus flood threats on certain localities and give the residents of others a false sense of security (Custers, 1993). There have been reports that flood impacts on some groups have actually increased since the construction of mitigation measures (protective banks, etc.). There may be unexpected benefits: protective banks may provide a refuge if the protected area floods and may improve year-round communications (factors often overlooked during planning) (Paul, 1997; Thompson and Sultana, 1996). SIA should be used to take stock of likely impacts; this will not be easy due to the different vulnerabilities associated with class, gender, age, culture and so on. It may be that, for some people who respond well to reliable flood warnings, communication systems and a system of refuges will be a better option than more costly coastal and river defences. SIA can provide indications of past impacts and human trends that may alter vulnerability and cause changes in flood adjustment.

Seismic, tsunami and volcanic events

Within a few years there should be a chance of better forecasting earthquakes, tsunami and volcanic eruptions, as well as improved knowledge of how they behave. Every once in a while there are massive losses of life, but history has shown that people soon choose to overlook the risk. Cities like Naples (Italy) should give volcanic threat a higher profile, given the size of population exposed to risk. In San Francisco, during the nineteenth century, earthquakes started catastrophic fires; building regulations have since been tightened. However, around the world, earthquake victims (and those who suffer other disasters) may be traumatized and pressed to reconstruct houses and livelihoods, and so may not stop to make rational decisions that might help should there be a future recurrence of disaster.

Social impact studies of how people respond to disaster are valuable. There have been a number of studies of the social impacts of post-1945 volcanic eruptions; for example, Mt Pinatubo (Philippines), Montserrat (Caribbean), Tristan da Cunha (South Atlantic), and Mt St Helens (USA) (Dillman *et al.*, 1983). Recent earthquakes in Japan and Turkey seem to have generated surprisingly few impact studies so far. Something that has become clear from past volcanic disasters is the need to establish the vulnerability of people to the hazard and the character of the risk (Dibben and Chester, 1999). The eruptions of Vesuvius (Italy) which buried Pompeii, Herculanium and other settlements in Roman times (AD 79), and more recently Mt Pelé, Martinique (early twentieth century) are examples of disasters where, had people been forced to evacuate, many lives would have been saved. Eruptions like those of Vesuvius and Mt Pelé (typical of volcanoes with viscous, acidic lava) throw up ash and relatively light debris for some time before occasional sudden, swift and deadly pyroclastic flows. People tend to shelter from the preceding fall-out, perhaps for hours or days, rather than evacuate and avoid the searing and poisonous eruption. Authorities must plan early warning and evacuation, and be prepared to have to force people to move through unpleasant or quite dangerous ash and pebble showers. There is likely to be traffic chaos, people may need protective shields or clothing, and civil defence may need to persuade or force people to move.

Whether caused by natural disasters, like earthquakes or volcanoes, or man-made, like building fires, terrorism or building collapse, it is vital that planners and the emergency services understand clearly how people respond to the stresses of disaster. Under stress, panic is a common response and leads to extremely irrational behaviour. Preparations and facilities that appear perfectly adequate may not be if they are made without reference to likely disaster responses (Donald and Canter, 1990; UNDRO, 1991).

Accurate and reliable early warning of exactly when earthquakes will occur, or how strong they will be has yet to be developed. The probability of occurrence and risk can reasonably be established, so that building legislation and contingency planning, and preparatory public education are possible. SIA can help in planning evacuations, and in showing how to prepare people though public education.

References

Alcamo, J., Leemans, R. and **Kreileman, E.** (eds) (1999) *Global Change Scenarios of the 21st Century: results from the IMAGE 2.1 Model*. Pergamon, Oxford.

Andrews, R.N. and **Clayton, R.** (1990) Environmental change and public health: an overview. *Environmental Impact Assessment Review* **10(4)**, 309–14.

Baker, E.J. (1995) Public response to hurricane probability forecasts. *Professional Geographer* **47(2)**, 137–47.

Behringer, W. (1999) Climate change and witch-hunting: the impact of the Little Ice Age on mentalities. *Climatic Change* **43(1)**, 335–51.

Benedict, J.B. (1999) Effects of changing climate on game-animal and human use of the Colorado high country (USA) since 1000 BC. *Arctic and Alpine Research* **31(1)**, 1–15.

Berke, P.R., Beatley, T. and **Bennett, E.** (1997) *After the Hurricane: linking recovery to sustainable development in the Caribbean*. Johns Hopkins University Press, Baltimore (MD).

Berz, G.A. (1993) Global warming and the insurance industry. *Interdisciplinary Science Reviews* **18(2)**, 120–5.

Chen, R.S., Boulding, E. and **Schneider, S.H.** (eds) (1983) *Social Science Research and Climate Change: an interdisciplinary approach*. D. Reidel, Dordrecht.

Custers, P. (1993) Bangladesh Flood Action Plan: a critique. *Economic and Political Weekly* **28(19–30)**, 1501–3.

David, D. and **Mellman, T.A.** (1997) Dreams following Hurricane Andrew. *Dreaming* **7(3)**, 209–14.

Dermeritt, D. and **Rothman, D.** (1999) Figuring the costs of climate change: an assessment and critique. *Environment and Planning A* **31(3)**, 389–408.

Dibben, C. and **Chester, D.K.** (1999) Human vulnerability in volcanic environments: the case of Furnas, São Miguel, Azores. *Journal of Vulcanology and Geothermal Research* **92(1)**, 133–50.

Dillman, D.A., Schwalbe, M.L. and **Short, J.F. Jnr** (1983) Communication behaviour and social impacts following the May 18th, 1980, eruption of Mt St Helen's, in S.A.C. Keller (ed.), *Mt St Helen's, One Year Later*. East Washington University Press, Cheney (Washington), 191–8.

Donald, I. and **Canter, D.V.** (1990) Behavioural aspects of the Kings Cross Disaster, in D.V. Canter (ed.), *Fires and Human Behaviour*. David Fulton, London, 15–30.

Dynes, R.R. (1974) *Organized Behavior in Disaster*. DC Heath & Co., Lexington (MA).

Erikson, K.T. (1976) *Everything in its Path: destruction of community in the Buffalo Creek flood*. Simon and Schuster, New York (NY).

Faupel, C.E. and **Styles, S.P.** (1993) Disaster education, household preparedness, and stress responses following Hurricane Hugo. *Environment and Behavior* **25(2)**, 228–49.

Flavin, C. (1994) Storm warnings – climate change hits the insurance industry. *World Watch* **7(6)**, 10–20.

Huntington, E. (1915) *Civilisation and Climate*. Yale University Press, New Haven (CT).

Kay, R.W. (1994) Geomagnetic storms – association with incidence of depression as measured by hospital admission. *British Journal of Psychiatry* **164**, 403–9.

McDonnell, S., Troiano, R.P., Barker, N., Noji, E., Hlady, W.G. and **Hopkins, R.** (1995) Long-term effects of hurricane Andrew: revisiting mental health indicators. *Disasters* **19(3)**, 235–46.

McGoodwin, J.R. and **Dyer, C.L.** (1993) Hurricane Andrew and South Florida's commercial fishing people: impacts and immediate needs *Mast* **6(1–2)**, 205–19.

McMichael, A.J., Haines, A., Stooff, R. and **Kovats, S.** (eds) (1996) *Climate Change and Human Health* (assessment by a task group on behalf of the WHO, WMO and UNEP). World Health Organization, Geneva.

Meggers, B. (1994) Archaeological evidence for the impact of mega-Niño events on Amazonia during the past 2 millennia. *Climatic Change* **28(4)**, 321–38.

Miller, M.L., Dale, R. and **Brown, T.** (eds) (1987) *Social Science in Natural Resource Management*. Westview, Boulder (CO).

Oppenheimer, S. (1998) *Eden in the East: the drowned continent of Southeast Asia*. Weidenfield and Nicolson, London.

Paul, B.K. (1997) Flood research in Bangladesh in retrospect and prospect; a review. *GeoForum* **28(2)**, 121–31.

Piotrowski, C. and **Armstrong, T.R.** (1999) Mass media preferences in a disaster: a study of Hurricane Danny. *Social Behavior and Personality* **26(4)**, 341–5.

Riad, J.K., Norris, F.H. and **Ruback, R.B.** (1999) Predicting evacuation in two major disasters: risk perception, social influence, and access to resources. *Journal of Applied Social Psychology* **29(5)**, 918–34.

Rotton, J., Dubitsky, S.S., Milov, A., White, S.M. and **Clark, M.C.** (1997) Distress, elevated cortisol, cognitive defects, and illness following a natural disaster. *Journal of Environmental Psychology* **17(2)**, 85–98.

Russell, G. (1999) Hurricane Mitch and human rights. *Development in Practice* **9(3)**, 322–4.

Sandner, V. (1999) Auswirkungen des hurrikans Mitch auf Zentralamerika. *Geographische Rundschau* **51(7–8)**, 418–23.

Schneider, R. (1974) *Applications of Meteorology to Economic and Social Development* (World Meteorological Organization Technical Notes No. 132). WMO, Geneva.

Smith, K.J. and **Belgrave, L.L.** (1995) The reconstruction of everyday life: experiencing Hurricane Andrew. *Journal of Contemporary Ethnography* **24(3)**, 244–69.

Smith, S.K. and **McCarthy, C.** (1996) Demographic effects of natural disasters: a case study of Hurricane Andrew. *Demography* **33(2)**, 265–75.

Taplin, R. and **Braaf, R.** (1995) Climate impact assessment, in F. Vanclay and D.A. Bronstein (eds), *Environmental and Social Impact Assessment*. Wiley, Chichester, 249–64.

Thompson, P.M. and **Sultana, P.** (1996) Distributional and social impacts of flood control in Bangladesh. *The Geographical Journal* **162(1)**, 1–13.

Tobin, G.A. and **Ollenburger, J.C.** (1996) Predicting levels of postdisaster stress in adults following the 1993 floods in the upper midwest. *Environment and Behavior* **28(3)**, 340–57.

UNDRO (1991) *Mitigating Natural Disasters: phenomena, effects and options, a manual for policy makers and planners*. United Nations, New York (NY).

West, C.T. and **Lenze, D.G.** (1995) Modeling the regional impact of natural disaster and recovery: a general framework and an application to Hurricane Andrew. *International Regional Science Review* **17(2)**, 121–50.

Zaman, M.Q. (1989) The social and political context of adjustment to riverbank erosion hazard and population resettlement in Bangladesh. *Human Organization* **48(3)**, 196–205.

Zeigler, D.J., **Brunn, S.D.** and **Johnson, J.H. Jnr** (1996) Focusing on Hurricane Andrew through the eyes of the victims. *Area* **28(2)**, 124–9.

14

THE FUTURE OF SIA

Before trying to foretell the likely development of SIA, or making any suggestions, it is important to assess how useful it has been so far.

Has SIA worked?

As with other fields of impact assessment there have been relatively few evaluations or ex-post audits of SIA (i.e. studies that look back to check whether an SIA was accurate, whether the procedures were cost-effective, and to see if recommendations were acted upon). There is more experience in auditing EIA; Sadler (1998), for example, audited environmental assessments on the basis of their utility of procedures, quality of results, and performance of the methods used. Nevertheless, SIA ex-post audits *can* be found. Deng and Altenhoefel (1997) conducted an audit of over 70 SIAs commissioned by US federal agencies, focusing on the methods used. Overall, the conclusion was that, in spite of shortcomings, SIA was most worthwhile. Macfarlane (1999) reviewed the effectiveness of 23 mining-related SIAs, first classifying them as either technocratic, participatory or integrative in approach. The latter, he concluded, was the most effective approach. There have been a few reviews of national SIA experience (e.g. Juslén, 1995).

The auditing of SIA differs a little from that of EIA, in that the results are not as precise and the units of measurement are less standardized. This makes it more difficult to review the performance of a given assessment through time, and also to compare one SIA with another (Murdock *et al.*, 1982 and 1984; Rakowski, 1995).

Possible and desirable future developments

SIA may prove a valuable tool in the quest to attain sustainable development. There appears to be growing interest in more comprehensive and integrated approaches to SIA, and especially in the methodologies evolved from SEA (*see* Chapter 4) (Dale and Land, 1994; Gramling and Freudenburg, 1992; McDonald, 1990; Rossini and Porter, 1983). Another possibility is to adapt a systems approach, using a river basin or socio-economic region as a physico-bio-socio-economic unit in which to assess socio-economic impacts. There may also be potential for adapting geographical information systems (GIS) for SIA; if complex and changing data on a variety of environmental variables can be stored and retrieved, then it should be possible to do similar things with demographic, health, cultural and other socio-economic variables.

While there is a need to improve and develop SIA, it is also clear that SIA could be much more widely used, especially given the role it could play in the quest for sustainable development. Many of the problems of SIA can be traced to problems faced by the social sciences in general, in particular the difficulty involved in making reliable future predictions about the behaviour of people. Reviewing the progress of the social sciences, Wilson (1998: 200–32), an eminent natural scientist interested in animal behaviour, concluded that, in spite of the resources that had been made available, there was less progress than one would have wished. This was not the usual physical-scientist-versus-social-studies trading of insults; Wilson had pondered how progress might be made and suggested that promising opportunities may lie in 'bridge-building' between the 'sciences'. One of the bridges identified by Wilson was contact between environmental and social science, and this he felt (1998: 214) offered the '. . . best way for the social sciences to gain in *predictive power* . . .' (my italics). Wilson saw potential in epigenetic approaches (epigenesis is the development of an organism under the joint influence of heredity and environment); and, more specifically, in the linking of psychology, biology, economics and social theory.

During recent field studies in the High Atlas Mountains of Morocco, it became apparent to a colleague and myself that similar communities in different valleys – endowed with broadly the same environment, natural resources and livelihood strategies – fared rather differently in the face of challenges such as structural adjustment measures and drought. The ability to withstand setbacks, and even to prosper in spite of them, seemed to be, at least in part, determined by a community's stock of social capital. Social capital is basically composed of the institutions, traditions and relationships which help to ensure that people co-operate and support each other in times of need or opportunity. It would be interesting to focus SIA on social capital to help identify when it is strong enough to encourage experimentation and innovation, and to warn of any weakening.

SIA has usefully been applied to social, economic and political changes – for example, structural adjustment programmes. Several fields seem to invite a greater application of SIA: an assessment of the ongoing effects of the end of the Cold War; the impact of environmental degradation; changes in the narcotics trade; and globalization.

Tentative recommendations

The shortcomings of SIA suggest a need for:

- more accurate prediction
- more emphasis on clear, concise, simple, relevant results
- procedures which ensure that SIA is used earlier on in the development or planning process
- the development of SIA that can be integrated with other impact assessment fields and fed into more 'strategic' planning
- SIA to be more widely seen to aid the quest for sustainability and better environmental management
- the wider use of SIA, which presupposes reliable methods, cheaper application, and minimal delay to development
- more skilled and experienced SIA practitioners
- the accreditation of SIA practitioners, the monitoring of their activities and greater control over the way in which SIA is commissioned and its results used.

References

Dale, A.P. and **Land, M.B.** (1994) Strategic perspectives analysis: a procedure for participatory and political social impact assessment. *Society and Natural Resources* **7(3)**, 253–67.

Deng, F. and **Altenhoefel, J.** (1997) Social impact assessment conducted by federal agencies. *Impact Assessment* **15(3)**, 209–31.

Gramling, R. and **Freudenburg, W.R.** (1992) Opportunity- threat, development and adaption: toward a comprehensive framework for social impact assessment. *Rural Sociology* **57(2)**, 216–34.

Juslén, J. (1995) Social impact assessment: a look at Finnish experiences. *Project Appraisal* **10(3)**, 163–70.

Macfarlane, M. (1999) *An Evaluation of Social Impact Assessment Methodologies in the Mining Industry*. PhD thesis, University of Bath, Bath (UK).

McDonald, G.T. (1990) Regional economic and social impact assessment. *Environmental Impact Assessment Review* **10(1–2)**, 25–36.

Murdock, S.H., Leistritz, F.L., Hamm, R.R., Hwang, S.S. and **Parpia, B.** (1984) An assessment of the accuracy of a regional economic-demographic projection model. *Demography* **21(3)**, 383–404.

Murdock, S.H., Leistritz, F.L., Hamm. R.R. and **Hwang, S.S.** (1982) An assessment of socioeconomic assessments: utility, accuracy and policy considerations. *Environmental Impact Assessment Review* **3(4)**, 333–50.

Rakowski, C.A. (1995) Evaluating a social impact assessment: short-term and long-term outcomes in a developing country. *Society and Natural Resources* **8(6)**, 525–40.

Rossini, F.A. and **Porter, A.L.** (1983) *Integrated Impact Assessment*. Westview, Boulder (CO).

Sadler, B. (1998) Ex-post evaluation of the effects of environmental assessment, in

A. Porter and J. Fittipaldi (eds), *Environmental Methods Review: retooling impact assessment for the new century*. AEPI, Fargo (ND).

Wilson, E.O. (1998) *Consilience: the unity of knowledge*. Little, Brown and Co., Boston (MA).

GLOSSARY

baseline data: data/information by which it is possible to judge/predict change that would happen with or without a proposed development happening.
BSE: bovine spongiform encephalopathy, a degenerative disease of cattle, also transmitted to humans, certain zoo animals, cats and possibly sheep. BSE has some similarities to a sheep disease – scrapie. Colloquially known in the UK as 'mad cow disease'.
CJD: Creutzfeldt-Jacob disease, a degenerative disease that affects the human nervous system, and is probably caused by prion-type agents transmitted in blood or food. Similar to **BSE**.
community: it is not easy to agree a general definition, indeed almost every source in the literature varies. It has been described as '. . . total ways of life, complexes of behaviour . . .'. There are clearly different types of community, e.g. regional, national, rural, urban, ethnic, status community. Also, there are planned communities, unplanned, stable growth communities, rapid growth communities, disrupted or disturbed communities, declining communities. It is generally agreed that a community, whatever the type, has: (a) distinctive space or territory; (b) a specialized authority system; (c) distinctive patterns of social interaction; (d) commonly held symbols and feelings that bind members. In short, a community has elements of territory and function. Making reliable predictions of community behaviour can be a challenge.
community cohesion: maintenance of a particular or special unit of character, the boundaries of which may be physical (e.g. an island community) or conceptual (e.g. 'cockney' in London or a neighbourhood), and often class- or employment-related. Through various mechanisms the people in a community maintain functional and effective ties; impacts or internal changes may damage these, causing stress and disintegration. Community cohesion may be difficult to measure.
culture: the total way of life of a population in an area.
empowerment: improving peoples' ability to secure their own survival and development, increasing their ability to participate in and exercise influence over crucial decisions affecting their survival.
ex-ante: conducted in advance (proactive).
ex-post: conducted after (retrospective).
feedbacks: factors that modify the process of change, possibly indirectly. A positive feedback is when change is reinforced; a negative feedback is when change is counteracted.
fiscal impact: change in costs and revenues that are likely to occur. The stress is on public service economics (costs and revenues).

iterative: adding depth and detail as the process proceeds.
monitoring: seeking to determine changes as they happen (as opposed to predicting in advance), usually by observing suitable indicators. Monitoring can update an SIA; SIA can be used to decide what to monitor.
normative: a goal-oriented approach (as opposed to, say, a predictive approach).
planning: a problem-solving process with various discernible stages.
policy: setting social goals and establishing strategy for further attainment.
primary data: data collected by study/research and which was not already available.
programme: plans of action devised for meeting specific objectives.
project: concrete actions devised for carrying out specific plans and reaching stated objectives.
secondary data: data already available, e.g. from a census, from academic journals, from expert opinion, published surveys, etc.
social context: an analysis of social context is a social and economic overview.
social impact: a significant improvement or deterioration in people's well-being or a significant change in an aspect of **community** concern.
social indicators: social indicators are standardized quantitative measures of specific social conditions that are periodically collected to help describe current conditions and ongoing changes (trends).
social profile: a comprehensive and systematic summary of the key characteristics of a **community** or region. Typically prepared by means of a desk study of the available literature, plus interviews with key informants.
society: society may be described as '. . . the means whereby cultural ends become realized'.
stakeholder analysis: analysis of the 'actors' involved in social impacts, so a useful technique for SIA.
structural adjustment: approach that seeks to control inflation and reduce imports by maintaining fiscal retrenchment policies and restraining the supply of money: currency devaluation (to make exports more competitive); diversification of production; efforts to improve economic growth. Between 1979 and 1995, about 67 countries had adopted structural adjustment policies. Cutbacks in state spending and privatization have, in some cases, led to widespread unemployment, static or falling wages, environmental degradation, increased poverty and rural–urban migration.
structural analysis: seeks to understand relationships between development and social change (a 'social structure' being a persistent pattern of relationships between elements of a society).

INDEX